the photoshop® CS2 book
for digital photographers

Scott Kelby

THE PHOTOSHOP® CS2 BOOK FOR DIGITAL PHOTOGRAPHERS

The Photoshop CS2 Book for Digital Photographers Team

CREATIVE DIRECTOR
Felix Nelson

TECHNICAL EDITOR
Polly Reincheld

COPY EDITOR
Veronica Martin

PRODUCTION EDITOR
Kim Gabriel

PRODUCTION MANAGER
Dave Damstra

PRODUCTION DESIGNERS
Taffy Orlowski
Dave Korman

ASSOCIATE DESIGNER
Christine Edwards

COVER DESIGNED BY
Felix Nelson

COVER PHOTOS BY
Scott Kelby and Dave Moser

STOCK IMAGES
The royalty-free stock images used in this book are courtesy of JupiterImages Corp.

PHOTOS.COM >>

Published by
New Riders / Peachpit

Copyright © 2005 by Scott Kelby

FIRST EDITION: April 2005

Composed in Cronos and Helvetica by NAPP Publishing

ISBN 0-321-33062-5

9 8 7 6 5 4 3 2 1

Printed and bound in the United States of America

www.peachpit.com
www.scottkelbybooks.com

For my amazing wife Kalebra,
for single-handedly making me
the luckiest guy in the world.

ACKNOWLEDGMENTS

Although only one name appears on the spine of this book, it takes a large, dedicated team of people to put a book like this together. Not only did I have the good fortune of working with such a great group of people, I now get the great pleasure of thanking them and acknowledging their hard work and dedication.

First, I want to thank the most amazing woman I've ever known, my absolutely beautiful and truly wonderful wife, Kalebra. She's equal parts savvy business woman, power negotiator, stand-up comic, super mom, gourmet chef, interior decorator, travel guru, motivational speaker, and rock star. I don't know what she's putting in her coffee, but let me tell you—it's workin'! She's the type of woman for whom love songs are written, and I am, without a doubt, the luckiest man alive to have her as my wife.

Secondly, I want to thank my 8-year-old son Jordan. God has blessed our family with so many wonderful gifts, and I can see them all reflected in his eyes. I'm so proud of him, so thrilled to be his dad, and I dearly love watching him grow to be such a wonderful little guy, who is blessed with his mom's compassion and her tender, loving heart. (You're the greatest, little buddy.)

I also want to thank my big brother Jeff for being such a positive influence in my life, for always taking the high road, for always knowing the right thing to say, and just the right time to say it, and for having so much of our dad in him. (I'm honored to have you as my brother and my friend.)

My heartfelt thanks go to the entire team at KW Media Group, who every day redefine what teamwork and dedication are all about. They are truly a special group of people who come together to do some really amazing things (on really scary deadlines), and they do it with class, poise, and a can-do attitude that is truly inspiring. I'm so proud to be working with you all.

Thanks to my compadre Dave Moser, whose tireless dedication to making everything we do better than anything we've done before is an inspiration to our whole team. He's an amazing individual, a great friend, and an awful lot of fun.

I owe a special thanks to my tech editor and adviser, Polly Reincheld. She puts every single technique in the entire book through the ringer to make sure that everything works the way it should, but she goes way beyond that, and her input, advice, perspective, and encouragement have made the book better than it would've been otherwise. I'm so happy to have her working on my books, and I'm so glad she's joined our team, despite the fact that she's constantly playing Shania Twain songs at her desk.

My thanks to Veronica Martin, the newest member of our team, who copyedited the book (and believe me, copyediting my books is no easy task).

Special thanks to my layout and production crew. In particular, I want to thank my friend and Creative Director Felix Nelson for his limitless talent, boundless creativity, input, and just for his flat-out great ideas. To Kim Gabriel for doing such an amazing job of keeping us all on track and organized—I can't thank you enough. Thanks and kudos to Dave Damstra (the best layout guy in the business) and his team for giving the book such a tight, clean layout.

Thanks to Jim Workman, Jean A. Kendra, and Pete Kratzenberg for their support, and for keeping a lot of plates in the air while I'm writing these books.

A special thanks to my wonderful Executive Assistant Kathy Siler for keeping me on track, focused, and juggling (okay, running) half a dozen different projects while I'm deep in "book land." She and I had a special bond this year, as both our NFL teams wound up at the bottom of their respective divisions, and I assume that bond will last until the Tampa Bay Buccaneers triumphantly return to form and mercilessly rout her beloved Redskins in Raymond James Stadium later this year. (I'm going to pay for that one.)

Many thanks to Dave Cross and Matt Kloskowski for their ideas and input on the book, and thanks to Chris Main and Barbara Thompson for being such an important part of our team.

I owe a special debt of gratitude to my friends Kevin Ames and Jim DiVitale for taking the time to share their ideas, techniques, concepts, and vision for a Photoshop book for digital photographers that would really make a difference. Extra-special thanks to Kevin for spending hours with me sharing his retouching techniques. Also my heartfelt thanks to Eddie Tapp and Taz Tally for their help and input on my color management chapter.

I want to thank all the photographers, retouchers, and Photoshop experts who've taught me so much over the years, including Jack Davis, Deke McClelland, Ben Willmore, Julieanne Kost, Vincent Versace, David Cuerdon, Robert Dennis, Helene DeLillo, Felix Nelson, Jim Patterson, Katrin Eismann, Doug Gornick, Manuel Obordo, Dave Cross, Dan Margulis, Peter Bauer, Joe Glyda, and Russell Preston Brown.

Also thanks to my friends at Adobe Systems, including Addy Roff, Julieanne Kost, Cari Gushiken, Gwyn Weisberg, Deb Whitman, John Nack, Kevin Connor, Mark Delman, Karen Gauthier, Russell Brady, Mark Dahm, Russell Preston Brown, and Terry "T-bone" White.

Thanks to Nancy Ruenzel, Scott Cowlin, and everyone at New Riders / Peachpit—they're really great people who continually strive to produce very special books.

My personal thanks go to Alan Meckler and Adrian Maynard at JupiterImages for enabling me to use some of their wonderful images here in the book.

Most importantly, I want to thank God, and His son Jesus Christ, for leading me to the woman of my dreams, for blessing us with such a special little boy, for allowing me to make a living doing something I truly love, for always being there when I need Him, for blessing me with a wonderful, fulfilling and happy life, and such a warm, loving family to share it with.

ABOUT THE AUTHOR

Scott Kelby

Scott is Editor-in-Chief and co-founder of *Photoshop User* magazine, Editor-in-Chief of Nikon's *Capture User* magazine, Editor-in-Chief of *Layers* magazine (the how-to magazine for everything Adobe), and is Executive Editor of *Photoshop Elements Techniques*.

He is President of the National Association of Photoshop Professionals (NAPP), the trade association for Adobe® Photoshop® users, and he's President of the software training and publishing firm, KW Media Group, Inc.

Scott is an award-winning author of more than 26 books on Photoshop, digital imaging, and technology, and is currently the world's No. 1 best-selling author of all computer and technology books. His other titles include *Photoshop Down & Dirty Tricks*, *Photoshop Photo-Retouching Secrets*, *Photoshop Classic Effects*, and *The Photoshop Elements Book for Digital Photographers*. Scott is also co-author of *Photoshop Killer Tips*, and he's creator and Series Editor for the entire *Killer Tips* series from New Riders.

Scott's latest books include *The iPod Book* and *The Book for Guys Who Don't Want Kids (How to Get Past the Fear of Fatherhood)*. In 2004, Scott was awarded the publishing industry's prestigious Benjamin Franklin Award for the previous edition of the book you're now reading.

Scott is Training Director for the Adobe Photoshop Seminar Tour, Conference Technical Chair for the Photoshop World Conference & Expo, and he is a speaker at digital imaging trade shows and events around the world. He is also featured in a series of Adobe Photoshop training DVDs and has been training Adobe Photoshop users since 1993.

For more background info on Scott, visit www.scottkelby.com.

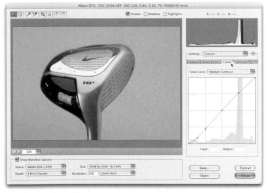

38 Special
Photographic Special Effects

Wide Receiver
Creating Panoramas

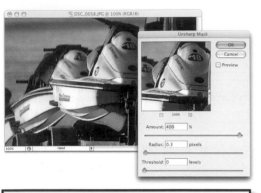

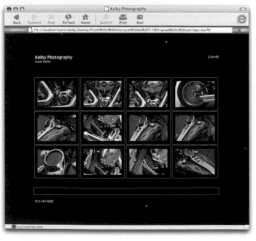

WARNING: SKIPPING THIS SECTION COULD SEVERELY DAMAGE YOUR COMPUTER

Before you do anything, do this first:

I know, I know—you want to jump right to Chapter 1 and dive into the tutorials, skipping this critically important section. That's probably because (a) it contains no photos or screen captures, so you're not interested, (b) you have a Napoleon complex (I have no idea what that means), (c) you're only used to reading things that appear in menus or dialogs, or (d) you have the patience of a hamster and therefore cannot possibly focus long enough to read this critically important message, even though it could save you from severely damaging your computer, which would cost you thousands of dollars (unless you have a really crappy computer, in which case you might only save a couple hundred bucks).

So, what is this critical thing that you must do first? You must read this entire section (some might call it an introduction, but I would never do that)—every letter, every word, even the ones that don't matter (like punctuation)—before you do anything. Why? There are two reasons:

(1) You paid good money for this book, and you deserve to get the most out of it (unless, of course, you shoplifted it, in which case you can turn right to Chapter 1 now).

(2) I haven't thought of a second reason yet, but I'm sure one will come to me before we're done.

Seriously though, there are things in this introduction, I mean "important section," that you'll want to know—like where to download the photos I used in the book, so you can follow right along using the same images (if you like). Now, I make the photos downloadable for every Photoshop book I write, but I always get letters from readers who complain, "Why don't you make the photos available for download, so we can follow along with the book?" Who are these people? People who don't read the introduction. I call them "goobers." Not to their face, mind you, but to close friends at my secret photo downloading parties (needless to say, only people who read my introductions are invited). Now, here's the good news: If you've read this far (and I know you have), you're no goober. In fact, you're clearly a person of a discerning virtue and impeccable taste. You're my kind of people (even if you are, in fact, just one person).

So, now that you've come this far (in other words, I hooked you with my "saving-you-from-damaging-your-computer" ruse), I can get down to business—giving you some important tips so you understand how and why the book was written, so you can get the most out of it. Rather than giving you a long, boring "it-was-the-book-that-had-to-be-written" kind of introduction, I thought I'd save you some time and interview myself. That's right, I thought I'd ask myself questions about the book, and by asking them to myself, and answering them myself, you'd not only get the answers you need, but you'd get to know a little about me, the person I'm always referring to as either "I" or "me" throughout the book. (Luckily, I find myself fascinating, so interviewing me, for me anyway, is a lot of fun. In fact, I can listen to me talk for hours, even about boring subjects. Even when droning on and on about some meaningless topic, I'm still quite interested to hear what I have to say.)

So, let me turn on the little tape recorder here. Okay, I'm ready. First question please:

Me: Scott, before we begin, I just have to say you're much taller and more handsome in person than I expected.
Me: Thanks. I hear that all the time.

Me: No seriously. You're totally buff.
Me: I know.

Continued

Me: This is the third edition of this book. Can you tell us what's different in this Photoshop CS2 version?

Me: Actually, this third edition is the biggest update of this book so far. In fact, it felt like I was writing a whole new book from the ground up, partly because Adobe added so many new features for digital photographers in CS2, and I had to cover them all. I thought CS added a lot for photographers, but CS2 goes way beyond that, so I felt I had to, too! Also, I've been taking a lot more time to shoot since I wrote the last book (I shot most of the photos used in this edition), and I've learned a lot more about Photoshop since the last edition too (which was published back in 2003).

Me: So what have you added, besides the new CS2 stuff?

Me: I included an entire chapter on Camera Raw (where the previous version just had about six pages on it). I think Camera Raw has become that important, and that powerful—so much so that it now needs its own chapter. Also, I set out to do something that I hadn't really seen anyone do in any Photoshop book yet, and that's really to demystify color management by letting you know exactly how to set it up, with everything shown step-by-step from beginning to end, so you can get what you see onscreen to match the print that comes out of your color inkjet. I devoted an entire chapter to it, and I'm really excited about how it turned out. I also included an entire chapter on creating panoramas, plus I took one of my most popular sessions from the Photoshop World Conference & Expo (my "How to Show Your Work Like a Pro" session) and turned it into a chapter in the book. Also, my "Photographic Special Effects" chapter is updated with the latest cutting-edge effects that I see some of the top pros using in their work, and I break everything down step-by-step. The whole book is riddled with new little tricks, new features, new tips, and some cool new techniques I've learned since the last book.

Me: So whom did you write this book for?

Me: It's aimed at professional and high-end prosumer photographers who either have gone digital or are just moving to digital. Since this book is for people who are already photographers, there's no discussions about f-stops, lenses, or how to frame a photo, and it starts at the moment your photo leaves the camera and comes into Photoshop. If you don't already know how to shoot, this book just isn't for you. (*Note:* There is nothing publishers hate more than when an author lists who the book "isn't" for. They want it to be for everybody, from soccer moms to *National Geographic* staff photographers, but sadly, this book just isn't for everybody—it's for people who are already serious about photography.)

Me: Is the book in a specific order?

Me: I put it in the order in which many pros actually manage the processing of their digital images. For example, a typical workflow might start with sorting the photos directly from your memory card, so I start with the Adobe Bridge (it's replacing the old File Browser of Photoshop 7 and CS). Then, I go right into Camera Raw, for people who are shooting in RAW. If they're not, then they'll jump to resizing and cropping, because that's generally what they'll do next. Then, before they do any color correction or dealing with image problems, we set up a real color management scheme. Then it's on to retouching, adding special effects, and then much later, on to sharpening (since pros apply the sharpening near the end of the whole process), then finally how to show your final work to your client. It's all pretty much following a typical workflow.

Me: So do the readers have to follow along in that order?

Me: Absolutely not—the book is designed so you can jump in anywhere. Although the chapters are in a workflow order, everything is spelled out in every chapter, so you can turn to the technique you want to learn and start right there—you'll be able to follow along, no sweat. Unless, of course, you're a goober, in which case, you missed all of this.

Me: How did you develop the content for the book?

Me: Each year I train thousands of professional digital photographers around the world at my live seminars, and although I'm doing the teaching, at every seminar I always learn something new. Photographers love to share their favorite techniques, and during the breaks between sessions, somebody's always showing me how they get "the job done." It's really an amazing way to learn. Plus, and perhaps most importantly, I hear right from their own lips the problems and challenges these photographers are running into in their own work in Photoshop, so I have a great insight into what photographers want to learn next. Plus, I'm also out there shooting, so I'm constantly fixing my own problems and developing new ways to make my digital imaging life easier. As soon as I come up with a new trick or if I learn a slick new way of doing something, I can't wait to share it. It's a sickness, I know.

Me: So what makes this book different from all the other Photoshop books out there?

Me: It's not another one of those Photoshop books that focuses on explaining every aspect of every dialog. I don't write "tell-me-all-about-it" books. Instead, I write "show-me-how-to-do-it" books. This is what makes it different. It shows photographers step-by-step how to do all those things they keep asking at my seminars, sending me emails about, and posting questions about in our forums—it simply shows them exactly "how to do it" without holding anything back. Plus, it does something that almost no other Photoshop book dares to do—it gives you the actual settings to use.

For example, almost every Photoshop book out there includes info on the Unsharp Mask filter. They all talk about what the Amount, Radius, and Threshold sliders do, and how those settings affect the pixels, blah, blah, blah. They all do that. But you know what they generally don't do? They don't give you any actual settings to use! Usually not even a starting point. Some provide numerical ranges to work within, but basically they explain how the filter works, and then leave it up to you to develop your own settings. I don't do that. I give you some great Unsharp Mask filter settings—the same settings used by many professionals, even though I know some Photoshop expert somewhere might take issue with them. I come right out and say, "Hey, use this setting when sharpening people. Use this setting to correct slightly out-of-focus photos. Use this setting on landscapes, etc." I give students in my live seminars these settings, so why shouldn't I share them in my book?

Plus, sharpening is much more than just using the Unsharp Mask filter, and it's much more important to photographers than the three or four pages every other book dedicates to it. I give you an entire chapter showing all the different sharpening techniques step-by-step, giving different solutions for different sharpening challenges. That's my thing—I want to be the guy that "shows them how to do it!" So, I did a whole chapter just on Camera Raw. Two chapters on all the amazing things the Bridge can do—and not just talking about it, but showing exactly how to do it all, with everything step-by-step from top to bottom but without all the techno jargon. The world doesn't need another "tell-me-all-about-it" book. It needs a "show-me-how-to-do-it" book, and that's my thing. It's who I am, and it's what this book is all about.

Me: This sounds like a lot of work. Did you have any help?

Me: When I developed the first edition of this book back in 2001, I got some incredible insights and advice from two of the industry's top digital photographers—commercial product photographer Jim DiVitale and fashion photographer Kevin Ames. These two guys are amazing—they both split their time between shooting for some of the world's largest corporations and teaching other professional digital photographers how to pull off Photoshop miracles at events such as Photoshop World, PPA/PEI's Digital Conference, and a host of other events around the world.

When they heard I was writing this book, they met with me and we spent hours hammering out which techniques would have to be included in the book, and I can't tell you how helpful and insightful their input was. This wasn't an easy task, because I wanted to include a range of techniques wide enough that they would be accessible to "prosumers" (the industry term to

Continued

describe serious high-end amateurs who use serious cameras and take serious shots, yet don't do photography for a living), but at the same time, I wanted high-end professionals to feel right at home with techniques that are clearly just for them, at their stage of the game.

For this edition, I also got advice and input for my new color management chapter from some of the leading color management experts in the industry, including Canon Explorer of Light and gifted instructor Eddie Tapp, who gave me some great insights, and I went back to my buddy Jim DiVitale to pick his brain as well. I also coaxed Photoshop guru Taz Tally (who teaches color management for a living) into taking a look at the final chapter, and he helped me tweak it even more to make it what it is today. I also got some great ideas from my home team, including Dave Cross and Matt Kloskowski, who work with me each day on *Photoshop User* magazine at the National Association of Photoshop Professionals.

Me: Does all this make the book too advanced?
Me: Absolutely not. That's because my goal is to present all these techniques in such a simple, easy-to-understand format that no matter where you are in your Photoshop skills, you'll read the technique, and rather than thinking, "Oh, I could never pull that off," you'll think, "Hey, I can do that."

While it's true that this book includes many advanced techniques, just because a technique is advanced doesn't mean it has to be complicated or "hard to pull off." It just means that you'll be further along in the learning process before you'd even know you need that technique.

For example, in the retouching chapter, I show you how to use the Healing Brush to completely remove wrinkles, and that's what many photographers will do—completely remove all visible wrinkles. But advanced Photoshop users might retouch the photo differently, because they know that a 79-year-old man's face shouldn't be as wrinkle-free as Ben Affleck's. When they do a similar retouch, they're not going to remove every wrinkle—instead they'll be looking for a way to just reduce the intensity of the wrinkles, so the portrait looks more natural (and the photo appears unretouched). To do that, they'll need something beyond the basic Healing Brush technique—they'll need a more advanced technique that may require a few more steps along the way, but produces far better results.

So, how hard is it to do the advanced "healing" technique we just talked about? It's simple—duplicate the Background layer, remove all the wrinkles using the Healing Brush, then lower that layer's Opacity a bit to bring back some of the original wrinkles from the layer underneath (see Chapter 10). It works like a charm, but really—how complicated is that? Heck, anyone who's used Photoshop for a week can duplicate a layer and lower the Opacity, right? Right. Yet few photographers know this simple, advanced technique. That's what this book is all about. If you understand that line of thinking, you'll really get a lot out of this book. You'll be able to perform every single technique—you'll be using the same advanced correction and retouching techniques employed by some of today's leading digital photographers; yet you'll make it all look easy, because it really is easy, and it's a lot of fun—once somebody shows you how to do it.

Me: So what's not in this book?
Me: I tried not to put things in this book that are already in every other Photoshop book out there. For example, I don't have a chapter on the Layers palette or a chapter on the painting tools or a chapter showing how each of Photoshop's 110 filters looks when applied to the same photograph. I just focused on the most important, most asked-about, and most useful things for digital photographers. In short—it's the funk and not the junk.

What does this "For Pros Only" logo mean?

 It means "Go away—this isn't for you!" (Kidding.) Actually, it's a heads-up to people who are further along in their skills and are looking for more advanced techniques. It isn't a "this is hard" warning. It just means that as you get better in Photoshop, these are the techniques you're going to want to consider next, because although they usually include more steps and take a little longer, they provide more professional results (even though the difference may be subtle).

Me: Is this book for Windows users, Mac users, or both?

Me: Because Photoshop is identical on Windows and on the Mac, the book is designed for both platforms. However, the keyboard on a PC is slightly different from the keyboard on a Mac, so anytime I give a keyboard shortcut in the book, I give both the PC and Mac keyboard shortcuts. See, I care.

Me: What would you say to people who are more advanced in their Photoshop skills?

Me: Actually, I would just tell them one thing to look out for. I wrote this book so anyone at any level of the Photoshop experience could jump right in, so if you've been using Photoshop for years, don't let it throw you that I spell everything out. For example, in the tutorials, rather than writing "Open Curves" (which a pro instinctively knows how to do), I usually write, "Go under the Image menu, under Adjustments, and choose Curves." That way, everybody can follow along, and this is particularly important for photographers who are just giving up film and switching to digital. Many of these traditional film photographers are brilliant, talented, amazing photographers, but since they're just now "going digital," they may not know anything about Photoshop. I didn't want to leave them out or make it harder for them, so I spell things out. I knew you'd understand.

Me: Okay, they've waited long enough. Where can they download the photos used in the book?

Me: The photos in this book come from three sources. Most of the photos I took myself over the past year, but I also asked my buddy, and fellow photographer, Dave Moser if I could use some of his wonderful work in the book as well. My third source was the great people at JupiterImages, who not only let me use some of their great royalty-free stock photos (this was especially helpful in the retouching chapter since I don't do much portraiture), but they allowed me to let my readers download low-res versions of their images that I used in the book. You can download all these photos from the book's companion website at **www.scottkelbybooks.com/cs2digitalphotographers**. Of course, the whole idea is that you'd use these techniques on your own photos, but if you want to practice on these, I won't tell anybody. By the way, if you're wondering why I chose JupiterImages, it's simple. I saw their stuff, I was really impressed with what they're doing, so I asked (okay, begged) them to let me use their royalty-free stock in the book. They've got a really interesting concept in royalty-free stock, so stop by their site (www.photos.com) and check them out. I know this sounds like a plug for JupiterImages, and it is. They didn't ask me to do it, but I'm so delighted to be using their images, I wanted to let them, and you, know.

Me: Well, Scott, this has just been great, and I have to admit, yours is the most fascinating, exciting, and insightful interview I've ever done.

Me: I knew you were going to say that.

Exposure: 1/10s | Focal Length: 105mm | Aperture Value: f/4.0

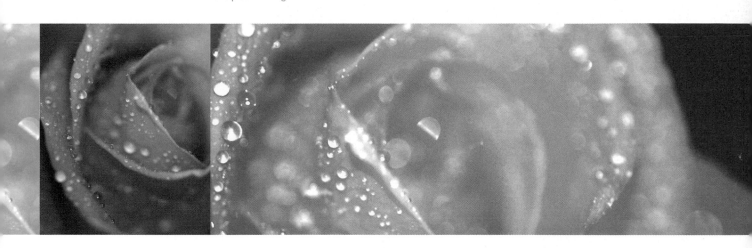

Love Can Build a Bridge
bridge essentials

Now, since the "fake title" I give each chapter is based on either a movie title, song title, or band name, the obvious name for a chapter on the new Adobe Bridge (which replaces the old File Browser) is "Bridge Over Troubled Water." However, that name stinks up the place for three reasons: (1) The song is kinda lame; (2) the "troubled water" part sounds negative; (3) the name is too obvious. And if you've read any of my books in the past, you already know that (a) I don't usually go for obvious names, (b) my chapter titles are just for fun—it's the subheads that appear below them that tell you what the chapter is really about, (c) you know that these chapter intros have little—if anything—to do with what's actually in the chapter; but, since the rest of the book is so "Step One, do this, Step Two, do that," if I don't get to write these chapter intros using my own writing "voice," I'll come unglued, and (d) you know that I like to list things using numbers and letters (like I'm doing here). Now, since I didn't use the painfully obvious "Bridge Over Troubled Water" as the title, why did I use The Judds' "Love Can Build a Bridge" as the title? I used it because it wasn't "Bridge Over Troubled Water," and honestly, that was good enough for me. Actually, I wanted to use the title *The Bridge on the River Kwai* (which is a brilliant movie), but the title was just a little too long to fit, so I went with the Judd duo instead. A lot of authors don't give you this type of inside look behind the scenes into what really goes on in the seedy world of publishing. But then, most authors' chapter intros make sense.

Saving Your Digital Negatives

Okay, I know this is the Adobe Bridge chapter, but before you even open the Bridge, you've got to save your digital negatives to CD. Don't open the photos, adjust them, choose your favorites, and then burn them to a CD; burn them now—right off the bat. These are your "digital negatives," which are no different from the negatives you'd get from a film lab after they've processed your film. By burning a CD now, before you enter the Bridge, you're creating a set of digital negatives that can never be accidentally erased or discarded—you'll always have these digital negatives. Here's how:

Step One:
On your computer's desktop, create a new blank folder (you don't have to name this folder). Now, plug your card reader (CompactFlash card, Smartcard, etc.) into your computer.

Step Two:
Double-click on your memory card's icon and locate the photos on your memory card. Shift-click the first image and the last image to select all the photos on your memory card, and then drag-and-drop them into that empty folder on your hard disk.

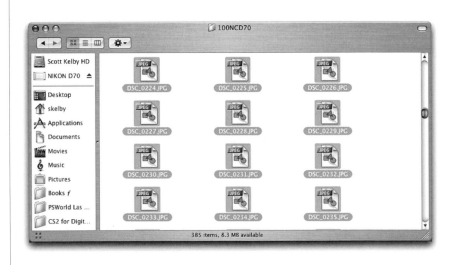

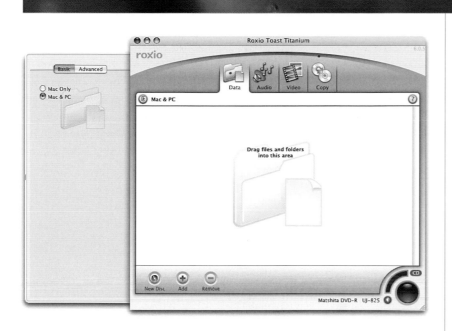

Step Three:

Insert a blank CD into your CD burner (today, it's almost impossible to buy a computer without a CD burner, but if by chance you don't have one, buy one now—it's that important). My personal favorite CD-burning software is Easy CD Creator for Windows or Roxio Toast Titanium for the Mac (its interface is shown here). Toast has become very popular, partially because its easy-to-use drag-and-drop interface is a real timesaver. Here's how it works: Launch your CD software (if it hasn't already launched), go to that folder of images on your hard disk, and then click-and-drag the whole folder into the CD data window.

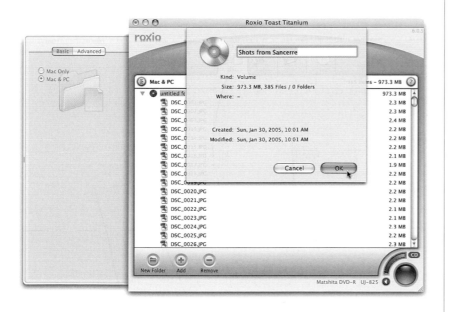

Step Four:

After your images appear in the CD software data window, double-click on the tiny CD icon in the window and give your disc a name (in Toast, a dialog appears in which you can type the disc's name). Then, simply click on the Record button and Toast does the rest, leaving you with a reliable, protected set of digital negatives. If you're the extra-careful type (read as "paranoid"), you can burn yourself another copy to keep as a second backup. There's no loss of quality, so burn as many copies as you need to feel secure (remember, just because you're paranoid, doesn't mean they're not out to get you).

Creating a Contact Sheet for Your CD Jewel Case

Okay, your CD of digital negatives is burned; but before you go any further, you can save yourself a lot of time and frustration down the road if you create a CD-jewel-case-sized contact sheet now. That way, when you pick up the CD, you'll see exactly what's on the disc before you even insert it into your computer. Luckily, the process of creating this contact sheet is automated, and after you make a few decisions on how you want your contact sheet to look, Photoshop takes it from there.

Step One:
You'll create your CD contact sheet using Photoshop's Contact Sheet II feature, so go ahead and launch Photoshop, and then go under Photoshop's File menu, under Auto-mate, and choose Contact Sheet II. You can also access the Contact Sheet II command from the Bridge by going under the Tools menu, under Photoshop, and choosing Contact Sheet II. However, choosing it there just launches Photoshop anyway, as Contact Sheet II is actually a part of Photoshop, not the Bridge. The Adobe Bridge is a separate application. (More on that later.) The Contact Sheet II dialog will appear onscreen.

Step Two:

Go under the Source Images section, select Folder in the Use pop-up menu, then click on the Choose button (or Browse button on a PC) and a navigation dialog will appear. Locate that untitled folder of photos (you know, the folder you just burned to CD in the previous tutorial) to choose those images.

Step Three:

The rest of the Contact Sheet II dialog is where you pick how you want your contact sheet to look. Under the Document section, enter the Width and Height of your jewel box cover. (The standard size is 4.75" x 4.75", but I recommend using 4.5" x 4.5"; otherwise, the contact sheet places the thumbnails too close to the edge. By making it ¹/₄" smaller, as you'll see later, you can add ¹/₄" of white space around it, making it look much better.) For the Resolution field, I usually choose a low resolution of 150 ppi because the thumbnails wind up being so small they don't need to be a high resolution (and the command runs faster with low-res images). I leave the Mode as RGB Color (the default), and I choose to Flatten All Layers; that way I don't end up with a large, multilayered Photoshop document. I just want a document that I can print once and then delete.

Continued

The Thumbnails section is perhaps the most important part of this dialog because this is where you choose the layout. Luckily, Adobe put a preview box on the far-right side of the dialog, where little gray boxes represent how your thumbnails will look. Change the number of Rows and Columns (try setting them both at 6), and this live preview will give you an idea of how your layout will look.

Then, at the bottom of the dialog, you can decide if you want to have Photoshop print the file's name below each thumbnail. I strongly recommend leaving this feature turned on. Here's why: One day you may have to go back to this CD looking for a photo. The thumbnail will let you see if the photo you're looking for is on this CD (so you've narrowed your search a bit), but if there's no name below the image, you'll have to launch Photoshop CS2 and use the Bridge to search through every photo to locate the exact one you saw on the cover. However, if you spot the photo on the cover and see its name, then you just have to search your hard disk (or in the Bridge) for that file's name. Believe me, it's one of those things that will keep you from ripping your hair out by the roots, one by one.

There's also a Font pop-up menu for choosing from a handful of fonts for your thumbnail captions, and then you choose a size from the Font Size pop-up menu (try 6 points for best results). The font choices are somewhat lame, but believe me, they're better than what was offered in the original Contact Sheet, so count your blessings.

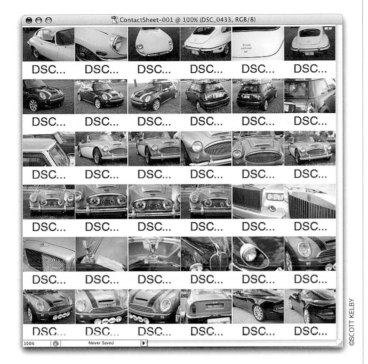

TIP: When you're choosing a font size for your contact sheet's thumbnail captions, make sure you decrease the default Font Size setting of 12 points to something significantly lower, like 6 points. You'll need to do this because of the long file names assigned to the images from your digital camera (otherwise, you'll only see the first three letters of the file name, making the contact sheet worthless, like the one shown here). So how small should you make your type? That depends. The more thumbnails you're fitting on your contact sheet, the smaller you'll need to make the font size.

Step Four:
Now it's time to let 'er rip! With all your settings in place, just click OK. Within a minute or two, you'll have a contact sheet. But notice how tight the thumbnails are to the top and side edges? That's what I was talking about earlier when I said it's better to make your contact sheet's size slightly smaller than you need, so later (actually, in the next step), you can add some white space around it, which makes it less crowded, easier to use, and it just plain looks better.

Continued

Step Five:

Here's where we add that ¼" of space back in, allowing some "breathing room" around the thumbnails in the contact sheet. Go under the Image menu and choose Canvas Size. When the dialog appears, ensure the Relative checkbox is on, enter 0.25 inches for the Width and Height fields, set the Canvas Extension Color pop-up menu to White, then click OK.

Step Six:

Here's the contact sheet now, after adding ¼" of white space around the top, bottom, and sides. Looks much better, doesn't it? (Contrast this with the previous contact sheets and you'll see the difference.)

This is the CD with these two shots. The top one is DCS_0473.JPG. The bottom one is DSC_0520.JPG

Step Seven:

This is more like a tip than a step, but a number of photographers add a second contact sheet to make it even easier to track down the exact image they're looking for. It's based on the premise that in every roll (digital or otherwise), there's usually one or two key shots—two really good "keepers" that will normally be the ones you'll go searching for on this disc. So what they do is make an additional contact sheet with just the two or three key shots on that CD, which they'll use either as the cover or the inside cover of their CD jewel case. They include a description of the shots, which makes finding the right image even easier. *Note:* If you're only using two or three images, you don't need to use Contact Sheet II— you can just create this second cover yourself by dragging the images into a blank Photoshop document using the Move tool (V) and adding file names, descriptions, etc., with the Type tool (T).

Step Eight:

Here's the final result, after the contact sheet has been printed and fitted into your CD jewel case.

Bridge Basics

Okay, we've backed up our originals and burned them to CD, we've created a contact sheet to keep track of all our images on that CD; so now we're going to open the images right from the CD using the Adobe Bridge (which is technically a separate application that we can use to sort and categorize our digital camera images). If you're familiar with the File Browser from previous versions, it's an evolution of it, but it has more features, and best of all, also manages images for use in other Adobe applications.

Accessing the Bridge:

There are three ways to access Photoshop CS2's Bridge: (1) In the Photoshop interface, click on the Go to Bridge icon on the far-right corner of the Options Bar, immediately to the left of where the Palette Well starts. (2) You can go under the File menu and choose Browse. (3) You can bring it up with the keyboard shortcut Command-Option-O (PC: Control-Alt-O).

©SCOTT KELBY

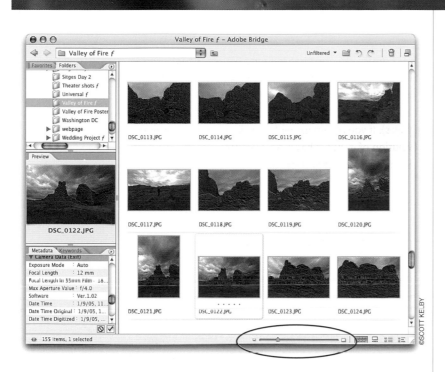

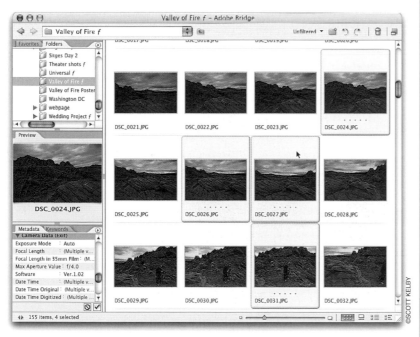

A thumbnail factory:

When you click on a folder of images (or a memory card, CD of images, etc.), the Bridge automatically displays full-color thumbnails of any photos or subfolders it finds. The Bridge is generally pretty quick about displaying these thumbnails, but the more images you have, the longer it will take to render the images. Also, it builds thumbnails from the top down, so even though you see thumbnails in your main window, if you scroll down, the thumbnails farther down could still be rendering—so you might have to be a little patient. To change the size of your thumbnails, drag the Thumbnail Size slider near the bottom right of the window area: dragging to the left makes thumbnails smaller, dragging to the right makes them larger.

Opening photos in Photoshop:

If you see a thumbnail of a photo you'd like to open in Photoshop, just double-click on it and it will open right up. (*Note:* You can also open it by double-clicking on the larger preview that appears in the Preview palette to the left of the thumbnails.) You can open multiple photos at the same time by clicking on the first photo you want to open, pressing-and-holding the Command (PC: Control) key, and then clicking on any other photos. Once you've got them all selected, just double-click on any one of them, and they'll all open in Photoshop, one after another. You can also open entire contiguous rows by clicking on the first thumbnail in a row, holding the Shift key, clicking on the last photo in a row, and then double-clicking on any selected thumbnail.

TIP: You can navigate from thumbnail to thumbnail by using the Arrow keys on your keyboard.

Navigating to Your Photos Using the Bridge

The Adobe Bridge has five built-in "layouts" for different working styles (Adobe calls them "workspaces"), and the default Bridge layout is divided into two main sections: (1) the main window that displays thumbnail versions of your photos; (2) a Panel area to the left of that (with palettes for navigating to your photos, for seeing larger previews of your thumbnails, and for viewing metadata and adding keywords). We'll look at this default layout and special built-in workspaces that have been designed to make navigating to your images even easier.

Navigating to your photos:

The left side of the Bridge is called the Panel area (although they're really palettes, they're just not "floating palettes"—like the rest of the palettes in Photoshop—because they have to stay within the Panel area). The top-left palette is the Favorites, which is designed to give you direct access to your most-used applications and image folders. Nested right behind this palette is the Folders palette, which you use to locate photos on your digital camera's memory card, on your hard drive, on a CD of images, a network drive—you name it. The idea behind this palette is simple: It gives you access to your digital camera images without having to leave the Bridge. To access the photos inside a folder from here, just click once on the folder.

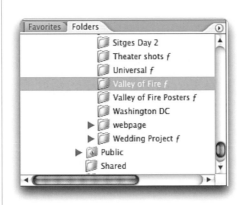

Saving your favorite folders:

If you find yourself going to a particular folder fairly often, you can save that folder as a "favorite" by either Control-clicking (PC: Right-clicking) on the folder (in the Folders palette or in the thumbnail window) and choosing Add to Favorites from the contextual menu that appears, or you can just drag-and-drop that folder from the thumbnail window right into the bottom area of the Favorites palette. Once you've saved a favorite folder, just click on it in your list of Favorites to get to it.

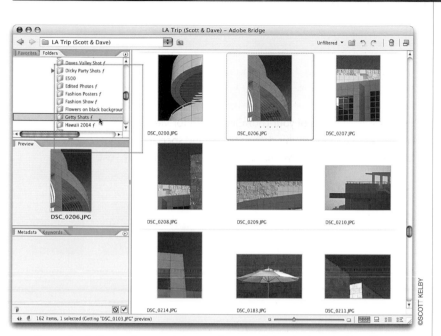

©SCOTT KELBY

Here we're clicking on the second photo at the top and dragging it to the Getty Shots folder on the left (you can see the square outline of the thumbnail while dragging it).

Moving photos from folder to folder:

Another nice navigation feature of the Bridge is that you can use it to move photos from one folder to another. You do this by dragging the thumbnail of the photo you want to move, then dropping that photo into any folder that appears in the Folders palette (when you move the dragged photo over a folder, a highlighted rectangle appears letting you know that you've targeted that folder). That photo will now be removed from the currently selected folder and placed into the folder you dragged-and-dropped it into.

TIP: If you press-and-hold Option (PC: Alt) as you drag, instead of moving your photo, the Bridge will place a duplicate of your photo into that folder, rather than moving the original.

The ideal workspace for navigation:

Adobe has pre-designed four workspaces that set the Bridge up in a configuration that works best for certain tasks. If you're going to be searching for photos, there's a workspace you'll want to know about: the File Navigator (surprisingly enough), and it's found by going under the Bridge's Window menu, under Workspace, and choosing File Navigator (or you can just press Command-F3 [PC: Control-F3]). This workspace reconfigures the Bridge with just the Favorites and Folders palettes visible on the left, making it easy to navigate and save folders as favorites.

Continued

The Lightbox workspace:

This workspace hides all the panels on the left side from view (which expands the main thumbnail viewing area), filling the Bridge with a digital lightbox that displays photo thumbnails in your currently selected folder. This is a great layout when you're sorting through photos, deciding which stay and which get deleted. You can choose this workspace from the Window menu, under Workspace, and select Lightbox, or simply press Command-F2 (PC: Control-F2).

TIP: By the way, if you ever want to quickly hide all the panels on the left side of the Bridge, just click on the double-headed arrow in the bottom left-hand corner of the Bridge.

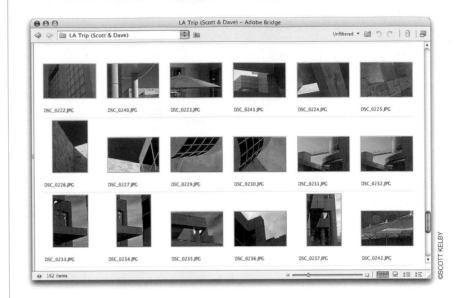

The Metadata Focus workspace:

This workspace puts the Metadata palette front and center by expanding its viewing area, placing it squarely in the center of the Panel area and shrinking the size of the thumbnail area. (After all, the focus here is viewing and editing your images' embedded metadata and/or adding keywords to make your photos easier to find when searching for them.) You choose this workspace from the Window menu, under Workspace, and select Metadata Focus, or press Command-F4 (PC: Control-F4).

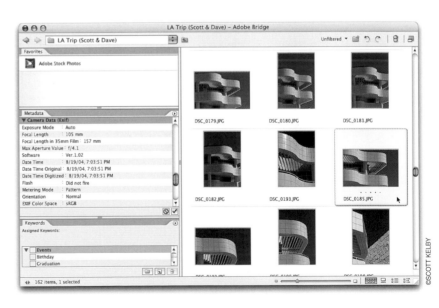

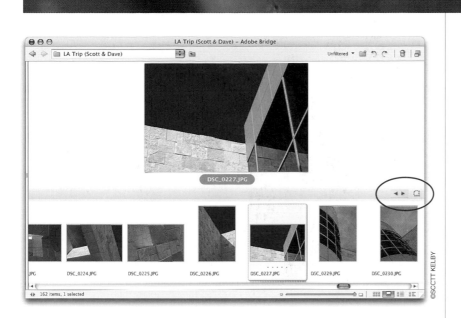

©SCOTT KELBY

The Filmstrip Focus workspace:

This workspace isn't so much about sorting—it's about viewing your photos—and it gives you a view that's similar to Windows XP's Filmstrip folder view, which places a row of thumbnails across the bottom, with a large preview of any selected thumbnail on top (by the way, if you'd prefer to have the thumbnails appear along the right side of the window, rather than the bottom, just click on the little odd-shaped icon [with dots in the shape of a capital "L"] in the bottom-right side of the preview area). You can move from thumbnail to thumbnail (kind of like a slide show) by clicking on the left/right arrow icons along the bottom right of the preview. You can choose this workspace from the Window menu, under Workspace, and select Filmstrip Focus, or just press Command-F5 (PC: Control-F5).

Make your own custom workspace:

Although Adobe ships Photoshop CS2 with four built-in workspaces (well, there are technically five if you count the ability to return to the Default Workspace by pressing Command-F1 [PC: Control-F1]), you can also make your own workspace. Stack palettes where you want them, resize your palettes' Panel area (by dragging the center tab on the divider bar left or right), and choose your desired thumbnail size from the Thumbnail Size slider in the bottom right-hand corner of the Bridge. When everything looks the way you want it, go under the Window menu, under Workspace, and choose Save Workspace. A dialog will appear in which you can name your workspace and give it a Function key shortcut. Click Save and your custom workspace will appear in the Workspace submenu.

Continued

A hidden advantage:

If you'd prefer to have a smaller version of the Bridge, you're in luck—just click on the Switch to Compact Mode icon located in the top-right corner of the Bridge (it's the second icon from the left), and the Bridge will literally shrink in size, leaving only your thumbnails visible (much like the Lightbox view). The "hidden advantage" of this workspace is that it "floats," meaning it's always floating in front of whichever applications are open (so if you're working in Photoshop CS2 or another Creative Suite application, the Bridge will appear just like a floating palette). By the way, if you like the Compact Mode but don't want this "floating" feature, turn off Compact Window Always On Top from the Bridge's flyout menu (it's the right-facing arrow in the top-right corner).

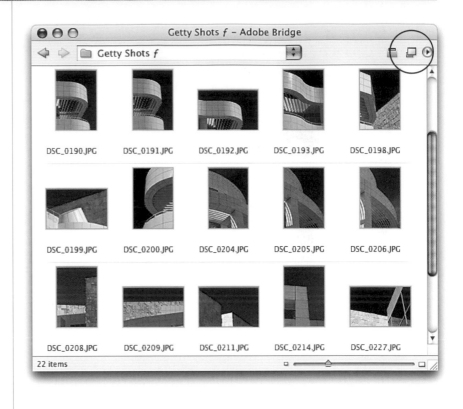

Even more compact:

If you like Compact Mode, you're gonna love Ultra-Compact Mode (believe it or not, that's it's real name—I love it!). First, switch to Compact Mode and then click on the Switch to Ultra-Compact Mode icon (it's the first icon in the top-right corner). This hides the thumbnail area, leaving just the drop-down navigation menu, the viewing mode icons, and an arrow so you can reach the Bridge's fly-out menu. I guess this mode is for people who want the Bridge temporarily out of the way, without closing it or actually minimizing it (operating-system-wise).

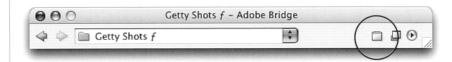

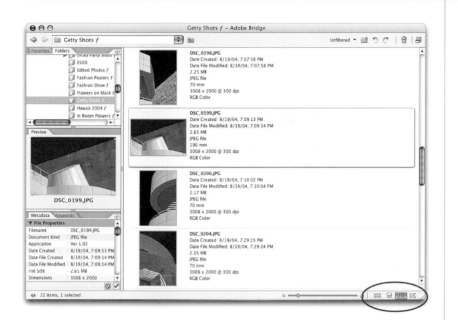

Other viewing options:

Besides the built-in workspaces (and ones you create yourself), there are some other views that you might find useful. For example, there's a view that gives you a photo thumbnail and some of the EXIF metadata on that photo. You access it by going under the Bridge's View menu and choosing Details.

TIP: If you just want to change only the thumbnail area (not the whole layout of the Bridge itself), check out the four icons in the bottom right-hand corner of the Bridge. The first (from the left) gives you the Lightbox thumbnail view; the second is Filmstrip Focus view; the third is Details; and the fourth is Versions and Alternate view. (The latter is only available in conjunction with Version Cue, Adobe's slick little Creative Suite application that helps network users find and track multiple versions of an image.) By the way, you can toggle through these different views by pressing Command-\ (PC: Control-\) (Backslash key).

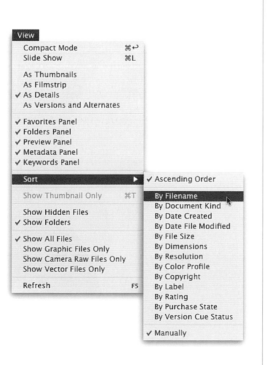

Sorting by file name, etc.:

Besides all the manual sorting (or using ratings, as you'll learn later), you have a wide variety of other ways to sort your photos by going under the View menu, under Sort, and choosing from the long list of options, which includes sorting alphabetically by name, by file type, by document size—you name it. Just choose an option from the list and your photos will immediately re-sort to your selection.

Customizing the Look of Your Bridge

Back in Photoshop CS, you had little control over the look of the File Browser, but with the Adobe Bridge, you've got a number of options for personalizing the look and feel. But not only that, you also have more control over what information will be displayed. Here's how to set up your Bridge your way:

Setting your background:
You have three basic choices for the background color that will appear behind your thumbnails: black, white, or some shade of gray. To set your background color, go under the Bridge menu (on a Mac) or the Edit menu (on a PC) and choose Preferences. When the Preferences dialog appears, with General selected (in the list on the left side of the dialog), you'll see the Background slider under the Thumbnails section. Just drag the slider where you want it (I chose a medium gray), and then click OK.

Which info do you want?
By default, the name of each file is displayed below the thumbnail, but you can add up to three additional lines of information (which are gathered from the EXIF data embedded in the file by your camera, plus the metadata added by Photoshop and the Bridge itself). First, press Command-K (PC: Control-K) to open the Preferences, and under the Thumbnails section in the General category, turn on the checkbox beside each of the three lines of info you want to add. Then, from the pop-up menus, choose which type of information you want to appear on each line.

TIP: So you can add up to three lines of extra information below your thumbnails, but what if you want to see just the thumbnails, and temporarily hide all that extra information? Just press Command-T (PC: Control-T) and only the thumbnails will be displayed. This is a handy shortcut, because all those extra lines of info take up space, and when you're displaying three extra lines, plus the file's name and perhaps even a rating, fewer thumbnails fit in the same amount of space.

Adding more panels:

Although the Bridge is designed to have three palette panels visible on the left-hand side, you can actually have more (or fewer). To add an additional panel to the Bridge, you first have to go up to the View menu and choose the palettes you want visible. Then, click directly on the palette's tab and drag slowly upward (or downward, if your palette is at the top of the Panel area) until a thin bar highlights between the two currently visible palettes. When you release your mouse button, a new panel section will appear. This way you can have all five palettes visible all the time (if that's your "thing").

Getting Bigger Previews

The Preview palette in the Adobe Bridge is designed to give you a larger preview of the thumbnail images that you click on in the main window. Although the Preview palette looks like a one-trick pony, there are a few hidden little features that can make it a much more useful tool.

Bigger previews are just a double-click away:

When you're in the Default Workspace (found in the View menu under Workspace), you'll see the Preview palette in the middle of the Panel area—and the preview is so small you're probably wondering why Adobe included it at all. It's because there's more to it than meets the eye (well, at least at first). You can make the preview much larger by double-clicking—not on the Preview tab—but instead directly on the Folders (or Favorites) tab above it. This will collapse (hide) the Folders palette (and the nested Favorites palette) so that only their tabs are visible, expanding the viewing area of the Preview palette upward. If you need the preview even bigger, then double-click on the Metadata (or Keywords) tab in the bottom left of the Panel area to collapse them, expanding the Preview palette even more. This works particularly well when you're viewing a portrait-oriented photo (tall rather than wide). However, when you have a photo in landscape orientation, to get the preview much larger you'll also have to expand the width of the Panel area by clicking on the center tab on the divider bar (along the right side of the Panel area) and dragging it to the right. (*Note:* To make any collapsed palette visible again, just double-click directly on its tab name.)

The Preview palette at default size

Collapsing the Favorites and Folders palettes

All the palettes collapsed except Preview

The view with both the top and bottom palettes collapsed and the divider bar dragged to the right to accommodate a photo in landscape orientation

The Metadata palette gives you access to information that's embedded into your photo by your digital camera at the moment you take the shot. By default, nested with the Metadata palette is the Keywords palette, which enables you to search for specific images by assigning keywords (that may sound complicated, but it's actually pretty simple). We'll start here with a simple look at how to access the embedded background information on your photos using the Metadata palette. (The next chapter has more in-depth info on using and editing metadata.)

Getting Info on Your Photos (Called Metadata)

Metadata	
▼ **File Properties**	
Filename	: DSC_0172a.jpg
Document Kind	: JPEG image
Application	: Adobe Photoshop CS2 (9.0x1...
Date Created	: 9/27/04, 11:24:32 AM
Date File Created	: Today, 3:45:47 PM
Date File Modified	: Today, 3:45:48 PM
File Size	: 491 KB
Dimensions	: 480 x 722
Resolution	: 72 dpi
Bit Depth	: 8
Color Mode	: RGB Color
Color Profile	: sRGB IEC61966-2.1
▶ **IPTC Core**	
▼ **Camera Data (Exif)**	
Exposure Bias Value	: +0.33
Exposure Mode	: Auto
Exposure Program	: Normal
Focal Length	: 60 mm
Focal Length in 35mm Film	: 90 mm
Max Aperture Value	: f/4.4
Software	: Adobe Photoshop CS2 (9.0x1...
Date Time	: Today, 3:45:47 PM
Date Time Original	: 9/27/04, 11:24:32 AM
Date Time Digitized	: 9/27/04, 11:24:32 AM
Flash	: Did not fire
Metering Mode	: Pattern
Orientation	: Normal
EXIF Color Space	: sRGB
Custom Rendered	: Normal Process
White Balance	: Auto
Digital Zoom Ratio	: 100 %
Scene Capture Type	: Standard
Gain Control	: 0
Contrast	: 0
Saturation	: 0
Sharpness	: Normal
Sensing Method	: One-chip sensor
File Source	: Digital Camera
Make	: NIKON CORPORATION
Model	: NIKON D70

Embedded info on your photo:
When you take a photo with today's digital cameras, at the moment you take the shot, the camera automatically embeds loads of information about what just took place—things like the make and model of the camera, the time the photo was taken, the exposure setting, the f-stop, shutter speed, etc. (This info is called EXIF data.) Once you bring the digital photo into Photoshop, more information is embedded into the photo (stuff like the file name, when it was last edited, the file format it was saved in, its physical dimensions, color mode, etc.). All this embedded info comes under the heading "metadata," and that's why it appears in the Metadata palette. At the top of the palette, under the heading File Properties, is the info Photoshop embeds into your file. The next category down is IPTC Core metadata, which is where you can embed your own customized info (stuff like copyright, credits, etc.) into the photo (this is covered in detail in the next chapter). The Camera Data (EXIF) category displays data embedded by your camera. If you find yourself using most of this information, you might be a...(hint: rhymes with "seek").

Finding Your Photos Fast by Adding Keywords

By default, nested with the Metadata palette is the Keywords palette. Keywords are important, because once you've applied one or more keywords to a photo, it's that much easier to find that photo again by using the Adobe Bridge's Find (search) function. For example, if you shoot flowers, you can add the keyword "calla lily" to every shot of a calla lily. Then, if later you wanted to quickly locate every shot you've taken of calla lilies—you just type "calla lily" in the Find dialog and all your calla lily photos appear in seconds. Did it seem like I just used the words "calla lily" a lot?

Step One:

To get to the Keywords palette, you have to first choose a workspace that enables the Panel area on the left side of the dialog, so go under the Window menu, under Workspace, and choose Reset to Default Workspace (or I guess you could choose the File Navigator workspace, then go under the Bridge's View menu and choose Keywords Panel, but that just seems like so much work). Now go to the bottom-left side of the Bridge and click on the Keywords tab to make the Keywords palette visible.

Step Two:

In the Keywords palette, you'll see a list of default keywords for some of the most common topics (for example, there's a set called Events, and within that are keywords for Birthday, Graduation, and Wedding). So, if you're working with photos from your child's birthday, you don't have to create a keyword—the keyword "Birthday" is already there waiting for you. There's a People set too, and if your kids are named Matthew or Ryan, you're in luck! However, my son's name is Ram Chip (Ram Chip Kelby, to be exact). Okay, his mother wouldn't let me name him that, but come on—would Ram Chip be a great name for a Photoshop user's kid or what?

Step Three:

Now, let's say you're lucky enough to have a kid named Ryan, and as luck would have it, you have photos visible in the Bridge and Ryan is in some of them. To tag these photos with the keyword "Ryan," hold the Command key (PC: Control key) and click on all the photos that have Ryan in them (or Shift-click the first and last images to select contiguous rows). Then, click on the checkbox that appears before the keyword Ryan (under the People category). This will bring up a scary-looking warning dialog telling you that you've selected multiple files (sure, it's risky, but go ahead). Click on the Yes button, and all those photos are instantly tagged with the invisible keyword Ryan. However, if your kid isn't named Ryan, this can be somewhat embarrassing.

Step Four:

So what if your kid isn't named Ryan? You're out of luck. This feature only works for photos of kids named Ryan or Matthew (kidding). Just go to the Keywords palette, Control-click (PC: Right-click) directly on the name "Ryan," and from the contextual menu that appears, choose Rename; then type in your kid's name instead (Ram Chip?) and press the Return (PC: Enter) key to lock in your name change.

Step Five:

Once you've added keywords to all of the photos that contain your kid, the hard part is done. Now you can use the keywords to find those photos—and just those photos—later. By the way, if you want to delete the default sets that Adobe put there, just click on the topic (like Events or People) and click on the Trash icon at the bottom of the Keywords palette. You can delete individual keywords the same way.

Continued

Step Six:

Okay, your keywords are assigned; now it's time to put them to use. Click on a folder of photos you want to search within, then press Command-F (PC: Control-F) to bring up the Bridge's Find (search) feature. When the dialog appears, go under the Criteria section and choose Keywords in the first pop-up menu (otherwise, by default the Bridge will only search the file's name, which may be something as descriptive as DCS_0434.NEF).

Step Seven:

From the second pop-up menu in the Criteria section, choose Contains, and then in the field to the right, enter your keyword (in this case, "Ram Chip"). Click Find and within a few seconds, just the photos that have been tagged with the keyword Ram Chip will appear in your thumbnail window (actually, by default they open in a separate browser window, but if you want them to open in the same window, replacing what's being viewed there now, just deselect the checkbox for Show Find Results in a New Browser Window). The new photo thumbnails are, in fact, the results of your search. In this instance, we searched in a particular folder of photos, but you can perform this search on your main folder of photos (or your whole hard disk if you want). In the Find dialog, just click on the Browse button to navigate to the folder you want to search. (Note: Be sure to turn on the Include All Subfolders checkbox so the Bridge searches the folders inside your main folder.)

©DAVE MOSER

Step Eight:

Okay, so all your photos appear in the thumbnail window. Now what? Well, you can edit them, sort them, etc., but if you think you'd like to have instant access to this exact group of photos again, you can create a "collection." To create a collection of just these photos, click on the Save As Collection button in the top-right corner of the thumbnail window. Name your collection in the resulting dialog and click Save. Now you can access this group of photos by clicking on the Collections icon in the Favorites palette. The name and date your collection was created will be visible with its icon. *Note:* Collections update "live," meaning whenever you assign criteria to a new image that matches the criteria you've saved in a collection, it will automatically add that new image to the collection. So if you give a new image the keyword Ram Chip, that image will be added to your saved Ram Chip collection.

Step Nine:

Now that you know how to use (and rename) the default sets of keywords, creating your own sets of keywords should be a no-brainer. Just click on the New Keyword Set icon at the bottom of the Keywords palette (it looks like a folder). The category will appear in your Keywords palette with its name already highlighted. Give your category a name (in this case, try "British Cars"), then press the Return (PC: Enter) key to lock in your name. Now, click on the category British Cars, and then click on the New Keyword icon at the bottom of the palette to add keywords to your British Car category. You name this keyword the same way you did the category. To add more keywords, just remember to click on the category first, then click on the New Keyword icon.

Renaming Individual Photos

If you want to rename an individual photo, it's fairly straightforward. Now there is also a way to actually rename every photo at once with names that make sense (to you anyway); but that, my friends, is in the next chapter. For now, here's how to rename one thumbnail image at a time (this is a great technique to employ if you charge by the hour).

Step One:
It's hard to imagine why someone wouldn't like such a descriptive name as DSC_1053.JPG, but if you're one of those people who enjoys names that actually describe what's happening in the photo, here's how it's done: With a thumbnail selected, click directly on the photo's name (in the thumbnail window) and the name will highlight, ready for you to type in a more descriptive name (like "DSC_1054"…kidding).

Step Two:
Once you've typed in your new name, press the Return (PC: Enter) key and the thumbnail updates with your new-and-improved name. (Here I changed the name of the file DSC_1053.JPG to Barcelona Daisies.JPG.)

©SCOTT KELBY

Rotating photos within the Adobe Bridge is as easy as clicking one button. However, when you rotate photos within the Bridge itself, you're only really rotating the thumbnail. This is handy, because when you're sorting photos with a portrait orientation (tall rather than wide), you want to be able to see them upright to make a sorting judgment call; but you have a separate decision to make if you want the actual photo rotated—not just the thumbnail. Here's how to do both:

Rotating Photos

Rotating thumbnails:

Rotating a thumbnail is a total no-brainer: Just click on the thumbnail you want to rotate, then click on one of the circular arrow rotation icons in the top-right corner of the Bridge. The left arrow icon rotates counterclockwise; the right arrow icon rotates clockwise. You can also use the shortcut Command-[(PC: Control-[) (Left Bracket key) to rotate counterclockwise, and Command-] (PC: Control-]) (Right Bracket key) to rotate clockwise.

Rotating the actual photo:

When you rotate a thumbnail, you're doing just that—the photo doesn't get rotated until you actually open it in Photoshop (go look in the image's folder on your hard drive, and you'll see from the file's thumbnail that the actual photo isn't rotated). So if you really want to rotate the original photo, double-click on the photo in the Bridge and the image will open in Photoshop with the rotation applied. Now you can choose Save from the File menu to make the rotation permanent.

Sorting and Arranging Your Photos

Ah, finally, we get to the fun part—sorting your photos. Adobe has been trying different sorting methods since they introduced the File Browser. Back in Photoshop 7, you had to rank each photo—and even then you didn't necessarily get them in the exact order you wanted. In CS, you could flag photos, and then just view the flagged images. Well, in Photoshop CS2, Adobe's taking things up a notch with a new rating scheme that's a mix of the best of the Photoshop 7 and CS versions, with some nice new bells and whistles.

Method One: Drag-and-Drop

Sorting is based on the simple premise that in every digital roll you have some good shots, some "just-okay" shots, and some completely lame shots (or "losers," as we call them). Generally, people want the good shots to appear at the top of the Bridge's thumbnail window, followed by the just-okay shots and the lame shots (if you keep them at all) at the bottom. You can do this manually by simply clicking-and-dragging the thumbnails into the order you want. For example, if you want a thumbnail in the second row to appear in the top row, just click on its thumbnail and drag it to that spot. A thick, vertical bar lets you know where the dragged thumbnail will land. You can drag photos around just like you would on your own personal lightbox, putting photos into the exact order you want them. Sorting this way works great when you're working with a small number of photos (like 24 or fewer), but when you start to sort a 1-GB memory card, dragging them around gets incredibly cumbersome—that's why now there's an improved "rating" system.

©SCOTT KELBY

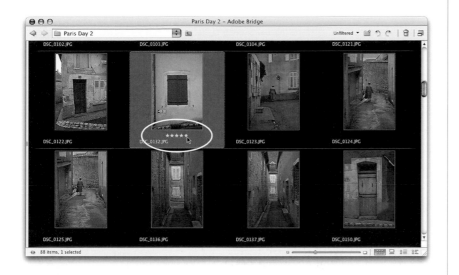

Method Two: Star Ratings

When you're sorting a large number of images, try rating them (rather than dragging them around). If you're an iPod user, you're probably familiar with how you rate songs on your iPod (or in iTunes), and this is very similar. You can rate your photos (from one star to five stars) by first clicking on the photo you want to rate. Five tiny dots will be visible directly beneath your thumbnail. Click-and-hold on the first dot and a star will appear. Drag to the right to add up to five stars. That's it—you've rated the photo. (By the way, you can just click directly on the dot you want; you don't have to drag.) You can also rate by clicking on the photo and pressing Command-5 (PC: Control-5), -4, -3, etc. To rate multiple photos at once (which is what you want to do), Command-click (PC: Control-click) on your best images, give just one of them a five-star rating, and all the other selected photos will receive the same rating. (*Note:* Files saved as read-only cannot be rated.)

Putting these ratings to use:

Once you've rated your photos, you can sort them fast. For example, to see just your best shots, click on the word "Unfiltered" in the upper right-hand corner of the thumbnail window. A drop-down menu will appear in which you can choose Show 5 Stars—only your five-star photos will be displayed. You can also use the keyboard shortcut Command-Option-5 (PC: Control-Alt-5) to see just your five-star rated images (or use the shortcut but press 4, 3, etc., to see those star ratings).

Continued

Method Three: Labeling Photos

Let's say you've rated your most recent import of photos, and you rated 37 of those photos with five stars. Within that five-star grouping, aren't there some that are better than others? I mean, isn't there a *best* five-star photo? And a second best? So, how do you separate your best five-star images from the pack? Why you'd label them with a color, of course (that way you can have a *red* five-star image!). Seriously, imagine how good a photo would have to be to be a *red* five-star photo. In fact, if you do rate one as a red five-star, a pop-up menu appears where you can choose Submit to National Geographic (kidding).

Step One:

To add color labels, Control-click (PC: Right-click) on your selected photos, and when the contextual menu appears, you'll see a submenu at the bottom called Label. Choose the label color you want. The label colors go from Red (which I assume would be the best) to Yellow, Green, Blue, and Purple. By the way, all the label colors have keyboard shortcuts (Command/Control-6, -7, etc.) except Purple (the label of shame), which has no shortcut. It should only be used for your worst best photos.

Step Two:

Once you've filtered your thumbnails (so only your five-star photos are showing), click on the word "Filtered" (notice it changed from "Unfiltered"). This time choose Show Red Label, and only the five-star, red-label photos (the best of the best) will be visible.

Here I lazily lowered the rating from five to four stars.

Lazy rating:

If you've rated a photo, and then realize that it doesn't have the proper rating, don't go back and drag over the little dots (that's so, I dunno, manual). Instead, to increase the rating of a selected image, just press Command-. (PC: Control-.) (that's the Period key by the way). If you want to make sure your photo never gets on the cover of a national magazine, decrease its rating by pressing Command-, (PC: Control-,) (oh, and that's the Comma key). *Note:* Another reason I called this "lazy rating" is that not only are you being lazy, but the Bridge is acting lazy as well, because it seems to change the rating at a much slower pace.

Clearing your ratings:

If you've applied a rating to a photo and you want to remove the rating, just click on the thumbnail and press Command-0 (zero) (PC: Control-0 [zero]). However, if this photo is labeled, as well as rated, this will not remove the label color. To do that, you have to Control-click (PC: Right-click) on the selected thumbnail, go under the Label submenu, and choose No Label. Now, why doesn't the No Label option have a shortcut? Perhaps it's the same reason Purple doesn't have a shortcut. These designations are for lame photos—photos other people take—not us, right? Right!

TIP: Although you can't change the label colors, you can change their names by going to the Preferences dialog (under the Bridge menu on a Mac; the Edit menu on a PC) and choosing Labels from the categories on the left of the dialog. Now you can just type in your new custom label names beside each color.

Continued

Live rating done backwards:

You'll probably find that it's helpful to sort your photos by rating. That way your five-star photos show up at the top of your Bridge, followed by the four-star, three-star, and so on, with the real dogs (the one-star photos) appearing at the bottom. Well, this actually takes two steps because of a default setting that just seems sort of backwards to me (maybe it's just me), but here's what you need to do: First, go under the View menu, under Sort, and choose By Rating. Now, your thumbnails are sorted according to the ratings you've applied to your photos, but here's the catch: By default, your five-star photos will actually appear at the bottom. Why? Because for some reason, by default, the Ascending Order sorting option is turned on. All you have to do is turn it off (it's at the top of the Sort submenu under the View menu). Now your five-star photos will appear up top, followed by your four-star, etc.

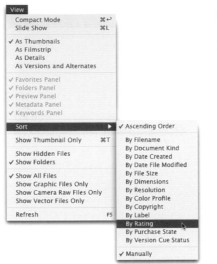

First choose to sort by rating

Then turn off Ascending Order

When you need to refresh:

If you plug in a memory card or insert a CD, it often shows up in the Folders palette on the left side of the Bridge. I say often, because if the Bridge is already open when you insert the card, it doesn't automatically update to show the card. But if the Folders palette is visible and you don't see your card (or CD, etc.), then just choose Refresh from the Folders palette's flyout menu (in its top-right corner). The Bridge will update your Folders palette to show your card.

Other Thumbnail Tips

There are a few little tips that aren't big enough for their own tutorial but are handy enough that I felt they needed to be included:

Selecting your unselected photos:

Let's say you've got six photos selected—meaning you've Command-clicked (PC: Control-clicked) on them. If you decided you want to select everything *but* those six, you can go under the Edit menu and choose Invert Selection.

Duplicating files:

Want to quickly duplicate any file? Just click on its thumbnail and press Command-D (PC: Control-D). You'll see the thumbnail of this duplicate appear in the Bridge next to the original (it adds the word "copy" to the file name so you'll be able to tell it apart from the original). To duplicate multiple files, just select them all first, and then use the shortcut.

Opening from your hard disk:

If you're working on your computer and you run across a folder of photos you'd like to open in the Bridge, just drag-and-drop the folder right into the Preview palette; the photos in that folder will open in the Bridge.

Deleting Files from within the Bridge

If you've backed up your digital negatives to a CD for safekeeping, of course you're going to want to delete shots that are terribly out of focus, etc., but beyond that, is there really a reason to keep one-star files on your computer? They just take up drive space and otherwise impede the national economy, so you might as well delete them and move on with your life. Here's a couple of ways to do just that:

Best Option:

If you burned a CD when you first inserted your memory card (and I know you did, because now you know how important it is to keep your digital negatives safely stored), then you can delete any photo from the Bridge that you don't want. This is as easy as clicking on the offending thumbnail and pressing Command-Delete (PC: Control-Backspace). You'll get a warning dialog telling you that if you continue this madness (by clicking OK), Photoshop will actually move this file from the folder where it resides and put it into the Trash (or Recycling Bin) until you choose to empty the Trash/Bin.

Next Best Option:

Another way to delete a file is to click on it, and then click on the Trash icon up in the Bridge's Options Bar.

Least Best Option:

And of course, there is (as always) the slow way—go under the Bridge's File menu and choose Move to Trash (or Send to Recycle Bin on a Windows PC).

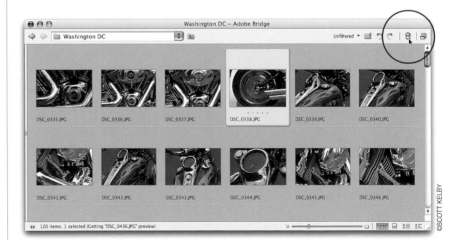

Give Me
the Bridge
advanced bridge techniques

Ah, you're back for more. I'm proud of you. Most people stop reading my chapter intros after Chapter 1, but not you my friend. You're not one of "them." You're one of us. You're edgy. An outsider. You don't follow the crowd. You're promiscuous and ambidextrous. You're synthetic yet not overly tolerant of lactose. I really have no idea what I'm saying here, yet you keep reading. You're my kind of people (meaning, you have multiple personalities). So, what is this chapter about? It's about advanced techniques for using the Adobe Bridge. A lot of people will be satisfied with just learning the basics, the essential stuff in Chapter 1. But you're not one of them, are you? You can't be constrained by normal conventions. You're a breed apart. (Here we go again.) You're elusive yet easy to find. You're a patriotic anarchist. You're loose with money. You're alluring, but with a grungy kind of neofascism that makes women want you and men want to be you (or vice versa, whatever that means). See, you could be learning techniques, important advanced techniques right now, right this very minute, but you can't turn the page. You're transfixed. You're mesmerized by the very thing that disgusts you most (and we've yet to determine what that is). But I do know this: when you do turn the page (and I have a feeling that will be very soon), you'll enter a world of garish delights that dare not speak its name (I can't believe my publisher lets me print this stuff). By the way, I kind of cheated on the chapter title "Give Me the Bridge." It's a line repeated numerous times in the song "Bustin' Loose" by Chuck Brown, and it just feels so "right" I had to use it. Forgive me.

Creating Full-Screen Slide Shows

One of my favorite features of the Adobe Bridge is the ability to play a full-screen slide show of my photos. It can run automatically, loop, or you can control it yourself. Perhaps best of all, it also lets you play photo editor while it's running, so if you need to rotate a shot, delete a shot, etc., you can, as your photos are displayed at a large enough size that making decisions like that is easy. All it's missing is a nice dissolve transition, but outside of that, it's not too shabby.

Slide shows:

First Command-click (PC: Control-click) on the photos in the Bridge you want to appear in your slide show. To enter Slide Show mode, just press Command-L (PC: Control-L), which amazingly does not bring up Levels. (Remember—although the Bridge is so tightly integrated it feels like you're still in Photoshop, in reality the Bridge is a separate application, so Adobe can get away with using Photoshop shortcuts.) The first selected photo appears full screen, but to start the show, you have to press the Spacebar. To quit the slide show, press the Escape key on your keyboard.

Automatic vs. manual:

Once you start your slide show, your photos will automatically advance one at a time until all your photos have been displayed at full screen. However, if you'd prefer to advance the slides manually, don't press the Spacebar. Instead, just press the Right (or Down) Arrow key on your keyboard. Every time you press it, the next slide will display until you've reached the last slide. To see a previous slide, press the Left (or Up) Arrow key. You can also click your mouse button to cycle through individual slides.

Adobe Bridge Slideshow Commands
Press the H key to show or hide these commands

General

Esc	Exit Slideshow	Space	Pause/Play
L	Loop on/off	W	Window mode on/off
C	Change caption mode	D	Change display mode
S/Shift+S	Increase/decrease slide duration		

Navigation

Left Arrow	Previous page	Right Arrow	Next page
⌘+Left Arrow	Previous document	⌘+Right Arrow	Next document

Editing

[	Rotate 90° counterclockwise	]	Rotate 90° clockwise
1–5	Set rating	6–9	Set label
, (comma)	Decrease rating	. (period)	Increase rating
0	Clear rating	' (apostrophe)	Toggle rating

The most important commands:
Once you enter Slide Show mode, if you press the H key on your keyboard, a menu of keyboard shortcuts will appear so you can control your slide show while it's running. One shortcut you might want to try out is the W key, which changes the slide show from a full-screen experience to one that fits nicely in its own floating window. Also, if you view high-res photos, you may find that the default display mode zooms in too close, so press the D key a time or two until your full image fits onscreen.

Adding background music:
I know what you're thinking: "Hey, cool, it lets you add background music!" Sadly, no. It doesn't. But that doesn't mean you can't have background music. Here's what I do—I open my computer's music player (I use Apple's iTunes), start the background music first, and then I switch to the Bridge and begin my slide show. Although it takes one additional step (starting the background music in iTunes), the effect is exactly the same—a slide show playing full screen with background music. By the way, if you want some ideas for background music for slide shows, I posted an iTunes Music Store "iMix" of cool slide show background music, which I called (oddly enough) "Scott's Slideshow Mix." It lists the songs, lets you listen to 30-second previews, and you can even download and buy the songs (for 99¢ each). If you have iTunes, check it out at http://phobos.apple.com/WebObjects/MZStore.woa/wa/viewPublishedPlaylist?id=222715 or just go to the iTunes Music Store and search for my iMix by its name, "Scott's Slideshow Mix."

Scott's Slideshow Mix — See all iMixes by this user — Tell a friend — Total Songs: 20 — $19.80 (BUY ALL SONGS) — How do I make an iMix?

Rating ★★★★★ ★★★★ ★★★ ★★ ★ (Submit)

iMix Notes This is the collection of songs I referenced in my book, that work well as background music behind slideshows. It's a wide range of musical styles, and they were chosen to not get in the way of the images, but to support them. Hope you like 'em! :-)

	Song Name	Artist	Album	Time	Price
1	Ariane	Acoustic Alchemy	The Very Best of Acous...	4:53	$0.99 BUY SONG
2	Heart of a Child	Jon Schmidt	August End	5:07	$0.99 BUY SONG
3	The Woods so Wild	Julian Bream	Ultimate Guitar Collecti...	2:07	$0.99 BUY SONG
4	Fireworks	Moby	18	2:13	$0.99 BUY SONG
5	Whipping the Horse's Eyes	Calexico	Feast of Wire	1:24	$0.99 BUY SONG
6	A Night to Remember	Yanni	Dare to Dream	5:46	$0.99 BUY SONG
7	Irish Boy (CAL)	Mark Knopfler	Screenplaying (Music fr...	4:38	$0.99 BUY SONG
8	Unomathemba	Ladysmith Black Mamba...	Shaka Zulu	3:47	$0.99 BUY SONG
9	The Sailor's Grave on the Prairie	Leo Kottke	6- and 12- String Guitar	2:33	$0.99 BUY SONG
10	Visiting	William Ackerman	A Windham Hill Retros...	6:08	$0.99 BUY SONG
11	Verbal	Amon Tobin & MC Deci...	Out from Out Where	3:55	$0.99 BUY SONG
12	Stars Fell on Alabama	Harry Connick, Jr.	20	4:52	$0.99 BUY SONG
13	The Bricklayer's Beautiful Daughter	William Ackerman	A Windham Hill Retros...	3:37	$0.99 BUY SONG
14	Signe	Eric Clapton	Unplugged	3:13	$0.99 BUY SONG
15	Family Portrait	Rachel's	Music For Egon Schiele	5:41	$0.99 BUY SONG
16	The Great Wall	David Arkenstone	Citizen of Time	4:46	$0.99 BUY SONG
17	Four Ton Mantis	Amon Tobin	Supermodified	4:46	$0.99 BUY SONG
18	Angela Smiled	W.G. Snuffy Walden & S...	Music by W.G. Snuffy W...	5:31	$0.99 BUY SONG
19	Canarios	Neal Hellman	Autumn in the Valley	3:51	$0.99 BUY SONG
20	The Fairy Queen	Clannad	Magical Ring	2:41	$0.99 BUY SONG

Getting and Editing a Photo's Metadata

Photoshop CS2's Bridge gives you direct access to information that is embedded into your photo by the digital camera itself, plus access to the info embedded by Photoshop once you open the file. This information is lumped together under the name "metadata," and here we'll take a brief look at the available metadata, but more importantly, we'll learn how to edit that metadata to embed your own custom info.

The Metadata palette:

The bottom-left panel in the Bridge displays the currently selected photo's metadata. There are two types of meta-data categories that are "read only," meaning the info has been put there by Photoshop or your camera and you can't edit it. First, there's File Properties (the information Photoshop adds to your photo, like the file size, when it was last edited in Photoshop, its physical dimensions, etc.); and second, the Camera Data (EXIF), commonly known as "EXIF data." (EXIF stands for Exchangeable Image File data, and rather than spelling it out, most people pronounce it "EX-IF".) This EXIF data is the info that's automatically embedded into your photo by your digital camera. It includes the make and model of the camera that shot the image, the exposure, shutter speed, f-stop, if your flash fired when the photo was taken, the focal length of your lens, and more than a dozen background details, many of which are incredibly boring, even to people with big, giant über-brains. The third type of metadata is IPTC, and it's editable, meaning you can embed your own info into your digital files (as long as they're not saved as read-only files).

The File Properties metadata is the info Photoshop embeds into your photo.

The Camera Data (EXIF) is the info embedded into your photo by your digital camera, while IPTC metadata is the custom info that you embed.

Metadata

▼ File Properties
Filename : DSC_0009.JPG
Document Kind : JPEG file
Application : Ver.1.02
Date Created : 1/20/05, 1:2
Date File Created : --
Date File Modified : 1/26/05...
File Size : 2.41 MB
Dimensions : 3008 x 2000
Resolution : 300 dpi
Bit Depth : 8
Color Mode : RGB Color

Find...

Increase Font Size
Decrease Font Size

Preferences...

Seeing all that tiny type:

Because there's so much metadata included in each photo, Adobe had to make the font's point size pretty darn small. That's not a problem if you're 14 years old, but if you're in your mid-20s (like me), it can actually seem too small, and then you get angry and start writing letters, circulating petitions, calling emergency meetings of the condo association board, etc. Luckily, in Photoshop CS2 you don't have to endure tiny metadata type because you can increase the font size. Just click on the Metadata palette's fly-out menu (in the top-right corner) and choose Increase Font Size. If it's still not big enough, choose it again. And again, until your neighbors can read it through your window.

Description
Camera Data 1
Camera Data 2
Categories
History
IPTC Contact
IPTC Content
IPTC Image
IPTC Status
Adobe Stock Photos
Origin
Advanced

Camera Data 1

Make: NIKON CORPORATION
Model: NIKON D70
Date Time: 2005-01-20T13:26:43.7-05:00
Shutter Speed:
Exposure Program: Normal program
F-Stop: f/4.2
Aperture Value:
Max Aperture Value: f/4.1
ISO Speed Ratings:
Focal Length: 105.0 mm
Lens:
Flash: Did not fire
No strobe return detection (0)
Unknown flash mode (0)
Flash function present
No red-eye reduction
Metering Mode: Pattern

Powered By
xmp

Cancel   OK

Accessing metadata another way:

You can also view a photo's metadata by clicking on the photo, going under either the Bridge's or Photoshop's File menu and choosing File Info. When the dialog appears, in the categories on the left, click on Camera Data 1 to display the most common EXIF data. Click on Camera Data 2 to display the stuff used only by high-level digital camera geeks and certain government officials. These two readouts are displayed in a nice, easily digestible format; but if you crave the full EXIF data dump, click on Advanced, and then click on the triangle (or plus sign on a PC) to the left of the words "EXIF Properties" to reveal it all.

Continued

Editing your metadata:

There's a special section of the metadata called IPTC (named for the International Press and Telecommunications Council) where you can actually embed your own custom metadata information. In the Metadata palette, click on the right-facing triangle to the left of the words "IPTC Core" to reveal its info. The little pencil icons to the right indicate which fields can accept your custom metadata. To enter your own info, click once on the item you want to edit. Then, directly after the colon next to the item, editable fields will appear in which you can enter your info.

Customizing your fields:

By default, there is a long list of IPTC fields you can add info into, but there are many more than the average person will ever need. Most folks limit this list to display only the fields they really want visible. To do this, click on the right-facing arrow in the top-right corner of the Metadata palette and choose Preferences from the flyout menu that appears. This brings up the Preferences dialog with the Metadata category selected. Scroll down to IPTC Core and you'll see the full list of available IPTC fields (scary, ain't it?). Only the fields with checkmarks by them will be visible, so to hide a field in the list, just click on the checkmark beside that field. Also, ensure the Hide Empty Fields checkbox is selected, so when you click OK, only the checked fields will be visible.

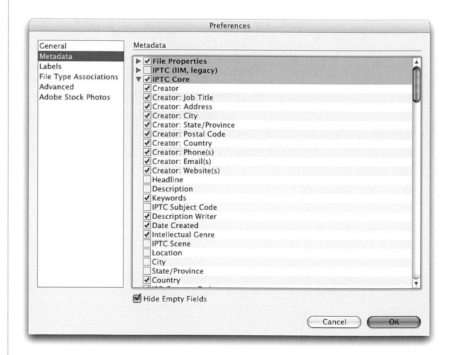

Adding metadata to many images:
If you want to apply your copyright info (or any other IPTC metadata) to a number of different photos, it could really take some serious time, but luckily there's a way to apply the same metadata to a number of different images at once. In the Bridge, click on the first photo you want to apply new metadata to, then press-and-hold the Command key (PC: Control key) and click on all the other photos you want to apply the same metadata to. (Just to keep things simple, we'll assume you're adding fresh copyright info to a group of just-imported photos.) Now go to the Metadata palette, scroll down to IPTC Core, and click on the words "Copyright Notice." When you do this, a warning dialog similar to the one shown here (okay, exactly like the one shown here) will appear warning you that you've selected to edit the metadata of multiple files (which in this case is what you want to do). Click on the Yes button, and then type your data in the active field. Now your custom metadata (your copyright info in this case) will be written to all your selected files. Pretty sweet, eh?

Batch Renaming Your Files

The Adobe Bridge has a feature that will automatically rename an entire folder full of images, so your digital camera photo names are no longer the cryptic DSC_0486.JPG, DSC_0487.JPG, and DSC_0488.JPG variety, but are names that will be more recognizable (which you choose), such as NY Street Scenes01, NY Street Scenes02, NY Street Scenes03, etc.—and best of all, the whole process is automated. Here's a step-by-step:

Step One:

First, you have to tell the Bridge which photos you want to rename. If it's just a certain number of images within your main window, you can hold the Command key (PC: Control key) and click on only the photos you want to rename. But a more likely scenario is that you'll want to rename all the photos open in your thumbnail window, so go under the Bridge's Edit menu and choose Select All, or press Command-A (PC: Control-A). All the photos in your main window will be highlighted. Now, go under the Bridge's Tools menu and choose Batch Rename.

Step Two:

When the Batch Rename dialog appears, you need to select a destination for these renamed photos by choosing an option. Will they just be renamed in the folder they're in now? Do you want them renamed and moved to a different folder, or do you want to copy them into a different folder? If you want to either move or copy them, you'll need to click on the Browse button. In the resulting dialog, navigate to the folder you want your photos moved (or copied) into after they're renamed. (This ability to copy files to another folder is new in CS2, which was met with considerable high-fiving in our office.)

Step Three:

Under the New Filenames section of the dialog, the first pop-up menu shows Current Filename by default. You want to click on this menu and instead choose Text. A text field will appear to the right of the menu, so just click within that field and type in your own custom file name (I entered "Buildings in Midtown"). At the bottom of the dialog, there's a live before-and-after preview of your custom file name so you can see how it will look. Don't click Rename yet.

Step Four:

So far, so good, but there's a problem: In your folder you can only have one photo exactly named "Buildings in Midtown," so you'll need to add something to the end of the file name (like a number). To use the built-in auto-numbering, click once on the small plus sign (+) to the right of the text field to add another customized set just below your original naming options. From the pop-up menu, choose Sequence Number (to have the Bridge automatically add a sequential number after the name); in the center text field, enter the number you want to start with (I typed the number one); then, from the pop-up menu on the far right, choose how many digits you want for your sequence (I chose Two Digits). Look at the preview at the bottom of the dialog to see how the name looks now: "Buildings in Midtown01.JPG."

Continued

TIP: If you want to take this a step further (this is totally optional by the way), you can click on that little plus sign again to add another set of naming options. In the first field choose Current Filename, which adds the original file name at the end of your new file name. Under the Options category, it's a smart idea to turn on the checkbox for Preserve Current Filename in XMP Metadata, just in case you have to go searching for the original file one day.

Step Five:

When you click on the Rename button, Batch Rename does its thing. If you choose to rename your files in the same folder, you can just take a peek at the Bridge, and you'll see that your selected thumbnails are now updated with their new names. If you choose to move all your files to a different folder and then click on the Rename button, the main window will be empty (that makes sense because you moved the images to a new folder and the main window is displaying the current folder, which is now empty). So, you'll need to go to the Folders palette in the Bridge and navigate your way to the folder in which you moved (or copied) all your photos (and best of all, they'll be sporting their new, more descriptive names).

Step Six:

Batch Renaming doesn't just change the thumbnails' names—it applies this name change to the actual image file. To check it out, leave the Bridge and go to the folder on your hard disk where these photos are stored. Open that folder and you'll see the new file names have been assigned there as well.

I'm pretty sure the last thing you want to do in the Adobe Bridge is spend a lot of time typing, but sometimes you've just gotta. You have to embed your copyright info, your contact info, your website, and on and on. That's why you'll want to know how to create a metadata template, which allows you to enter all that info only once, then you can embed it all automatically with a click of a mouse.

Creating Metadata Templates

Step One:
You'll need to start with a photo to base your template on, so navigate to a folder of images within the Bridge that you'd like to assign some copyright and contact info to, then click on one of the thumbnail images in that folder.

Step Two:
Go under the Bridge's File menu and choose File Info. In the resulting dialog, you'll see a list of metadata info categories on the left-hand side. Under the Description category, in the various fields, enter the information that you'd like to turn into a template. All the info you enter will be applied to the other images in this same folder. Don't click OK yet.

Continued

Step Three:

Click on the little right-facing arrow in the top-right corner of the File Info dialog, and when the flyout menu appears, choose Save Metadata Template.

Step Four:

When you select Save Metadata Template, a dialog will appear where you can name your template. Give it a descriptive name, click on the Save button, and then click OK in the File Info dialog.

Step Five:

Now that you've created your template, it's time to put it to use. Go under the Bridge's Edit menu and choose Invert Selection—now every photo will be selected except the one that you just added the metadata to (in Step 2).

Step Six:
To add your custom info to these photos, rather than typing it all in, you'll use that metadata template you saved. Just go under the Bridge's Tools menu, under Append Metadata, and choose your template's name from the submenu (in this example, my template was named "Nikon Safari Shots").

Step Seven:
Because you'll be adding this information to all your selected photos in this folder, you'll get the "You-have-selected-multiple-files" warning dialog. Obviously, you'll want to click on Yes; but what the heck, while you're here, click on that Don't Show Again checkbox, and that's the last time you'll have to see that annoying warning dialog. Once you click Yes, your copyright info, contact info, etc., will be immediately embedded into each selected image.

TIP: I didn't have room to mention this in Step 6, but when we chose Append Metadata, which adds our metadata to the photo, the info will appear only in fields that have no metadata already assigned. In our example, no metadata had yet been assigned to the other photos, so we could choose Append Metadata. If you already have metadata in place for a photo, you can choose Replace Metadata instead, which overwrites the old metadata with the new metadata from your template.

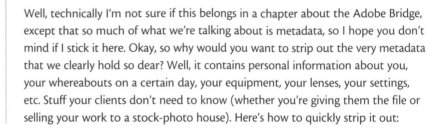

Stripping Out Metadata from Your Photos

ADVANCED
FOR PROS ONLY!
TECHNIQUES

Well, technically I'm not sure if this belongs in a chapter about the Adobe Bridge, except that so much of what we're talking about is metadata, so I hope you don't mind if I stick it here. Okay, so why would you want to strip out the very metadata that we clearly hold so dear? Well, it contains personal information about you, your whereabouts on a certain day, your equipment, your lenses, your settings, etc. Stuff your clients don't need to know (whether you're giving them the file or selling your work to a stock-photo house). Here's how to quickly strip it out:

Step One:
In the Bridge thumbnail window, click on the photo for which you want to strip out the metadata. Then, in the Metadata palette, scroll down to the Camera Data (EXIF) category—that's what we're going to strip out. Now you can double-click on that photo to open it in Photoshop CS2.

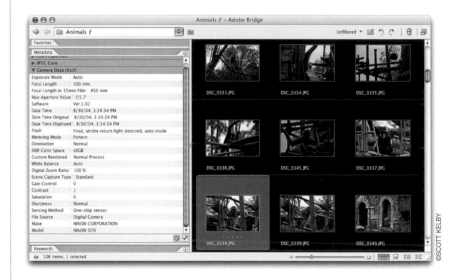

Step Two:
Once the photo is open in Photoshop, go under the File menu and choose New. When the New dialog appears, (while the dialog is open onscreen) return to the menu bar, choose Window, and at the bottom of the Window menu you'll see the name of your open photo. Select that photo's name, and the exact Width, Height, Resolution, and Color Mode settings from your open photo will be copied into the New dialog's fields. All you have to do is click OK and a new document with the same specs as your open photo will appear onscreen.

Step Three:

Once your new blank document is open in Photoshop CS2, switch back to your original photo. Press V to get the Move tool, press-and-hold the Shift key, then click-and-drag your photo onto the blank document. Because you're holding the Shift key, the photo will appear in the exact position as it did in the original. However, this dragged copy is on its own separate layer, so press Command-E (PC: Control-E) to merge this layer with the Background layer (this basically flattens the document).

Step Four:

If you want to check the metadata before you leave Photoshop, just go under the File menu and choose File Info. On the left side of the resulting dialog, click on Camera Data 1 and Camera Data 2—you'll see that the fields are blank. If you want to check the metadata in the Bridge, choose Save from the File menu, then look at the Metadata palette in the Bridge—you'll see that the entire main Camera Data (EXIF) has been stripped away. By the way, if you find yourself doing this a lot, this is an ideal thing to record as an action (more on actions later).

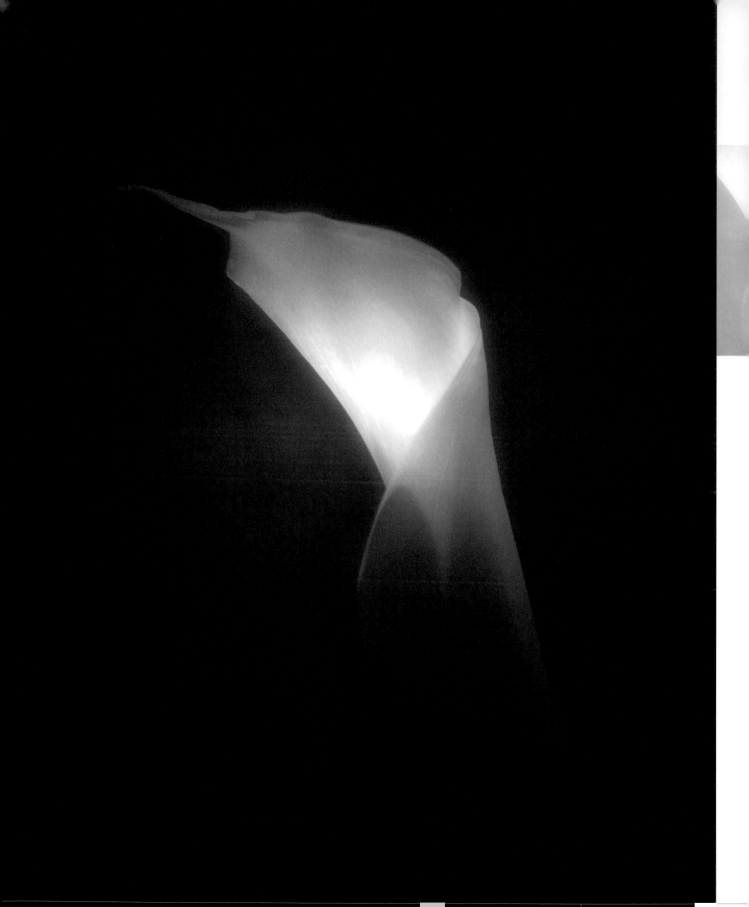

Exposure: 0.8s   Focal Length: 40mm   Aperture Value: *f*/4.3

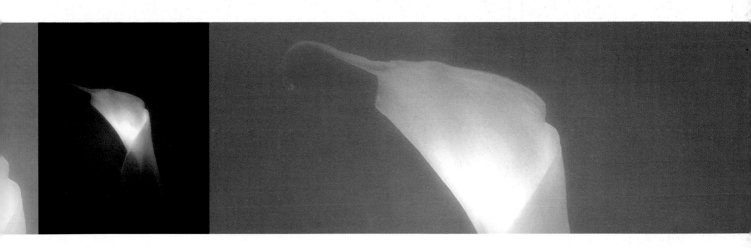

Raw Hide
mastering camera raw

This is the first version of this book to have an entire chapter devoted to Camera Raw. So why a whole chapter? Three reasons: (1) Camera Raw is that important, has that many new features in CS2, and I felt I needed to cover them all; (2) I needed the extra pages to get my page count up; (3) I really didn't need the page count, but you can't be sure of that. Now, is this chapter for everybody? No. It's really only for people who shoot in RAW format (you'll know if your digital camera can shoot in RAW, because the salesman who sold you the camera would've been totally naked at the time of your purchase). Okay, I'm going to get serious for just a moment (and for only a moment, so don't get excited—especially with that naked salesman around). Camera Raw isn't for everybody. For example, if you're

a seasoned pro that gets the exposure dead-on every time and never has white balance issues, go ahead and shoot in a high-quality JPEG format. But for everyone else, RAW lets us fix all sorts of things after the fact, in Photoshop, and because it's all happening within the data from the camera, we can tweak the exposure, white balance, and a dozen other settings to create a new, perfectly balanced "original" from our digital negative. This is very powerful stuff. Now, back to the crazy crap. See the title for this chapter, "Raw Hide"? You're thinking it's that old western TV show, right? Well, I'm thinkin' it's the theme song from that old western TV show. Come on, sing with me: "Head 'em up, move 'em out, Rawwwww Hidddeeeeeeee!" (Note to editors: Insert whip sound effect here.)

Camera Raw Essentials

If you take a photo with a traditional film camera and send the film to a lab for processing, they produce an original print from the negative you gave them (and the negative remains intact). Well, Photoshop's Camera Raw lets you be the lab, by letting you import an unprocessed RAW original (your "digital negative") and process it yourself, just like the lab. You can adjust everything—from exposure to white balance and more—to create your own original print to open in Photoshop, while the RAW file remains intact. Of course, the first step is shooting in RAW mode (luckily almost all of today's digital cameras can shoot in RAW mode).

Step One:

You can open a Camera Raw image in several ways—right from within the Adobe Bridge by either double-clicking on a RAW image or pressing Command-R (PC: Control-R) with the image selected, or you can also open it using the standard Open command from Photoshop CS2's File menu. Regardless, a RAW image automatically opens in the Camera Raw interface (shown in the next step).

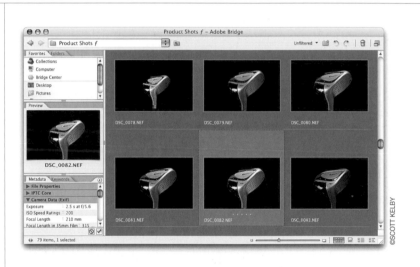

Step Two:

If you want to open multiple RAW photos from the Bridge, Command-click (PC: Control-click) on all the images you want to open in Camera Raw; then, once they're selected, double-click on any one of the selected photos. The photo you double-clicked on will appear in the preview window ready for editing, and the other photos you selected will appear along the left side of the Camera Raw dialog. To edit one of the images listed on the side, just click once on the one you want to edit.

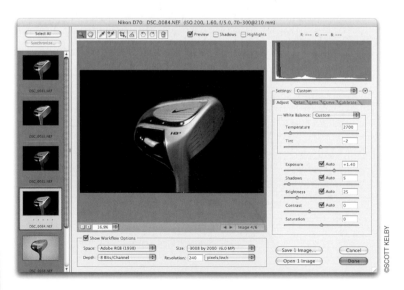

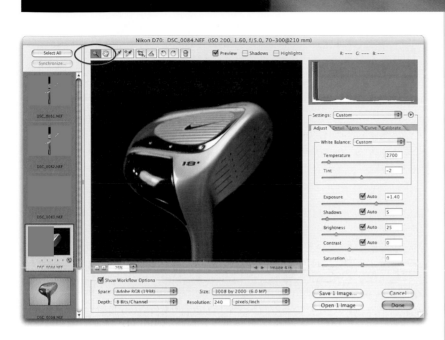

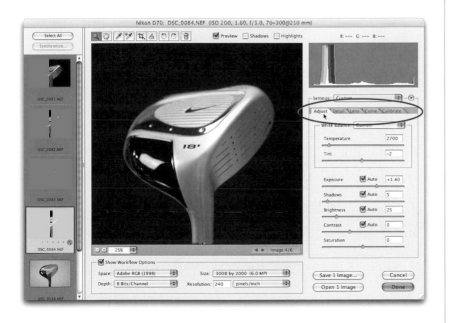

Step Three:

To take advantage of that large preview area, here are some quick preview short-cuts: There's a Zoom tool that works just like the one in Photoshop. If you double-click on it (in the top-left corner above the preview), it zooms up to a 100% view. When you're zoomed in tight, press-and-hold the Spacebar on your keyboard to get the Hand tool, then just click-and-drag in the preview window to move around the image. To quickly fit your entire photo in the preview area, double-click on the Hand tool above the preview or press Command-0 (zero) (PC: Control-0). You can also press Command–+ (Plus key) (PC: Control–+) to zoom in and Command–- (Minus key) (PC: Control–-) to zoom out. Also, you can rotate a photo left or right by pressing L or R, respectively.

Step Four:

You do your photo processing in the right column of the Camera Raw interface. There are five "tabs" with different sets of controls under each, but all the basic essential adjustments are found under the Adjust tab (make sure it's visible by clicking on its tab).

TIP: I'm sure you've noticed that the Auto checkboxes are "on" by default, but if you really want to turn them off for good, here's what you do: Open a RAW file, turn off all the Auto checkboxes, and then go to the Settings flyout menu (it's the right-facing arrow to the right of the Settings pop-up menu) and choose Save New Camera Raw Defaults. Now, when you open a RAW image, all the Auto checkboxes will be off by default.

Continued

Step Five:

We'll start by looking at the White Balance setting. When you open a photo in Camera Raw, Photoshop looks at the White Balance setting that was used when the photo was taken, and it displays that setting in the White Balance pop-up menu. If the white balance looks good to you, you can leave it set as-is. If the white balance was set correctly (or if you just want to see if you can come up with a setting that looks better to you), you can apply a preset setting by choosing one from the White Balance pop-up menu. When you choose a new white balance, the preview updates so you can see how this new setting will affect your photo.

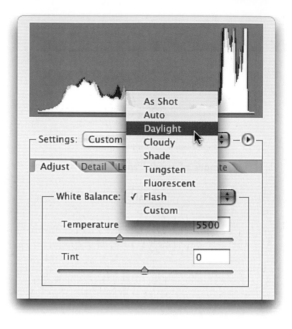

Step Six:

Besides using these default White Balance settings, you can tweak them manually to create your own custom white balance. You do this using the Temperature and Tint sliders. To make your white balance more blue, drag the Temperature slider to the left. To add more yellow, drag it to the right. The Tint slider basically does the same thing, just with different colors: dragging to the left brings more green into your photo and dragging to the right brings in more red. By using these two sliders, you can pretty much create whatever white balance situation you prefer (this is totally a personal preference thing).

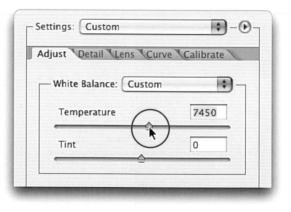

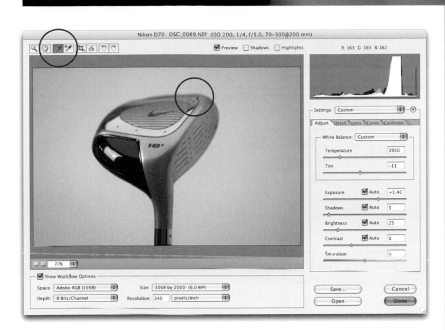

Step Seven:

There's another way to set your white balance: use the White Balance tool (found at the top of the Camera Raw dialog—it looks like the regular Eyedropper tool). You just press the letter I to get that tool, then click it once in a neutral area of your photo (you don't want to click in a perfectly white area with no detail; you want an area that's off-white or light gray with some detail).

TIP: To help you find this neutral color in your images, I've included a black/gray/white swatch card for you in the back of this book (it's perforated so you can tear it out). Just put this card into your RAW shot, take the shot, and when you open the RAW file in Camera Raw, you can then click the White Balance tool on the neutral gray swatch on the swatch card. When you're done, just crop the card out of the image. (See Chapter 6 for more information on how to use this handy card.)

Step Eight:

Now let's move on to your tonal adjustments (which are located just below the White Balance section). The top slider (and probably the most widely used slider in all of Camera Raw) is for adjusting the exposure of your photo (you can increase the exposure up to four f-stops and decrease it up to two f-stops. So, an Exposure slider setting of +1.50 would be an increase of a stop and a half). One way to make this adjustment is to "eye" it: Just drag the slider, then look at the preview to see how your image looks. But there are some other features to help you make more informed exposure decisions.

Continued

Step Nine:

To get some help with setting your exposure, there's now an Auto checkbox in CS2 that will attempt to automatically set the exposure for you. It often does a pretty darn good job, so it's worth seeing how it looks (you can see an instant preview as soon as you click the checkbox on/off). Leaving the Auto Exposure checkbox on increased the Exposure to +1.40 for this image. If that doesn't look good to you, there's another popular way to set the right exposure....

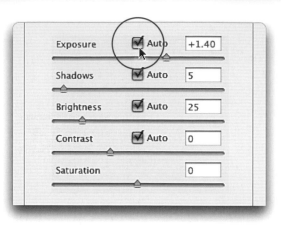

Step Ten (Exposure):

The method I use to set the exposure is to have Camera Raw tell me how far I can go (either increasing or decreasing the Exposure setting), so I get the best possible exposure, without clipping off any highlights or shadows. To do this, press-and-hold the Option (PC: Alt) key and click on the Exposure slider (by the way, moving a slider automatically turns off the Auto checkbox for that slider). When you do this, the screen will turn black. If anything shows up in white (or red, green, or blue), that's a warning that the highlights are clipping (basically, that means there will be *no* detail in that area, which may actually be okay—clipping areas like a bright reflection on a car's bumper or the center of the sun isn't a problem). So, as long as important areas aren't clipped off, I keep clicking-and-dragging to the right (with Option/Alt held down) until some real clipping starts to appear. In this case, I pushed it to +1.50, whereas Auto only went to +1.40. I can go with that or something less, but if I push it any further, I'm going to lose important detail.

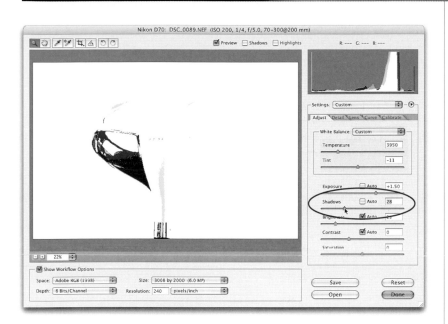

Step Eleven (Shadows):

Now that your Exposure is set (and you protected your highlights from clipping), what about the shadows? Well, there's a slider for that too—it's called (surprisingly enough) the Shadows slider. Sliding it to the right increases the shadows in your photo. Again, there's an Auto checkbox (and you should give that a try), but you can also use the Option-drag (PC: Alt-drag) trick on the Shadows slider. This time, the preview will show shadow areas (with no detail) in pure black (meaning these areas are getting clipped—white areas are not clipped). If you see other colors (like red, green, or blue), they're getting clipped a bit too, but not as significantly as the overall shadows, so I'm not as concerned about a little bit of clipping in color. If there's significant clipping, drag to the left to reduce the amount of shadows. If not, drag to the right until you start getting some clipping.

TIP: In CS2, Adobe added a very helpful feature to keep you from clipping either your highlights or shadows. At the top of the Camera Raw dialog, there are two checkboxes: one for highlights, one for shadows. When you turn them on, any-time highlight areas start getting clipped (regardless of which slider you're using), the clipped areas will appear in solid red, while clipped shadow areas will appear in blue, giving you an instant visual warning exactly where clipping is occurring. Not bad, eh?

Continued

Step Twelve (Brightness):

The next adjustment slider down is Brightness. Since you've already adjusted the highlights (with Exposure) and shadows (with the Shadows slider), the Brightness slider adjusts everything else (I always relate this slider to the midtones slider in the Levels dialog, so that might help in understanding how this slider differs from Exposure or Shadows). There is an Auto checkbox for Brightness, but I'm not too crazy about this particular Auto setting, as it seems (to me anyway) to give the photo a flat look, but hey—that's just me. Turn Auto on/off and see if you agree—or just drag the slider to the right (above 50) to lighten the midtones or to the left (below 50) to darken them.

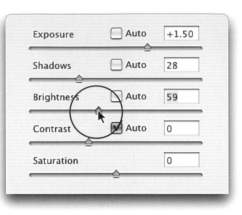

Step Thirteen (Contrast):

The Contrast slider does pretty much what you'd expect it to—adds or reduces contrast (depending on which way you drag it). If you drag to the right, it increases the contrast in the image (so you can imagine you'll probably be dragging right most of the time), or if you want to reduce the contrast in your image (making it look flat), drag to the left. There's also an Auto checkbox here, but to me it never seems to add enough contrast, so I usually wind up adjusting this one myself while looking at the preview (and the histogram) as a guide.

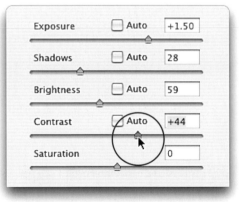

Step Fourteen (Saturation):

The Saturation slider makes the colors in your RAW photo either more saturated and colorful (by dragging to the right) or less saturated and flat (by dragging to the left). This is my least-used slider in Camera Raw, as I normally wait until I'm in Photoshop, because I view adding saturation as a special effect, and not generally something I do when I'm just trying to create a nicely exposed, well-balanced image. In fact, I only adjust this setting if some of the other changes I made in Camera Raw make my colors look flat. Otherwise, I ignore that slider, but that's just me; if you want more saturated photos, go for it (I won't tell anybody). By the way, there's no Auto checkbox for Saturation. I call that an act of mercy.

Step Fifteen:

Let's say that you've got a studio set up, so you have pretty controlled lighting. If that's the case, you might want to save these correction settings (for this particular camera, used in this particular lighting situation). That way, the next time you're processing images taken with this camera in your studio, you can quickly call up these same settings. To do this, just click on the right-facing arrow to the right of the Settings pop-up menu and choose Save Settings from the flyout menu that appears. Give your settings a descriptive name, and then click Save. Now this group of settings will appear in the Settings pop-up menu.

Sizing and Resolution in Camera Raw

Since you're creating and processing your own images, it only makes sense that you get to choose what resolution, what size, which color space, and how many bits per channel your photo will be, right? Adobe calls these "workflow" decisions, which is why in order to make these decisions you have to turn on the checkbox for Show Workflow Options. Once you do that, the workflow options are revealed. Here's how to know what to put where:

Step One:

Once you've made all your exposure and tonal settings, fixed any lens-related problems, and generally have the photo looking the way you want it to in the Camera Raw dialog, it's time to fine-tune your resolution, size, etc. (In the bottom left of the dialog, make sure the Show Workflow Options checkbox is turned on.) First we'll start with choosing your size. By default, the size that appears in the Size pop-up menu is the original size dictated by your digital camera's mega-pixel capacity (in this case it's 2560x1920 pixels).

Step Two (Size):

If you click-and-hold on the Size pop-up menu, you'll see a list of image sizes that Camera Raw can generate from your RAW original. The ones with a plus sign (+) by them indicate that you're scaling the image up in size. The minus sign (-) means the image will be smaller than the original size taken by the camera, which quality-wise isn't a problem. The number in parentheses shows the equivalent megapixels that size represents. Usually, it's fairly safe to increase the size to the next largest choice—anything above that and you risk having the image look soft or pixelated.

Step Three (Resolution):

Just under the Size pop-up menu, you'll see the Resolution field. The topic of resolution is something entire training DVDs are dedicated to, so we won't go in-depth about it here, but I'll give you some quick guidelines. If your photo will wind up on a printing press, use 300 ppi (you don't really need that much, but many print shops still think you do, so just play it safe at 300 ppi). If you're printing 8x10" or smaller to an inkjet printer, you can also use 300 ppi (or even 360 if you're really picky). For larger prints (like 13x19"), you can get away with 240 ppi or less (I've used as little as 180). Either way, you're not locked in because you can always change the size and resolution in Photoshop.

Step Four (Space and Depth):

The color space choice is easy: Choose Adobe RGB 1998. It's the most popular choice with photographers because the range (gamut) of colors it supports is greater than sRGB (giving you more color), and it's big enough to get the most out of your inkjet prints (unlike ProPhoto RGB, which lets you add colors your printer can't reproduce). As for the Depth pop-up menu, generally choose 8 Bits/Channel. Although some high-end photographers insist on 16-bit, you don't get the full use of Photoshop's tools and features, plus the file sizes are approximately double in size, which makes Photoshop run a lot slower (not to mention they take up more room on your hard disk).

Cropping within Camera Raw

Photoshop CS2 is the first version to enable you to crop your images right within Camera Raw, but it does it a little differently than the regular cropping in Photoshop CS2, so here's a quick look at how it works.

Step One:

Once your image is open in Camera Raw, you use the Crop tool to crop the image (no big shock there), but it works differently than the regular Crop tool. First, click-and-hold on the Crop tool in the Toolbox (along the top of the preview area) and a pop-up menu will appear. If you choose Normal, you'll get the standard "drag-it-where-you-want-it" cropping, or you can use one of the cropping presets. When you drag out any cropping border, the Size pop-up menu (in the Show Workflow Options section in the bottom of Camera Raw) changes into a Crop Size pop-up menu, which displays the pixel dimensions of the currently selected crop and gives you the equivalent megapixels.

Step Two:

If you want an exact size for your cropped image (like 6x4", 8x10", etc.), you can click-and-hold on the Crop tool in the Toolbox, and then choose Custom from the pop-up menu. When the Custom Crop dialog appears, change the Crop pop-up menu to Inches, then type in the size you want in the fields. You can enter exact pixel sizes, centimeters, or a custom ratio.

Step Three:

If you go with one of the preset ratio crops, you can drag either horizontally or vertically and the border will maintain that ratio. However, if you drag out a cropping ratio vertically, and then instead want that crop ratio to be horizontal, just grab a corner point and drag up (or down, depending on which corner point you select) and the cropping border will flip horizontally. Also, you can change to any other ratio by Control-clicking (PC: Right-clicking) within the cropping border and choosing a new ratio from the contextual menu. You can also clear the current crop by pressing the Escape key on your keyboard or by pressing Delete (PC: Backspace).

Step Four:

Once you click on the Open button in Camera Raw, the image is cropped to your specs and opened in Photoshop. If you click on the Done button in Camera Raw, the cropping border remains with the file, but the image itself isn't cropped—if you reopen the RAW file, you'll see the cropping border still in place.

Continued

CROPPING TIP 1: If you have a crop border in place and click Save in the Camera Raw dialog, a Save Options dialog will appear. If you choose Photoshop in the Format pop-up menu, a new option will appear called Preserve Cropped Pixels. Select that option and click Save. When you later open this cropped image, it will appear cropped, but the image will be on an editable layer (not the Background layer), and the rest of the original image is still available. Just press V to get the Move tool and drag it into view within the document window.

CROPPING TIP 2: If you have multiple photos open in Camera Raw, you can crop them all at one time. Here's how: Click on the Select All button above the row of thumbnails along the left side of the Camera Raw dialog, and then use the Crop tool to create your cropping border on your image in the preview area. If you look at the other images along the side, you'll see they all have a tiny Crop icon in the bottom-left corner of their thumbnail, indicating that they'll all be cropped to match (when they're opened or saved).

CROPPING TIP 3: If you have a cropping border in place, you can zoom your cropped area to fit within the entire preview window by simply double-clicking on the Crop tool.

Adobe added a timesaving method for straightening photos within Camera Raw (in fact, in CS2 it's now easier to straighten RAW photos than it is to straighten simple 8-bit images). What I like best about this technique is that it's pretty much a one-click trick. What's really weird, though, is that the hardest part is learning how to cancel a straightening (especially because once you use the Straightening tool, that straightening info stays with the RAW file, even if you just click Done).

Straightening Photos within Camera Raw

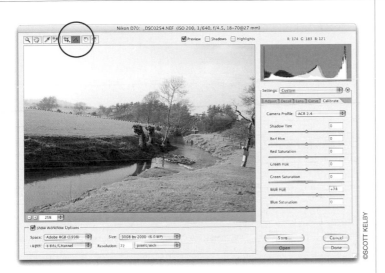

Step One:

Start by opening the RAW photo that needs to be straightened in Camera Raw (needless to say, it must be a photo taken in RAW format. So, if it was needless to say, why did I say it? I have issues). In the Camera Raw Toolbox, choose the Straightening tool (it's immediately to the right of the Crop tool). Now, click-and-drag it along the horizon line in your photo.

Step Two:

When you release your mouse button, the preview shows you how the photo will be rotated and straightened. It doesn't actually rotate the photo at this point—that doesn't happen until you open the file in Photoshop itself. For now, you just get a border that shows you how it will be rotated. Now, if you click Save or Done, the straightening information is saved along with the file, so if you open this file again in Camera Raw, that straightening crop border will still be in place.

TIP: If you want to cancel your straightening, click on the Crop tool in Camera Raw's Toolbox. Then, press the Escape key on your keyboard, and the straightening border will go away. However, if you want to keep your straightening, click the Open button, and the photo will be straightened and cropped perfectly to size, ready for editing in Photoshop.

Automating Your Camera Raw Processing

One of the coolest things about Camera Raw in Photoshop CS2 is the level of automation. By that I mean that when you apply changes to one image, you can easily and quickly apply that same set of changes to a host of other images—even while you're working on other things, it's still processing in the background. Sweeeet!

Method One:

This first one might really surprise you: You can edit multiple RAW images and apply settings to all of them at once, without ever having Photoshop open. That's right, you can do it all from the Adobe Bridge. Just Command-click (PC: Control-click) on the thumbnails you want to edit, press Command-R (PC: Control-R), and those photos will open in Camera Raw (right from the Bridge, without even launching Photoshop). Click on the Select All button in the top-left corner of the Camera Raw dialog to select all your open photos. Now, any changes you make to your main image will be applied to all open images.

TIP: When you click the Save Images button (and choose your settings in the resulting Save Options dialog), Camera Raw will batch process the files while you're correcting your images. A status link will appear above the Save Images button. Click on the link to see the status of your processed images.

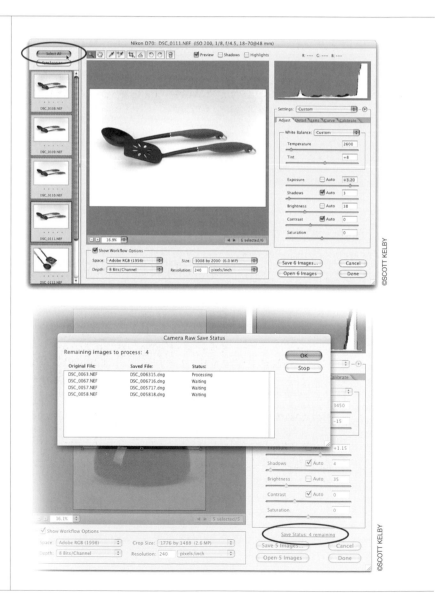

©SCOTT KELBY

Method Two:

If you've made an adjustment to one photo that was taken using a particular camera under a particular lighting situation (like a Nikon D70 in direct sunlight), you can save those changes and apply them in one click to other RAW images from right within the Bridge. First, save your settings by going under the Settings flyout menu (it's the little right-facing arrow to the right of the Settings pop-up menu) and choosing Save Settings. To apply those settings to another image(s), click on that photo in the Bridge, go under the Edit menu, under Apply Camera Raw Settings, and choose your saved setting.

Method Three:

If you've made changes to a RAW file, you can instantly return to your camera's original default settings by clicking on the photo in the Bridge, going under the Edit menu, under Apply Camera Raw Settings, and choosing Clear Camera Raw Settings. This removes your edits (or the default Camera Raw settings) and replaces the original default settings from your camera.

Continued

Method Four:

If you've applied some Camera Raw adjustments to a file, you can copy-and-paste those adjustments to any other files in the Bridge you like. Start by clicking on the thumbnail of an adjusted RAW photo. Then, go under the Bridge's Edit menu, under Apply Camera Raw Settings, and choose Copy Camera Raw Settings. Now Command-click (PC: Control-click) on the thumbnails of any other RAW photos that you want to have those same settings, and then go back under the Edit menu, under Apply Camera Raw Settings, and choose Paste Camera Raw Settings. This brings up a dialog asking which of those copied settings you want applied: everything or just certain settings. Choose what you want from the Subset pop-up menu or click on the checkboxes to turn on/off the items you want, and then click OK. Those checked settings will be applied to your selected images. How cool is that?

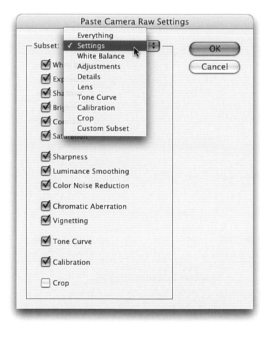

Sharpening within Camera Raw

ADVANCED TECHNIQUES
FOR PROS ONLY!

Although Camera Raw enables you to sharpen your image at this early stage in the correction process, you have to decide if this is something you really want to do. I've heard arguments for sharpening at this stage, but many more against it, so like most corrections, it'll come down to your own personal preference. If you do decide to sharpen now (or if you want to turn off the sharpening that's on by default), here's how:

Step One:
When you open an image in Camera Raw, by default it applies a small amount of sharpening to your photo. You can see how much by going to the Detail tab (along the right side of the dialog) and looking at the Sharpness slider. To add additional sharpness, drag the slider to the right (if you do this, first make sure to set your view to 100% in the bottom left of the preview so you can see the effect of sharpening).

Step Two:
Now that you know how to apply more sharpness (I hate to tell you this), I recommend setting the Sharpness at 0% (essentially turning it off). I recommend this for two reasons: First, because there's just one slider, so you basically have to take what it gives you. Second, I feel sharpening should be done right before you save the file, not when you're initially creating it, so it does the minimum amount of damage to the image. However, if you'd like to see what the "sharpened" image would look like, you can sharpen just the preview, not the actual file. Just press Command-K (PC: Control-K) while the Camera Raw dialog is open, and in the Camera Raw Preferences dialog, choose Preview Images Only in the Apply Sharpening To pop-up menu.

Adjusting Color (Calibrating)

So far, everything in Camera Raw has been about adjusting the exposure, or the brightness, or the sharpness, or the white balance…and that's all well and good, but what if your photo is too red, or what if the white balance looks right, but something in the photo is still too blue? Here's what to do:

Step One:

Let's say after setting the exposure, brightness, etc., there's a part of your image that has too much red. To remove that red, go to the Calibrate tab (along the right side of the Camera Raw dialog) and drag the Red Saturation slider to the left, lowering the amount of red in the entire photo. If the red simply isn't the right shade of red (maybe it's too hot and you just want to tone it down a bit), drag the Red Hue slider until the red color looks better to you (dragging to the right makes the reds more orange).

Step Two:

If all the images from your digital camera have this problem with red, you may want to save these calibration settings by choosing Save Settings Subset from the Settings flyout menu (it's the right-facing arrow to the right of the Settings pop-up menu). When the Save Settings Subset dialog appears, uncheck everything but Calibration (or choose it from the Subset pop-up menu), and then click Save. Now you can apply these settings to other images shot with that digital camera by choosing your saved subset from the Settings pop-up menu. *Note:* You can adjust your blues and greens in the same way.

Noise Reduction in Camera Raw

While you're processing your image, if you notice that your image has digital noise (those annoying red-and-green spots or splotchy patches of color), you can reduce that noise—especially the color part—from right within Camera Raw.

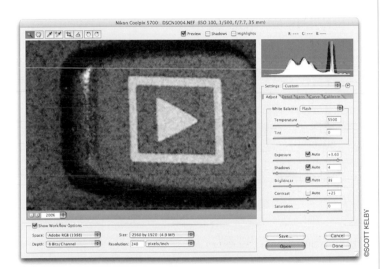

©SCOTT KELBY

Step One:
Open a RAW image in Camera Raw that has a digital noise issue, press Z to get the Zoom tool, and zoom in tight so the noise is easily visible. There are two types of noise you can deal with in Camera Raw: (1) high ISO noise, which often happens when you're shooting in low-light situations, especially when using a high ISO setting (hence the name); and (2) color noise, which can happen even in normal situations (this noise is more prevalent in some cameras than others).

Step Two:
Click on the Detail tab along the right side of the dialog. To decrease the amount of color noise, drag the Color Noise Reduction slider to the right. As you can see, it does a pretty fair job of removing the color noise, though it does tend to desaturate the overall color just a bit. That's why it's good to zoom out to see the preview so you don't wash out the photo. If the problem is mostly in shadow areas (high ISO noise), you can use the Luminance Smoothing slider in the same way—drag to the right to reduce the noise—but use this carefully, because it can tend to make your photo look a bit soft.

Bracketing with Camera Raw

FOR PROS ONLY!
ADVANCED TECHNIQUES

If you forgot to bracket in the camera itself, you can use Camera Raw to create multiple exposures, and then open those images in Photoshop, where you can composite them together to create an image that one exposure alone couldn't capture. Here's how it's done:

Step One:
Open the RAW image you want to apply a bracketing technique to. In this example, the kettle is too dark, but the background the kettle was shot on looks fairly good, so we're going to expose this first image for the highlights. Start by increasing the Exposure and Brightness settings by dragging the sliders to the right, and then lower the Shadows by dragging its slider to the left (the Auto checkboxes will be deselected automatically). Now the kettle, which was quite dark in the original RAW file, is fairly well exposed, so it's time to click on the Open button at the bottom of the Camera Raw dialog to open this version in Photoshop.

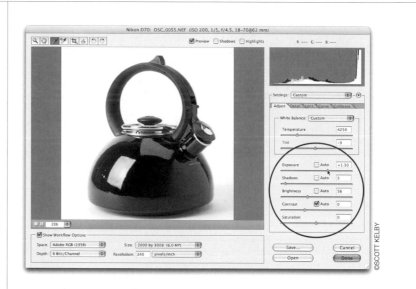

Step Two:
Now go back to the Adobe Bridge (or wherever the original image is), and reopen the same RAW file in Camera Raw. This time, we're going to expose it for the shadows, so reduce the Exposure setting, increase the Shadows, decrease the Brightness, and decrease the Contrast to create an image with deep, rich shadow areas that still have some detail and the nice gray background. Once it looks good in the preview, click on the Open button to open this shadow-heavy version in Photoshop.

Step Three:
Now you should have both versions open in Photoshop: the brighter one exposed for the highlights (to bring out the kettle) and the darker one exposed for the shadows (to bring out the gray background and the shadows below the kettle). Arrange the windows so you can see both onscreen at the same time.

Step Four:
Press V to get the Move tool, press-and-hold the Shift key, and drag-and-drop the darker version on top of the lighter version. The key to this part is holding down the Shift key while you drag, which perfectly aligns the dark copy (that now appears on its own layer in the Layers palette) with the lighter version on the Background layer. (This exact alignment of one identical photo over another is referred to as being "pin registered.") You can now close the shadow document without saving, as both versions of the image are contained within the lighter version.

Continued

Step Five:

Go to the Layers palette, hold down the Option (PC: Alt) key, and click on the Add Layer Mask icon at the bottom of the Layers palette. This puts a black mask over your darker image, covering it so you only see the lighter image on the Background layer.

Step Six:

Now you get to "reveal" the darker parts, but only where you want them. Here's how: Press the letter B to get the Brush tool, and then click on the down-facing arrow next to the word "Brush" in the Options Bar and choose a medium-size, soft-edged brush from the Brush Picker. Now, press the letter D to set your Foreground color to white, and start painting over the areas of the photo that you want to be darker (in this case, the base of the kettle). As you paint with white directly on that black mask, the white reveals the dark version beneath the mask.

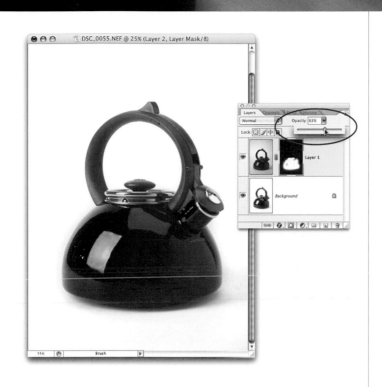

Step Seven:

Keep going until you've painted the dark areas that you want back in (in this case, you get a composite where the kettle is from the darker bracketed version, while the background and shadows beneath the kettle are from the lighter bracket). If the dark areas seem too intense, slightly lower the Opacity in the Layers palette. So what you wind up with is an image like the one shown here—one where the object and background are perfectly exposed—it's the best of two photos combined.

Fixing Chromatic Aberrations (That Colored-Edge Fringe)

ADVANCED TECHNIQUES FOR PROS ONLY!

Chromatic aberrations is a fancy name for that thin line of colored fringe that sometimes appears around the edges in photos. Sometimes the fringe is red, sometimes green, sometimes blue, but all the time it's bad, so we might as well get rid of it. Luckily, Camera Raw has a built-in fix that does a pretty good job.

Step One:

Open the RAW photo that has signs of chromatic aberrations (colored-edge fringe), and then press Z to get the Zoom tool in the Camera Raw dialog. Zoom in on an area where the fringe is fairly obvious. In the example shown here, I zoomed directly in on a newspaper in the photo that had a red-edge fringe along one side.

Step Two:

To remove this fringe, click on the Lens tab along the right side of the Camera Raw dialog to bring up the Chromatic Aberration sliders. They're pretty self-explanatory: The top one fixes red or cyan fringe; the bottom fixes blue or yellow fringe.

TIP: Before you begin fixing any chromatic aberrations, you may want to click on the Detail tab and lower the Sharpness amount to 0%, because sharpening can also cause color fringes to appear (and you want to make sure you're curing the right problem).

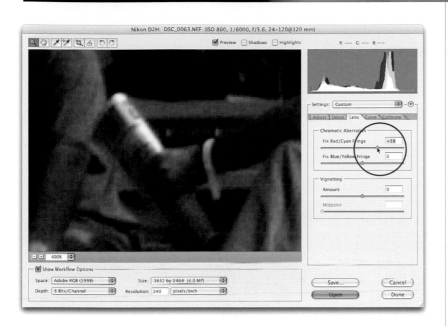

Step Three:
Since the fringe in this particular case is red, move the top Chromatic Aberration slider to the right (toward Cyan), which removes the red fringe.

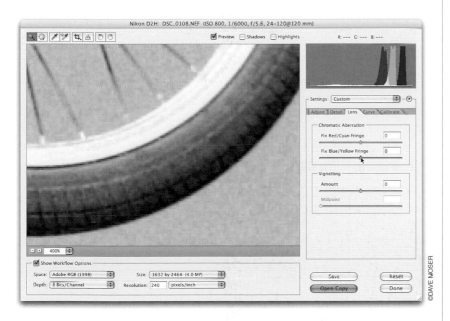

TIP: Here's a tip to help you more easily see where the fringe is (and if your corrections are really working). If you Option-click (PC: Alt-click) on one of the sliders, the preview will change to display just those two colors (Red/Cyan or Blue/Yellow) in your image. For example, this photo has a purple fringe around the base of the wheel, but by Option/Alt-clicking on the Blue/Yellow slider, it's easier to isolate the fringe, so I can now drag to the left (away from Yellow) to neutralize the purple fringe. The preview helps you see if the fringe is really going away while you're correcting it.

Adjusting Contrast Using Curves

Okay, besides the Contrast slider we talked about earlier (which is rather limited), in Photoshop CS2 you can actually create your own custom contrast curves. This gives you a much larger level of control over the contrast in your image, and you can use the built-in presets or create (and save) your own curve settings manually.

Step One:
Open the image in Camera Raw whose contrast you want to adjust using curves. Then click on the Curve tab along the right side of the Camera Raw dialog to make the curves visible. The default Tone Curve is set to Medium Contrast, which provides a medium amount of contrast (you can see only a slight angle in the curve).

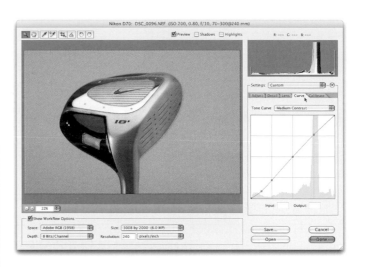

Step Two:
If you want to create much more dramatic contrast within your image, choose Strong Contrast from the Tone Curve pop-up menu, which creates a much steeper curve.

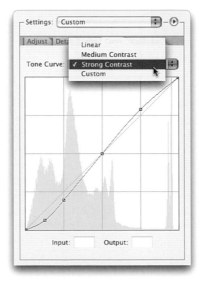

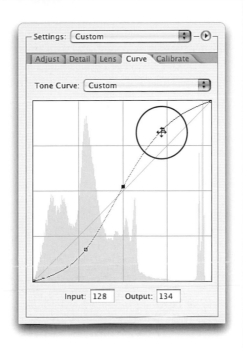

Step Three:

If you're familiar with curves and want to create your own custom curve, start by editing any one of the preset curves by simply clicking-and-dragging any adjustment points. Doing this immediately changes the Tone Curve pop-up menu to Custom, meaning you're free to adjust the curve any way you'd like. If you'd prefer to start from scratch, choose Linear from the Tone Curve pop-up menu, which gives you a flat curve. To add adjustment points, just click along the curve. To remove a point, just click-and-drag it right off the curve (drag it off quickly, like you're pulling off a Band-Aid).

Step Four:

If you create a contrast curve that you'd like to be able to apply again, unfortunately you're not able to add it to the Tone Curve pop-up menu; however, you can save that setting by going up to the Settings flyout menu (it's the right-facing arrow to the right of the Settings pop-up menu) and choosing Save Settings Subset. This brings up a dialog that lets you choose which controls you want to save. In this case, from the Subset pop-up menu choose Tone Curve. Click Save, name your file, and from now on you can choose to load your custom curve from the Settings pop-up menu.

Fixing (or Creating) Edge Vignetting

If you're looking at a photo and the corners of the photo appear darker, that's lens vignetting. This is either a problem or a cool effect, depending on how you view it. Generally, I look at it this way—if it's just the corners, and they're just a little bit dark, that's a problem and I fix it. However, sometimes I want to focus the viewer's attention on a particular area, so I create a vignette, but I expand it significantly beyond the corners so it looks like an intentional effect, not a lens problem. Here's how to fix (or create) vignettes:

Step One:
In the RAW photo shown here, you can see the hard areas in the corners (the vignetting I was talking about). This vignetting is normally caused by the camera's lens, so don't blame yourself (unless you bought a really cheap lens—then feel free to give yourself as much grief as you can bear).

Step Two:
To remove this vignetting from the corners, click on the Lens tab (along the right of the Camera Raw dialog) to bring up the Vignetting options. Click on the Amount slider and drag it to the right until the vignetting disappears (dragging to the right essentially brightens the corners, which hides the vignetting). Once you begin moving the Amount slider, the Midpoint slider beneath it becomes available. That slider determines how wide the vignetting repair extends into your photo (in other words, how far out from the corners your repair extends), so drag it to the right for even more lightening.

Step Three:

Now for the opposite: adding vignetting to focus attention (by the way, in the Photographic Special Effects chapter, I also show you how to get the same effect outside of Camera Raw). This time, in the Vignetting section, drag the Amount slider to the left, and as you drag you'll start to see vignetting appear in the corners of your photo. But since it's just in the corners, it looks like the bad kind of vignetting, not the good kind, so you'll need to go on to the next step.

Step Four:

To make the vignetting look more like a soft spotlight falling on your subject, drag the Midpoint slider to the left, which increases the size of the vignetting and creates a soft, pleasing effect. That's it—how to get rid of 'em and how to add 'em. Two for the price of one!

Saving RAW Files in Adobe's Digital Negative (DNG) Format

At this point in time, there's a concern with the RAW file format because there's not a single, universal format for RAW images—every digital camera manufacturer has its own. That may not seem like a problem, but what happens if one of these camera companies stops developing or supporting a format and switches to something else? Seriously, what if in a few years from now there was no easy way to open your saved RAW files? Adobe recognized this problem and created the Digital Negative (DNG) format for long-term archival of RAW images.

Step One:

As of the writing of this book, no major digital camera manufacturer has built in the ability to save RAW files in Adobe's DNG format (although we believe it's only a matter of time before they do); so for now what you can do is save your RAW file to Adobe DNG from right within the Camera Raw dialog, which you do by hitting the Save button. This brings up the Save Options dialog, and at the bottom of the dialog is where you choose your file format. To save in DNG, choose Digital Negative from the Format pop-up menu.

Step Two:

You have some additional options: You can choose to embed the original RAW file into your DNG (making the file larger, but your original is embedded for safekeeping in case you ever need to extract it—and if you have the hard disk [or CD space]—go for it!). There's a compression option (and it's "lossless," meaning you don't lose quality like you do with JPEG compression). You can also choose to include a JPEG preview with your DNG file. That's it—click Save and you've got a DNG archival-quality file that can be opened by Photoshop (or the free DNG utility from Adobe).

HDR and Exposure Merge

While Photoshop CS2 is the first version to compile High Dynamic Range (HDR) 32-bit images, you kind of have to think of this as more of a "technology preview" than a tool that will get a lot of use (at this point anyway), because thus far there are no monitors that can truly display HDR images or printers that can print the range of colors they possess. But there will be one day (and we'll all fly around with jet packs, too). Here's how to mess around with HDR and impress your photographer friends:

Step One:
The magic of HDR is that it lets you merge multiple shots of the same scene (using a tripod), but you vary the exposure time for each shot (not the f-stops—the exposure time). Then these are merged together to create one "megaphoto" with a dynamic range far exceeding what humans, printers, or displays can reproduce. However, dogs can see HDR and they love it! (Kidding.) So that's step one: Shoot multiple shots of the same scene and vary the exposure value (Adobe recommends two exposure-time value settings between shots, like 1/100, 1/250, 1/500, etc.). Once you've taken your shots, you can open them from the Adobe Bridge by navigating to them on your hard disk, then going under the Tools menu, under Photoshop, and choosing Merge to HDR.

Step Two:
When the Merge to HDR dialog appears, you'll see the results of the merge (and the photos used are displayed on the left side of the dialog). At this point, there's only one slider, which you can move to adjust the white point. You also get to choose the bit-depth, but if you leave it at the default 32-bit and open it in Photoshop CS2, there's a very limited number of tools or features that work on 32-bit images.

Exposure: 1/60s   Focal Length: 120mm   Aperture Value: *f*/5.7

Super Size Me
resizing and cropping

Now, you're probably thinking, "Scott, do we really need a full chapter on resizing and cropping?" Absolutely! Well, we definitely need a chapter on resizing (the different strategies for maintaining image quality when resizing are critical), and the cropping stuff just seemed like a natural fit here (because it's not a natural fit anywhere else). So, I thought I'd put these two great topics together to create a "super-sized" chapter. Okay, that was clearly a lame attempt to draw a connection between the chapter title and the real title of this chapter (which is the subhead beneath it). Actually, I think it works because this chapter is about resizing, and the chapter title is from the award-winning documentary *Super Size Me* (see the "sizing" connection?), which is about a guy who eats breakfast, lunch, and dinner at a McDonald's fast-food restaurant for like 40-something days until he gets so sick that he finally switches to Wendy's (or something like that). Anyway, back to our story. We know that learning different strategies about how and when to resize is important, but do we really need an entire chapter on cropping? No. But we do need at least a third of a chapter (which is about what you'll get, because most of this chapter is about resizing) to learn all the cool cropping things you need to know. Now, when I say "we do need at least a third of a chapter," who is the "we" I'm referring to? Anytime I say "we" in this book, I either mean: (a) me, (b) you and me, or (c) we. I sometimes mean (d) all of the above. Hey, I never said this would be easy.

Cropping Photos

After you've sorted your images in the Adobe Bridge, one of the first editing tasks you'll probably undertake is cropping a photo. There are a number of different ways to crop a photo in Photoshop CS2. We'll start with the basic garden-variety options, and then we'll look at some ways to make the task faster and easier.

Step One:
Press the letter C to get the Crop tool (you could always select it directly from the Toolbox, but I only recommend doing so if you're charging by the hour).

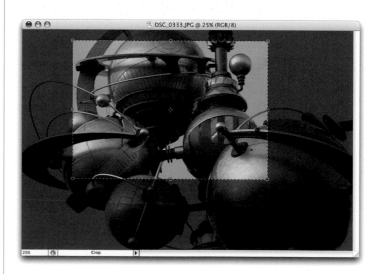

Step Two:
Click within your photo and drag out a cropping border. The area to be cropped away will appear dimmed (shaded). You don't have to worry about getting your crop border right when you first drag it out, because you can edit the border by clicking-and-dragging the points that appear in each corner and at the center of each side.

TIP: If you don't like seeing your photo with the cropped-away areas appearing shaded (as in the previous step), you can toggle this shading feature off/on by pressing the Backslash key on your keyboard. When you press the Backslash key, the border remains in place, but the shading is turned off.

Step Three:
While you have the crop border in place, rotate it by moving your cursor outside the border (when you do, the cursor will change into a double-headed arrow). Just click-and-drag and the cropping border will rotate in the direction you choose (this is a great way to save time if you have a crooked image, because it lets you crop and rotate at the same time).

Continued

Step Four:
After you have the cropping border where you want it, just press the Return (PC: Enter) key to crop your image.

TIP: If you've dragged out a cropping border, and then decide you don't want to crop the image, you can either press the Escape key on your keyboard, click on the "No" symbol in the Options Bar, or just click on a different tool in the Toolbox, which will bring up a dialog asking if you want to crop the image. Click on the Don't Crop button to cancel your crop.

ANOTHER TIP: Another popular way to crop is to skip the Crop tool altogether and just use the Rectangular Marquee tool (M) to put a selection around the area of your photo you want to keep. With your selection in place, go under the Image menu and choose Crop. The areas outside your selection will be cropped away instantly. Press Command-D (PC: Control-D) to deselect.

The "rule of thirds" is a trick that photographers sometimes use to create more interesting compositions. Basically, you visually divide the image you see in your camera's viewfinder into thirds, and then you position your horizon so it goes along either the top imaginary horizontal line or the bottom one. Then, you position the subject (or focal point) at the center intersections of those lines. But if you didn't use the rule in the viewfinder—no sweat! Here's how to use Photoshop CS2 to crop your image using the rule of thirds to create more appealing compositions:

Cropping Using the "Rule of Thirds"

Step One:
Open the photo you want to apply the rule-of-thirds cropping technique to (the shot here is poorly composed, with the horizon in the center of the image—it just screams "snapshot!"). Since this is a cropping technique, you realize that the dimensions of your photo are going to get smaller, right? Good. So create a new document that is somewhat smaller than the photo you want, but using the same resolution and color mode (this is *very* important, otherwise your image won't fit properly in this new document). In the example here, my original photo is 12x8", so the new document I created is only 8x6"; that way, there's room to play with my cropping (you'll see how in just a moment).

Step Two:
While your new document is active, go under the Photoshop menu (PC: Edit menu), under Preferences, and choose Guides, Grid & Slices. In the resulting dialog, under the Grid section, enter 33.3 in the Gridline Every field, and then choose Percent from the pop-up menu on the right. In the Subdivisions field, change the default setting of 4 to just 1, and then click OK. You won't see anything in your document yet.

Continued

Step Three:

Go under the View menu, under Show, and choose Grid. When you do this, the nonprinting grid you created in the previous step (the one divided into horizontal and vertical thirds) will appear in your image area as a visual representation of the rule-of-thirds grid, which you'll use for visual composition cropping.

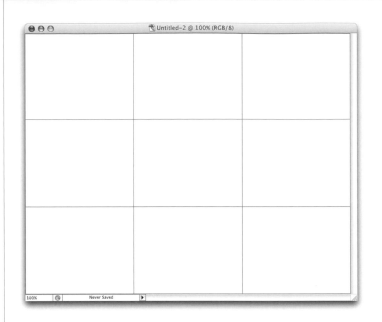

Step Four:

Return to your image document, press V to switch to the Move tool, and click-and-drag your image onto your blank document. Here's where you create a better composition: Using the Move tool, position your image's horizon along one of the horizontal grid lines (here I used the bottom line), and be sure your focal point (the boat, in this case) falls on one of the intersecting points (the bottom-left intersection in this example). Because your image is larger than the new document, you have plenty of room to position your photo.

Step Five:
You can now crop away the sides of your image. Press the letter C to switch to the Crop tool and click-and-drag around your entire image. With your crop border in place, press Return (PC: Enter) to complete your crop. Now just hide the grid lines by returning to the View menu, under Show, and deselect Grid—then enjoy your new, cropped image.

Cropping to a Specific Size

If you're outputting photos for clients, chances are they're going to want them in standard sizes so they can easily find frames to fit their photos. If that's the case, you'll find this technique handy, because it lets you crop any image to a predetermined size (like 5x7", 8x10", and so on).

Step One:

Let's say our portrait measures 15x10", and we want to crop it to be a perfect horizontal 10x8". First, press the C key to get the Crop tool, and up in the Options Bar on the left you'll see Width and Height fields. Enter the size you want for width, followed by the unit of measurement you want to use (e.g., "in" for inches, "px" for pixels, "cm" for centimeters, "mm" for millimeters, etc.). Next, press the Tab key to jump over to the Height field and enter your desired height, again followed by the unit of measurement.

Step Two:

Click within your photo with the Crop tool and drag out a cropping border. You'll notice that as you drag, the border is constrained to a horizontal shape and no side points are visible—only corner points. Whatever size you make your border, the area within that border will become a 10x8" photo. In this example, I dragged the border so it almost touched the top and bottom to get as much of the subject as possible.

Step Three:

After your cropping border is onscreen, you can reposition it by moving your cursor inside the border (your cursor will change to an arrow). You can now drag the border into place, or use the Arrow keys on your keyboard for more precise control. When it looks right to you, press Return (PC: Enter) to finalize your crop, and the area inside your cropping border will be 10x8". (I made the rulers visible by pressing Command-R [PC: Control-R] so you could see that the image measures exactly 10x8".)

TIP: Once you've entered a Width and Height in the Options Bar, those dimensions will remain in place until you clear them. To clear the fields (so you can use the Crop tool for freeform cropping to any size), just go up in the Options Bar and click on the Clear button (while you have the Crop tool active, of course).

COOLER TIP: If you already have a photo that is the exact size and resolution that you'd like to apply to other images, you can use its settings as the crop dimensions. First, open the photo you'd like to resize, and then open your "ideal-size-and-resolution" photo. Get the Crop tool, and then in the Options Bar, click on the Front Image button. Photoshop CS2 will automatically input that photo's dimensions into the Crop tool's Width, Height, and Resolution fields. All you have to do is crop the other image, and it will share the exact same specs as your "ideal-size" photo.

The Trick for Keeping the Same Aspect Ratio When You Crop

Okay, let's say you want to crop a photo down in size, but you want to keep the aspect ratio the same as the original photo from your camera (so when you crop, the photo will be smaller in size, but it will have the exact same width-to-height ratio as the original photo). You could pull out a calculator and do the math to figure out what the new smaller size should be, but there's a faster, easier, and more visual way. (By the way, although the Crop tool within Camera Raw in CS2 gives you a menu of preset ratios, you can only use those presets on a RAW image, but this technique works on *any* photo.)

Step One:
Open the photo you want to crop. Press Command-A (PC: Control-A) to put a selection around the entire photo.

Step Two:
Go under the Select menu and choose Transform Selection. This lets you resize the selection itself, without resizing the photo within the selection (which is what usually happens).

Step Three:
Press-and-hold the Shift key, grab a corner point, and drag inward to size the selection area. Because you're holding the Shift key as you scale, the aspect ratio (the same ratio as your original photo) remains exactly the same. Once you get the selection near the size you're looking for, move your cursor inside the bounding box, and then click-and-drag to position your selection where you want to crop. Then, press Return (PC: Enter) to complete your transformation.

Step Four:
Now that you've used your selection to determine the crop area, it's time to actually crop, so go under the Image menu and choose (no big surprise here) Crop.

Step Five:
Once you choose Crop, the image is then cropped to fit within your selection, so just press Command-D (PC: Control-D) to deselect. Because you followed the steps shown here, your cropped image maintains the same aspect ratio as your original photo.

Creating Your Own Custom Crop Tools

Although it's more of an advanced technique, creating your own custom tools isn't complicated. In fact, once you set it up, it will save you time and money. We're going to create what are called "tool presets." These tool presets are a series of tools (in this case, Crop tools) with all our option settings already in place. So we'll create a 5x7", 6x4", or whatever size Crop tool we want. Then, when we want to crop to 5x7", all we have to do is grab the 5x7" Crop tool preset. Here's how:

Step One:

Press the letter C to switch to the Crop tool, and then go under the Window menu and choose Tool Presets to bring up the Tool Presets palette (or click on it in the Palette Well on the right side of the Options Bar, where it's nested by default). You'll find five Crop tool presets are already there, all set at 300 ppi. That's great if you need these sizes at 300 ppi; but if you don't, you might as well drag these tool presets into the Trash icon at the bottom of the palette. (Also, make sure that Current Tool Only option is checked at the bottom of the palette so you'll see only the Crop tool's presets, and not the presets for every tool.)

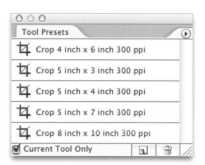

Step Two:

Go up to the Options Bar and enter the dimensions for the first tool you want to create (in this example, we'll create a Crop tool that crops to a wallet-size image). In the Width field, enter 2. Press the Tab key to jump to the Height field and enter 2.5. *Note:* If you have the Rulers set to Inches under the Units section in Photoshop's Units & Rulers Preferences (Command-K [PC: Control-K]), then when you press the Tab key, Photoshop will automatically insert "in" after your numbers, indicating inches.

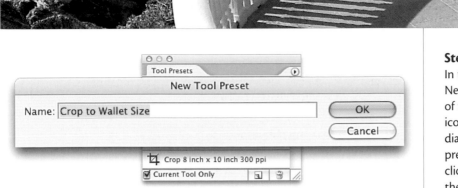

Step Three:
In the Tool Presets palette, click on the New Tool Preset icon at the bottom of the palette (to the left of the Trash icon). This brings up the New Tool Preset dialog, in which you can name your new preset. Name it "Crop to Wallet Size," click OK, and the new tool is added to the Tool Presets palette.

Step Four:
Continue this process of typing in new dimensions in the Crop tool's Options Bar and clicking on the New Tool Preset icon until you've created custom Crop tools for the sizes you use most. Make the names descriptive (for example, add "Portrait" or "Landscape").

TIP: If you need to change the name of a preset, just double-click directly on its name in the palette, and then type in a new name.

Continued

Step Five:

Chances are your custom Crop tool presets won't be in the order you want them, so go under the Edit menu and choose Preset Manager. In the resulting dialog, choose Tools from the Preset Type pop-up menu, and scroll down until you see the Crop tools you created. Now just click-and-drag them to wherever you want them to appear in the list, and then click Done.

Step Six:

Now you can close the Tool Presets palette because there's an easier way to access your presets: With the Crop tool selected, just click on the Crop icon on the left in the Options Bar. A pop-up menu of tools will appear. Click on a preset, drag out a cropping border, and it will be fixed to the exact dimensions you chose for that tool. Imagine how much time and effort this is going to save (really, close your eyes and imagine…mmmm…tool presets…yummy…).

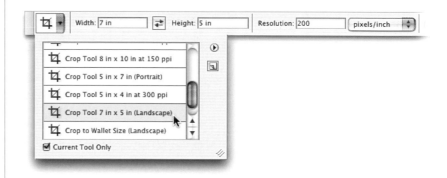

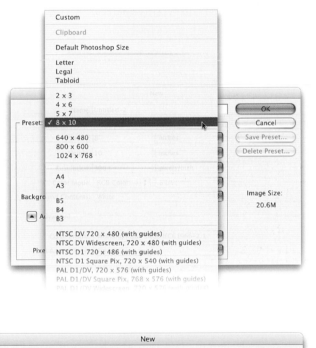

Photoshop's dialog for creating new documents has a pop-up menu with a list of preset sizes. You're probably thinking, "Hey, there's a 4x6", 5x7", and 8x10"—I'm set." The problem is there's no way to switch the orientation of these presets (so a 4x6" will always be a 4" wide by 6" tall, portrait-oriented document). That's why creating your own custom new document sizes is so important. Here's how:

Custom Sizes for Photographers

Step One:
Go under the File menu and choose New. When the New dialog appears, click on the Preset pop-up menu to reveal the list of preset sizes. The preset sizes for photographers are the set just below the Tabloid preset, and they include 2x3", 4x6", 5x7", and 8x10". The only problem with these is that their orientation is set to portrait and their resolution is set to 300 ppi by default. So, if you want a land-scape preset at less than 300 ppi, you'll need to create and save your own.

Step Two:
For example, let's say that you want a 5x7" set to landscape (that's 7" wide by 5" tall). First enter 7 inches in the Width field, 5 inches in the Height field, choose your desired Color Mode, and then enter a Resolution (I entered 212 ppi, which is enough for me to have my image printed on a high-end printing press). Once your settings are in place, click on the Save Preset button.

Continued

Step Three:

This brings up the New Document Preset dialog. You can toggle on/off which parameters you want saved, but I use the default setting to include everything (better safe than sorry, I guess).

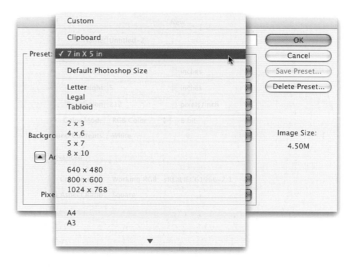

Step Four:

Click OK and your new custom preset will appear in the Preset pop-up menu. You only have to go through this once. Photoshop CS2 will remember your custom settings, and they will appear in this Preset pop-up menu from now on.

Step Five:

If you decide you want to delete a preset, it's simple—just open the New dialog, choose the preset you want to delete from the Preset pop-up menu, and then click on the Delete Preset button. A warning dialog will appear asking you to confirm the deletion. Click on Yes, and it's gone!

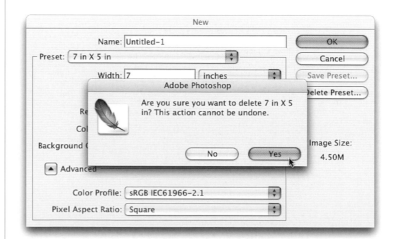

Resizing Digital Camera Photos

If you're used to resizing scans, you'll find that resizing images from digital cameras is a bit different, primarily because scanners create high-res scans (usually 300 ppi or more), but the default settings for many digital cameras produce an image that is large in physical dimensions, but lower in pixels-per-inch (usually 72 ppi). The trick is to decrease the physical size of your digital camera image (and increase its resolution) without losing any of its quality. Here's the trick:

Step One:
Open the digital camera image that you want to resize. Press Command-R (PC: Control-R) to make Photoshop's rulers visible. As you can see from the rulers, the photo is nearly 28" wide by nearly 42" high.

Step Two:
Go under the Image menu and choose Image Size (or press Command-Option-I [PC: Control-Alt-I]) to bring up the Image Size dialog. Under the Document Size section, the Resolution setting is 72 ppi. A resolution of 72 ppi is considered "low resolution" and is ideal for photos that will only be viewed onscreen (such as Web graphics, slide shows, and so on), but it's too low to get high-quality results from a color inkjet printer, color laser printer, or for use on a printing press.

Continued

Step Three:

If we plan to output this photo to any printing device, it's pretty clear that we'll need to increase the resolution to get good results. I wish we could just type in the resolution we'd like it to be in the Resolution field (such as 200 or 300 ppi), but unfortunately, this "resampling" makes our low-res photo appear soft (blurry) and pixelated. That's why we need to turn off the Resample Image checkbox (it's on by default). That way, when we type in a Resolution setting that we need, Photoshop automatically adjusts the Width and Height of the image down in the exact same proportion. As your Width and Height come down (with Resample Image turned off), your Resolution goes up. Best of all, there's absolutely no loss of quality. Pretty cool!

Step Four:

Here I've turned off Resample Image and I entered 150 in the Resolution field for output to a color inkjet printer. (I know, you probably think you need a lot more resolution, but you usually don't.) This resized my image to about 13x20", so with a little bit of cropping I can easily output a 13x19" print (which happens to be the maximum output size for my Epson 2200—perfect!).

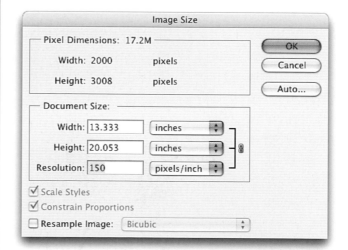

Step Five:

Here's the Image Size dialog for our source photo, and this time I've increased the Resolution setting to 212 ppi for output to a printing press. (Again, you don't need nearly as much resolution as you'd think.) As you can see, the Width of my image is no longer 28"—it's now just over 9". The Height is no longer 42"—now it's just over 14".

Step Six:

When you click OK, you won't see the image window change at all—it will appear at the exact same size onscreen—but look at the rulers. You can see that it's now about 9" wide by about 14" high. Resizing using this technique does three big things: (1) It gets your physical dimensions down to size (the photo now fits easily on an 11x17" sheet); (2) it increases the resolution enough so you can output this image on a printing press; and (3) you haven't softened, blurred, or pixelated the image in any way—the quality remains the same—all because you turned off Resample Image. *Note:* Do not turn off Resample Image for images that you scan on a scanner—they start as high-res images in the first place. Turning Resample Image off is only for photos taken with a digital camera.

Automated Saving and Resizing

Back when Photoshop CS was fairly new, Russell Preston Brown (Adobe's in-house evangelist and Photoshop madman) introduced a pretty slick little utility called Dr. Brown's Image Processor, which would let you take a folder full of images and save them in various formats (for example, it could open a PSD file and automatically make a JPEG and a TIFF from it, and resize each along the way). It became a cult hit, and now in CS2, an updated version of it is included (but sadly, they dropped the "Dr. Brown" part, which I always thought gave it its charm).

Step One:

Go under the File menu, under Scripts, and choose Image Processor. By the way, if you're working in the Adobe Bridge (rather than Photoshop), you can Command-click (PC: Control-click) on all the photos you want to apply the Image Processor to, then go under the Tools menu, under Photoshop, and choose Image Processor. That way, when the Image Processor opens, it already has those photos pegged for processing. Sweet!

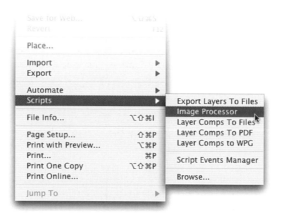

Step Two:

When the Image Processor dialog opens, the first thing you have to do is choose the folder of photos you want it to "do its thing" to by clicking on the Select Folder button, then navigate to the folder you want and click Choose. If you already have some photos open in Photoshop, you can click on the Use Open Images radio button (or if you choose Image Processor from the Bridge, the Select Folder button won't be there at all—instead it will list how many photos you have selected in the Bridge). Then, in the second section, decide whether you want the new copies to be saved in the same folder or copied into a different folder. No big whoop (that's a technical term).

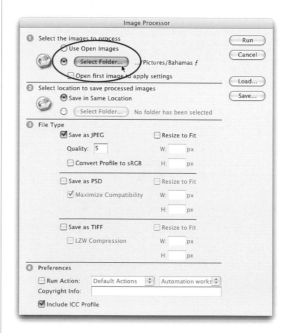

Step Three:

The third section is where the fun begins. This is where you decide how many copies of your original you're going to wind up with, and in what format. If you turn on the checkbox for Save as JPEG, Save as PSD, and Save as TIFF, you're going to create three new copies of each photo. If you turn on the Resize to Fit checkboxes (and enter a size in the Width and Height fields), your copies will be resized too (in the example shown here, I chose a small JPEG of each file, then a larger TIFF, so in my folder I'd find one small JPEG and one larger TIFF for every file in my original folder).

Step Four:

In the fourth section, if you've created an action that you want applied to your copies, you can also have that happen automatically. Just turn on the Run Action checkbox, then from the pop-up menus choose which action you want to run. If you want to automatically embed your copyright info into these copies, type your info in the Copyright Info field. Lastly, there's a checkbox that lets you decide whether to include an ICC profile in each or not (of course, I'm going to try to convince you to include the profile, because I wrote a whole chapter on how to set up color management in Photoshop). Click the Run button, sit back, and let it "do its thing," and before you know it, you'll have nice, clean copies aplenty.

Rule-Breaking Resizing for Poster-Sized Prints

This is a resizing technique I learned from my friend (and world-famous nature photographer) Vincent Versace. His poster-sized prints (24x36") always look so sharp and crisp—but we're both shooting with the same 6-megapixel camera—so I had to ask him his secret. I figured he was using some scaling plug-in, but he said he does the whole thing in Photoshop. My thanks to Vinny for sharing his simple, yet brilliant technique with me, so I could share it with you.

Step One:

Open the photo you want to resize, then go under the Image menu and choose Image Size. By the way, in Photoshop CS2 there's now *finally* a keyboard shortcut to get to the Image Size dialog: Command-Option-I (PC: Control-Alt-I).

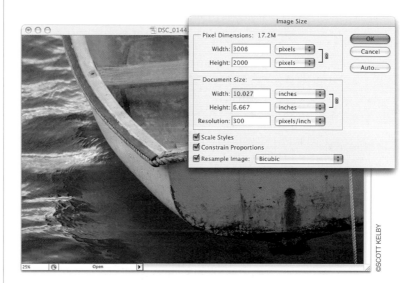

©SCOTT KELBY

Step Two:

Type in the dimensions you want as your final print size. My original width for my 6-megapixel image is just a hair over 10", so when I type 36" for the Width, the Height field will automatically adjust to around 24" (the Width and Height are linked proportionally by default—adjust one and the other adjusts in kind). Of course, not all images scale perfectly, so depending on how many megapixels your camera is, you may not be able to get exactly 24" (and in fact, you may not want to go that big, but if you do, you might need to enter more than 36" to make your Height reach 24", and then you can go back and crop your Width down to 36" [see the "Cropping to a Specific Size" technique earlier in this chapter]).

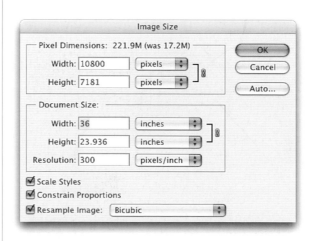

Step Three:

Once your size is in place, you'll need to adjust your resolution upward, so go to the Resolution field and enter 360. Now, you know and I know that this goes against every tried-and-true rule of resolution, and breaks the "never-just-type-in-a-higher-number-with-the-Resample-Image-checkbox-turned-on" rule that we all live and die by, but stick with me on this one—you've got to try it to believe it. So, type it in, grit your teeth, but don't click OK yet.

Step Four:

Back in Photoshop CS, Adobe introduced some new sampling algorithms for resizing images, and according to Vincent's research, the key to this resizing technique is to *not* use the sampling method Adobe recommends (which is Bicubic Smooth), and instead to choose Bicubic Sharper in the Resample Image pop up menu, which actually provides better results—so much so that Vincent claims that the printed results are not only just as good, but perhaps better than those produced by the expensive, fancy-schmancy upsizing plug-ins.

Step Five:

I've tried this technique numerous times, and I have to say—the results are pretty stunning. But don't take my word for it—click OK, print it out, and see for yourself. Here's the final image resized to 36x24" (you can see the size in the rulers by pressing Command-R [PC: Control-R]).

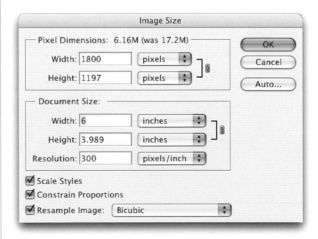

Making Your Photos Smaller (Downsizing)

There's a different set of rules we use for maintaining as much quality as possible when making an image smaller, and there are a couple of different ways to do just that (we'll cover the two main ones here). Luckily, maintaining image quality is much easier when sizing down than when scaling up (in fact, photos often look dramatically better—and sharper—when scaled down, especially if you follow these guidelines).

Downsizing photos where the resolution is already 300 ppi:

Although earlier we discussed how to change image size if your digital camera gives you 72-ppi images, with large physical dimensions (like 24x42" deep), what do you do if your camera gives you 300-ppi images at smaller physical dimensions (like a 10x6" at 300 ppi)? Basically, you turn on Resample Image (in the Image Size dialog under the Image menu), then simply type in the desired size (in this example, we want a 6x4" final image size), and click OK (don't change the Resolution setting, just click OK). The image will be scaled down to size, and the resolution will remain at 300 ppi. IMPORTANT: When you scale down using this method, it's likely that the image will soften a little bit, so after scaling you'll want to apply the Unsharp Mask filter to bring back any sharpness lost in the resizing (go to Chapter 13 to see what settings to use).

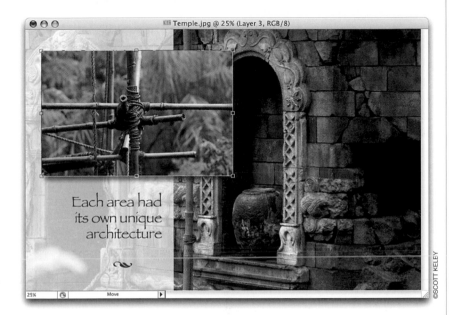

©SCOTT KELBY

Making one photo smaller without shrinking the whole document:

If you're working with more than one image in the same document, you'll resize a bit differently. To scale down a photo on a layer, first click on that photo's layer in the Layers palette, then press Command-T (PC: Control-T) to bring up Free Transform. Pressing-and-holding the Shift key (to keep the photo proportional), grab a corner point and drag inward. When it looks good to you, press the Return (PC: Enter) key. If the image looks softer after resizing it, apply the Unsharp Mask filter (again, see Chapter 13).

©SCOTT KELBY

Resizing problems when dragging between documents:

This one gets a lot of people, because at first glance it just doesn't make sense. You have two documents, approximately the same size, side-by-side onscreen. But when you drag a 72-ppi photo (of a tiger, in this case) onto a 300-ppi document (Untitled-1), the photo appears really small. Why is that? Simply put: resolution. Although the documents appear to be the same size, they're not. The tip-off that you're not really seeing them at the same size is found in the title bar of each photo. For instance, the tiger image is displayed at 100%, but the Untitled-1 document is displayed at only 25%. So, to get more predictable results, make sure both documents are at the same viewing size and resolution (check in the Image Size dialog under the Image menu).

Smart Resizing with Smart Objects

Each time you resize an image in Photoshop, you lose some quality. For example, if you make a photo larger, your image quality takes a pretty big hit. If you scale the photo down, you don't lose as much, but you still lose some. However, in CS2 Adobe introduced Smart Objects, which enable you to place a photo into an open document, resize it at will, and not lose any quality (as long as you don't resize larger than the original image). It does this by embedding the original photo into your layered document, so when you resize, it calls upon the original high-res photo to create the exact size you want.

Step One:

To create a Smart Object layer, you have to have a document already open (so you'll generally use this technique when you're combining multiple photos in the same document). Or, to create a Smart Object, all you have to do is go under the File menu and choose Place (you can place a regular photo, a RAW photo, or even a vector file, such as an Adobe Illustrator EPS file).

Step Two:

When the placed Smart Object image appears in your document, it appears with a bounding box around it so you can rotate and resize the image. Hold the Shift key, grab a corner point, and resize the photo to fit within the filmstrip frame, rotate it, and then press Return (PC: Enter) to complete your resizing, which creates the Smart Object layer.

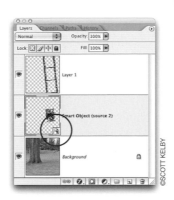

©SCOTT KELBY

Step Three:

If you look in the Layers palette, you'll see your Smart Object layer. You'll know it's a Smart Object layer because a tiny page icon will appear in the bottom-right corner of the layer's thumbnail.

Step Four:

Now, we're going to change our mind and take that small-sized photo we just placed into our layout and rotate it back so it's straight again. Then, we're going to increase the size until it's large enough to use as our background. Press Command-T (PC: Control-T) to bring up Free Transform. Rotate your image, and then hold the Shift key, grab one of the top corner points, and drag upward to increase the size of your placed photo. When you press Return (PC: Enter), Photoshop CS2 calls on your original image (which is actually embedded into your document), so your upsizing happens without losing quality. Remember: If you make a Smart Object larger than the original image's actual size, you *will* lose quality.

Step Five:

The example shown here gives you some idea of how incredibly cool Smart Objects are. The first photo was added using the Place command, then I used Free Transform to scale it up to fit within the background, which worked perfectly as a Smart Object. The second photo was a high-res image that was dragged-and-dropped into the background (rather than using the Place command). Then, I used Free Transform to scale it up to fit within the entire background, which pretty much destroyed the photo.

Sizing up as a Smart Object

Sizing up as a regular image

Continued

Step Six:
Another incredibly handy thing about Smart Object layers is that you can easily swap photos—replacing a new photo for one you already have in place—and still have them fully scalable. First, in the Layers palette, Control-click (PC: Right-click) on your Smart Object layer's name (in this example, we're going to replace the center photo with a different headshot). When the contextual menu appears, choose Replace Contents.

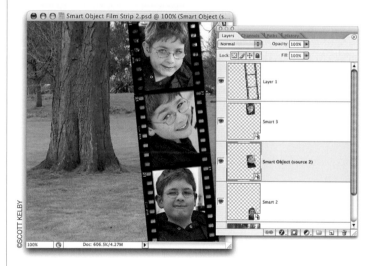

Step Seven:
This brings up the standard Place dialog. Navigate your way to the photo you want to insert to replace your existing Smart Object, and then click the Place button. When you do, the image you just chose will replace your original Smart Object photo, and it will appear in the same size and position. Since it too is a Smart Object, you'll be able to size it up (to the full original size of the high-res file, but no larger) without loss of quality.

Step Eight:
You can also place RAW images as Smart Objects. The advantage (besides the whole resizing thing) is that you can edit your Smart Object layer by going back to Camera Raw to create entirely new versions of your RAW photo. Here's how: Go under the File menu and choose Place. Locate your RAW photo and open it in Camera Raw so you can process the photo. When you click Open, it appears within your document as a Smart Layer. To re-edit (reprocess) this file from the RAW original, just double-click on the Smart Object's thumbnail.

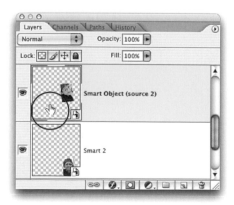

Step Nine:
When the Camera Raw dialog appears, you can reprocess the original RAW data. When you click OK, a new image is processed (at the size you want), and your Smart Object layer is updated with this newly reprocessed image. *Note:* After you've resized a photo, you can see the scaling percentage by looking at the Width and Height in the Options Bar when you have Free Transform active.

Step Ten:
If your photo is *not* a RAW image, you can still edit it separately—and have your edits update in your main document—by double-clicking on the Smart Object layer's thumbnail to open the original (embedded) document in Photoshop so you can make your edits. To have your changes appear in the Smart Object layer, you have to choose Save (from the File menu) when you're done editing the original image.

Step Eleven:
If you're completely done resizing, and you want to perform some regular edits (like cropping), you'll need to convert your layer from a Smart Object layer into a regular layer (which will reduce your file size considerably, as a full version of your original photo is embedded into your working file), so just go under the Layer menu, under Smart Objects, and choose Convert to Layer.

Resizing and How to Reach Those Hidden Free Transform Handles

What happens if you drag a large photo onto a smaller photo in Photoshop? (This happens all the time, especially if you're collaging or combining two or more photos.) You have to resize the photo using Free Transform, right? Right. But here's the catch: When you bring up Free Transform, at least two—or more likely all four—of the corner handles you need to resize the image are out of reach. You see the image's center point, but not the handles you need to reach to resize. Here's how to get around that hurdle quickly and easily:

Step One:

For the purpose of this example, create a new document in Photoshop's default size of 7x5". Now open a photo that's larger than your 7x5" document (in other words, open most any photo from your digital camera because it'll be larger than that). The photo shown here is roughly 10x6".

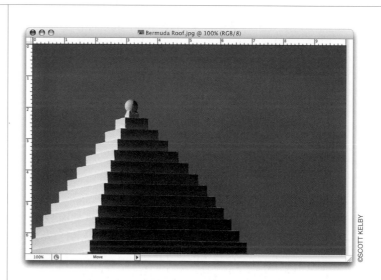

Step Two:

Press V to get the Move tool and click-and-drag this photo on top of your 7x5" document (the photo that you drag appears on its own layer automatically). Since the photo you added was larger than the document you dragged it into, the photo extends off the sides and top quite a bit. So, to make it fit comfortably in this new document, you'll need to scale the photo down.

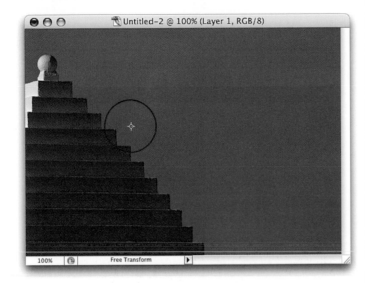

Step Three:
Press Command-T (PC: Control-T) to bring up Free Transform. Here's where the problem begins—you need to grab the Free Transform corner points to scale the photo down, but you can't even see the Free Transform handles in this image (you see the center point, but there's no way to reach the corner handles to scale the image down to size).

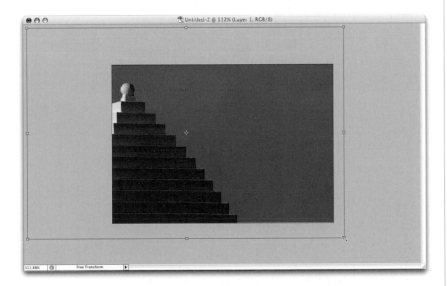

Step Four:
Here's the trick: Once you have Free Transform in place (and can't see the handles), just press Command-0 (PC: Control-0). Photoshop will automatically resize your document window and your image, so you can reach all the handles—no matter how far outside your image area they once were. Two things: (1) This trick only works once you have Free Transform active, and (2) it's Command-0 (PC: Control-0)—that's the number zero, not the letter O.

Using the Crop Tool to Add More Canvas Area

I know the heading here doesn't make much sense—Using the Crop Tool to Add More Canvas Area? How can the Crop tool (which is designed to crop photos to a smaller size) actually make the canvas area (white space) around your photo larger? That's what I'm going to show you.

Step One:

Open the image that you want to add white canvas area to. Press the letter D to set your Background color to its default color of white. Now press Command–- (Minus key) (PC: Control–- [Minus key]) to zoom out a bit (so your image doesn't take up your whole screen), and then press the letter F. This lets you see the gray desktop area that surrounds your image. (*Note:* In the Layers palette, ensure the Background layer is active if you have more than one layer.)

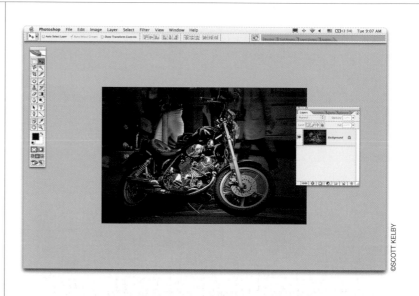

©SCOTT KELBY

Step Two:

Press the letter C to switch to the Crop tool and drag out a cropping marquee border to any random size (it doesn't matter how big or little the marquee is at this point).

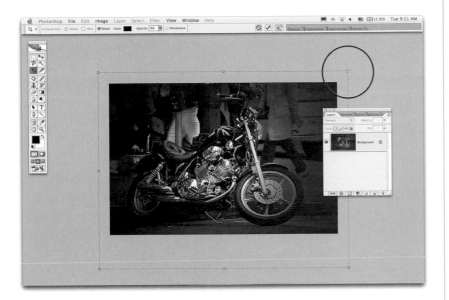

Step Three:
Now, grab any side handle or corner point and drag outside the image area, out into the gray desktop area that surrounds your image. The gray area that your cropping border selects outside the image will be added as white canvas space in the next step, so position the border where you want to add the canvas space.

Step Four:
Press the Return (PC: Enter) key to finalize your crop, and when you do, the gray area outside your image will become white canvas space. In the example shown here, I added some text in the bottom canvas area using the Type tool (T). The headline is set in the font Adobe Garamond Condensed, as is the address and contact info. The store's name is set in the font Futura Extra Bold (also from Adobe).

Straightening Crooked Photos

If you handheld your camera for most of your shots rather than using a tripod, you can be sure that some of your photos are going to come out a bit crooked. Here's a quick way to straighten them accurately in just a few short steps:

Step One:

Open the photo that needs straightening. Choose the Measure tool from Photoshop's Toolbox (it looks like a little ruler, and it's hidden behind the Eyedropper tool, so just click-and-hold for a moment on the Eyedropper tool until the Measure tool appears in the flyout menu).

Step Two:

Try to find something in your photo that you think is supposed to be straight (the ledge in the bottom left, in this example). Click-and-drag the Measure tool horizontally along this straight edge in your photo, starting from the left and extending to the right. As soon as you drag the tool, you can see the angle of the line displayed in the Info palette (found under the Window menu) and up in the Options Bar, but you can ignore them both because Photoshop is already taking note of the angle and placing that info where you'll need it in the next step.

Step Three:
Go under the Image menu, under Rotate Canvas, choose Arbitrary, and then the Rotate Canvas dialog will appear. Photoshop has already put the proper angle of rotation you'll need to straighten the image (based on your measurement), and it even sets whether the image should be rotated clockwise or counterclockwise.

Step Four:
All you have to do now is click OK, and your photo will be perfectly straightened (check out the ledge in the photo shown here—it's now nice and straight).

Step Five:
After the image is straightened, you might have to re-crop it to remove the extra white canvas space showing around the corners of your photo, so press C to switch to the Crop tool, drag out a cropping border, and press the Return (PC: Enter) key.

TIP: When you use the Measure tool, the line it draws stays on your photo until you rotate the image. If you want to clear the measurement and remove the line it drew on your image, click on the Clear button in the Options Bar.

Automated Cropping and Straightening

Since nearly everybody (digital or not) has a shoebox full of family photos up in the attic, I wanted to include a tutorial on the Crop and Straighten Photos automation. Its name is a bit misleading, because it does much more—it lets you scan multiple photos at one time (on your flatbed scanner), then it straightens every photo and places each into its own separate window (saving you the trouble).

Step One:
Place as many photos as will fit at one time on the scanning bed of your desktop scanner and scan them in. They'll all appear in one large document in Photoshop. As you can see, these photos were crooked when placed on the scanning bed, so naturally they appear crooked in the Photoshop document.

©SCOTT KELBY

Step Two:
Go under the File menu, under Automate, and choose Crop and Straighten Photos.

Step Three:
No dialog will appear. Instead, Photoshop will look for straight edges in your photos, straighten the photos, and copy each into its own separate window.

TIP: If you've scanned a number of photos, but decide you only want certain ones to be cropped and placed into their own separate documents, just put a selection around those photos using any selection tool, and then hold the Option (PC: Alt) key before you choose Crop and Straighten Photos.

Step Four:
This automation also works on single, crooked images. (Since the one shown here was taken with a digital camera, you're probably wondering how it got so crooked. I rotated it. Don't tell anybody.)

Step Five:
When you choose Crop and Straighten Photos, Photoshop will crop and straighten this one photo, but it still duplicates the image into a separate document. Hey, it's not perfect. Speaking of not perfect, it seems to work best when the photos you scan as a group have similar tonal qualities. The more varied the colors of the photos are, the harder time it seems to have straightening the images.

Anger Management
color management
step-by-step

Okay, there are entire books written on the subject of color management in Photoshop, so how am I going to condense everything you need to know into one chapter? It's easy—I'm not. You see, color management is like quicksand—the more you try to understand it, the deeper it sucks you down into the muck. What we need (you, me, us, we, you again, then me) is *less* about color management. That's right, this chapter puts a new spin on color management by actually giving you "less." Less about all the different color spaces (in fact, I don't even mention them), less about color gamuts (same here), less about soft proofing (I don't cover that at all), less about profiles, less about warnings, less about theory (there is none), less graphs and charts (there are none), and less about all the stuff you really don't care about. In fact, not only do we need a chapter that has less pages, we need one with less words, less ink, less spell checking, less editing, less royalties (less royalties?), less paper fiber, and less binding—and doggoneit, I'm just the guy to do it. (For the record, I've never used the phrase "doggoneit" in print before. This is the kind of groundbreaking stuff I'm talking about.) Anyway, here's my plan: If it's not a part of Photoshop's color management (that you're not directly going to change, adjust, or otherwise mess with in some meaningful fashion), I'm just gonna ignore it. That way, we can focus on just one thing: setting Photoshop up so the prints that come out of your personal color inkjet printer match exactly what you see onscreen. One thing. That's it. See, less is more. More or less. I think.

Configuring Your Camera for the Right Color Space

Although there are entire books written on the subject of color management in Photoshop, in this chapter we're going to focus on just one thing—getting what comes out of your color inkjet printer to match what you see onscreen. That's what it's all about, and if you follow the steps in this chapter, you'll get prints that match your screen. Now, I'm not going into the theory of color management, or CMYK soft proofing, or printing to multiple network printers, etc. It's just you, your computer, and your color inkjet printer. That, my friends, we can do.

Setting your camera to the right color space:

One of the key themes of proper color management is consistency. If you want to get consistent color from your camera, to Photoshop, to your printer, you'll want everybody speaking the same language, right? That's why I'm recommending, right from the start, that if your camera is set to shoot either JPEG or RAW+JPEG, you may be able to change your camera's color space from the default sRGB, which is an ideal space for images designed to be viewed on the Web, to Adobe RGB (1998), which is an ideal space for photographers whose final prints will come from a color inkjet printer. Now, if you only shoot in RAW, you can skip this because you'll assign the color space in Photoshop's Camera Raw dialog, but if you shoot in JPEG, you'll need to do it now. As an example of what I mean, here's how to set up a Nikon D70 to tag your photos with the Adobe RGB (1998) color profile.

Nikon D70

Step One: On the back of the camera, on the left side, press the Menu button to bring up the user menus in the LCD window.

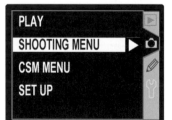

Step Two: Scroll down to the Shooting Menu and press the right arrow button on the back of the camera.

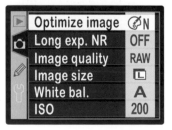

Step Three: When the Shooting Menu options appear, choose Optimize Image and press the right arrow button again.

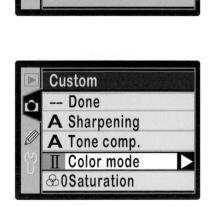

Step Four: In the Optimize Image menu, scroll down to Custom and press the right arrow button again.

Step Five: When the Custom menu appears, scroll down to Color Mode and press the right arrow button again. (*Note:* The "I" symbol before the words "Color Mode" tells you the current setting is sRGB.)

Step Six: When the Color Mode menu appears, scroll down to II: Adobe RGB, then press the right arrow button again to choose OK.

Step Seven: When you press the right arrow button, it returns to the Custom screen, but now there's a "II" before Color Mode, indicating you're now using Adobe RGB (1998).

Setting up other cameras:
I'm showing the setup here for a Nikon D70; however, I've put together these same steps for a number of other popular cameras, including the Nikon D2x (which is the camera I'm currently shooting with), the Nikon D100, and the setup for some of the most popular Canon digital cameras as well. These step-by-step tutorials are found on this book's companion website at www.scottkelbybooks.com/cs2digitalphotographers. If you have a digital camera that's not covered on my site, it's time to dig up your manual and find out how to "make the switch" to Adobe RGB (1998) or visit the manufacturer's website.

Configuring Photoshop for Adobe RGB (1998)

Once you've got your camera set to the right color space, it's time to set up Photoshop that way too. Back in Photoshop 5.5, when Adobe (and the world) were totally absorbed with Web design, they switched the color space from Monitor RGB to sRGB (which some pros refer to as "stupid RGB"). It was great for graphics that were destined for the Web. At that time, digital photography hadn't caught hold like it has today, so it seemed like the right thing to do, and at that time, it probably was. However, now we have to change the color space to something that's more appropriate for photography: Adobe RGB (1998).

Step One:

Before we do this, I just want to reiterate that you only want to make this change if your final print will be output to your own color inkjet. If you're sending your images out to an outside lab for prints, you should probably stay in sRGB—both in the camera and in Photoshop—because most labs are set up to handle sRGB files. Your best bet: Ask your lab which color space they prefer. Okay, now on to Photoshop: Go under the Edit menu and choose Color Settings.

Step Two:

This brings up the Color Settings dialog. By default, it uses the settings called North America General Purpose 2. Now, does anything about the term "General Purpose" sound like that's a good space for photographers? Didn't think so. The tip-off is that under Working Spaces, the RGB space is set to sRGB IEC61966–2.1 (which is the longhand technical name for what we simply call sRGB). In short, you don't want to use this group of settings.

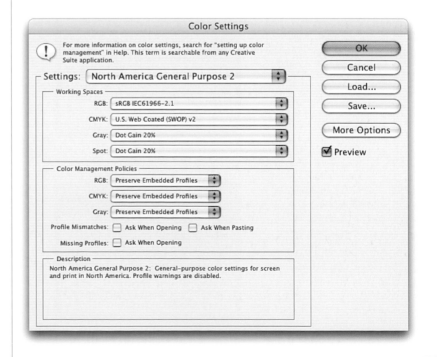

Step Three:

To get a preset group of settings that's better for photographers, from the Settings pop-up menu, choose North America Prepress 2. This automatically changes your RGB working space to Adobe RGB (1998) and sets up the appropriate warning dialogs to help you keep your color management plan in action when opening photos from outside sources or other cameras. Don't let it throw you that we're using prepress settings here—they work great for color inkjet printing because it uses Adobe RGB (1998) and because it turns on warnings for you, so you can deal with photos that you open with different or missing color profiles (more on this later).

Step Four:

Before you click OK, just for fun, temporarily change the Settings pop-up menu to North America Web/Internet and you'll see that the RGB working space changes back to sRGB, because sRGB is best suited for Web design. Makes you stop and think, doesn't it? Now, switch back to North American Prepress 2, click OK, and Photoshop is configured with Adobe RGB (1998) as your working RGB space. *Note:* If you're actually going to a printing press, where your final output is in the limited color range of CMYK, many pros prefer to use the ColorMatch RGB workspace (which you choose from the RGB Working Spaces pop-up menu) rather than Adobe RGB (1998), because it's closer to the range of colors that CMYK printing presses use.

Continued

Step Five:

One of the benefits of choosing North America Prepress 2 is that it turns on warnings (for example, it looks for a profile mismatch) and gives you the opportunity to fix it. For example, if you set your camera to shoot in Adobe RGB 1998, and Photoshop is set that same way too, they match, so it's smooth sailing—no warnings appear. However, if you open a photo you took six months ago, it will probably be in sRGB, and that doesn't match your Photoshop workspace (it's a mismatch). So, I recommend that you reopen the Color Settings dialog, go under Color Management Policies, and change your default setting (from the RGB pop-up menu) to Convert to Working RGB. Then, for Profile Mismatches, turn off the Ask When Opening checkbox. That way, your old photos will automatically update to match your current working space when you re-open them in Photoshop.

Step Six:

Okay, so what if a friend emails you a photo, you open it in Photoshop, and the photo doesn't have any color profile at all? Well, once that photo is open in Photoshop CS2, you can convert that "untagged" image to Adobe RGB (1998) by going under the Edit menu and choosing Assign Profile. When the Assign Profile dialog appears, click on the Profile radio button, ensure Adobe RGB (1998) is selected in the pop-up menu, and then click OK.

Calibrating Your Monitor (The Cheapo Freebie Method)

If you have any hope of getting what comes out of your color inkjet printer to match what you see onscreen, you absolutely, positively *have* to calibrate your monitor. It's the cornerstone of color management, and basically there are two ways to do this: (1) Buy a hardware calibration sensor that calibrates your monitor precisely; or (2) use the free built-in system software calibration, which is better than nothing, but not by much because you're literally just "eyeing" it. We'll start here with the built-in freebie calibration, but if you're really serious about this stuff, turn to the next technique and learn the hardware method.

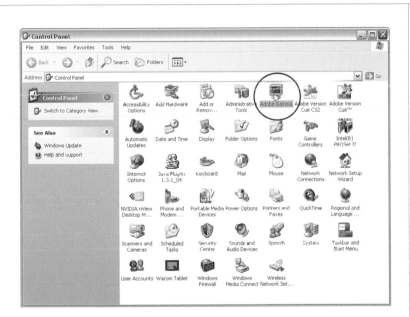

Freebie Calibration:
First, we'll look at the worst-case scenario: You're broke (you spent all available funds on the upgrade to CS2 and Clay Aiken's new CD), so you'll have to go with the free built-in system software calibration (which, as I mentioned, is better than not calibrating at all, but not by a whole bunch). Macintosh computers have calibration built into the system, but Windows PCs use a separate utility from Adobe called Adobe Gamma, so we'll start with that, and then we'll do the Mac freebie calibration. To get to Adobe Gamma on your Windows PC (if you're using Windows XP), go under the Start menu from the Taskbar, and then go to the Control Panel. Click on Adobe Gamma.

Step One (PC):
This brings up the Adobe Gamma dialog. Choose Step By Step (Wizard), which will lead you through the steps for creating a pretty lame calibration profile. (Hey, I can't help it—that's what it does. Do you really want me to sugarcoat it? Okay, how's this? "It will lead you through the steps for proper calibration" [cringe].) *Note:* Results will vary depending on whether your monitor is a CRT, LCD, etc.

Continued

Step Two (PC):

Click the Next button and you'll be asked to name the profile you're about to create. Now, it's possible that when you first hooked up your monitor a manufacturer's profile was installed at the same time. Although that canned factory profile won't do the trick, it can save you some time because it will automatically answer some of the questions in the dialog, so it's worth a look to see if you have one. Click on the Load button, then navigate your way to the ICC profiles in your system (you should be directed to them by default). If you see a profile with your monitor's name, click on it and then click OK to load that profile.

Step Three (PC):

From here on out, you'll be prompted with various directions (some with little square graphics with sliders beneath them). It asks you to move the sliders and then judge how the colors look. This is the very essence of the term "eyeing it," and it's why pros avoid this method. Everyone sees color and tone differently, and we're all viewing these "test squares" under different lighting conditions, etc., so it's highly subjective. But hey—it's free.

Step Four (PC):

The questions will continue (along the lines of the Spanish Inquisition) until it completes the calibration process, and then it offers you a before and after. You can pretty much ignore the Carmen Miranda before/after photo—that's just for looks—your before and after will be nothing like that, but after you're prompted to save your profile, you're done.

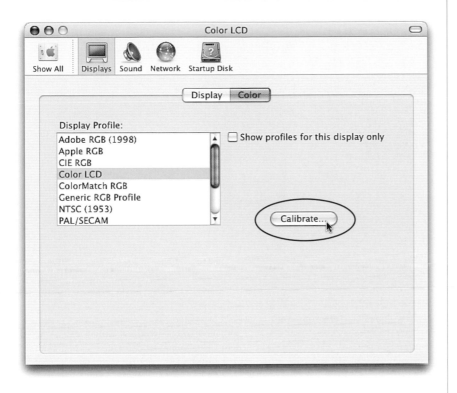

Step One (Mac):

Now for the freebie calibration on the Macintosh: To find Apple's built-in monitor calibration software, go under the Apple menu and choose System Preferences. In the System Preferences dialog, click on the Displays preferences, and when the options appear, click on the Color tab. When the Color options appear, click on the Calibrate button to bring up the Display Calibrator Assistant window (shown in the next step).

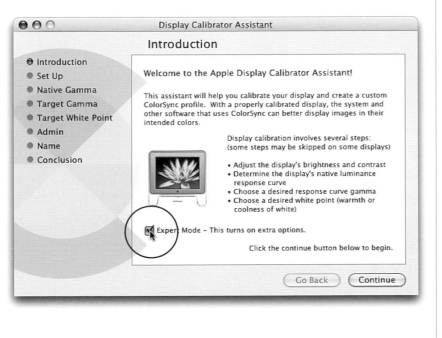

Step Two (Mac):

Now, at first this seems like a standard Welcome screen, so you'll probably be expecting to just click the Continue button, but *don't* do that until you turn on the Expert Mode checkbox. I know what you're thinking: "But I'm not an expert!" Don't worry, within a few minutes you'll be within the top 5% of all photographers who have knowledge of monitor calibration, because sadly most never calibrate their monitor. So turn on the checkbox and click the Continue button with the full confidence that you're about to enter an elite cadre of highly calibrated individuals (whatever that means).

Continued

Step Three (Mac):

The first section has you go through a series of five different windows, and each window will ask you to perform a simple matching test using a slider. It's a "no-brainer," as Apple tells you exactly what to do in each of these five windows (it's actually the same for all five windows, so once you've read the first window's instructions, you're pretty much set). So, just follow Apple's easy instructions to get through these five windows, then I'll join you right after.

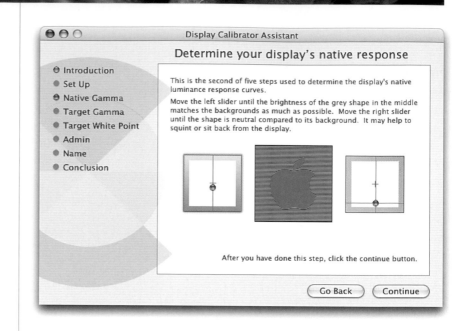

Step Four (Mac):

Okay, so you survived the "five native response windows of death." Amazingly easy, wasn't it? (It even borders on fun.) Well, believe it or not, that's the hard part—the rest could be done by your 5-year-old, provided you have a 5-year-old (if not, you can rent one from Apple's website). So here we are at a screen asking you to Select a Target Gamma (basically, you're choosing a contrast setting here). Apple pretty much tells you "it's best to use the Mac Standard of 1.8," but it has no idea that you're a photographer and need something better. Most digital imaging pros I know recommend setting your gamma to 2.2 (the PC Standard), which creates a richer contrast onscreen (which tends to make you open the shadows up when editing, which is generally a good thing detail-wise). Drag the slider to PC Standard and see if you agree, then click Continue.

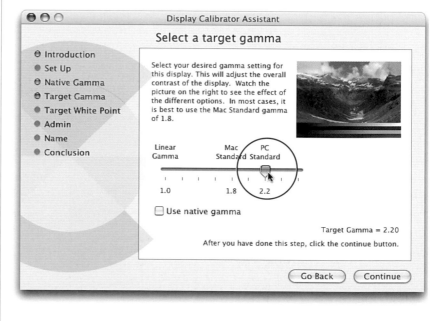

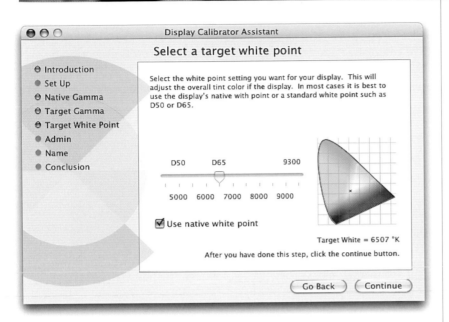

Step Five (Mac):
Now it asks you to select a white point. I use D65 (around 6500 Kelvin, in case you care). Why? That's what most of the pros use, because it delivers a nice, clean white point without the yellowish tint that occurs when using lower temperature settings. With the slider set at D65, you can click the Continue button. The next window just asks if you're sharing your computer with other users, so I'm skipping that window, because if you are, you'll click the checkbox; if you're not, you won't. Snore.

Step Six (Mac):
When you click Continue again, you'll be greeted with a window that lets you name your profile. Type in the name you want for your profile, and click the Continue button. The last window (which there's no real reason to show here) just sums up the choices you've made, so if you made some egregious mistake, you could click the Go Back button, but seriously, what kind of huge mistake could you have made that would show up at this point? Exactly. So click the Done button and you've created a semi-accurate profile for your monitor (hey, don't complain—it's free calibration). Now, you don't have to do anything in Photoshop for it to recognize this new profile—it happens automatically (in other words, "Photoshop just knows." Eerie, ain't it?).

Calibrating Your Monitor the Right Way

Hardware calibration is definitely the preferred method of monitor calibration (in fact, I don't know of a single pro using the freebie software-only method). With hardware calibration, you're measuring your particular monitor and building a real profile for the real world, and it makes a huge difference. I use ColorVision's Spyder2PRO hardware calibration, which is popular with many pros because it's easy to use, works well, and it's affordable. Although I personally use the Spyder2PRO, other hardware calibrators I would recommend are GretagMacbeth's Eye-One Display 2 and Monaco Optix XR.

Step One:

After you install the Spyder2PRO software, plug the Spyder2PRO colorimeter sensor into your computer's USB port, then launch the Spyder2PRO software. Like the freebie calibration software, it will ask you a series of questions (like do you have a tube-CRT monitor or a flat-panel LCD monitor) and a host of other boring questions, similar to what the freebie software asks. What separates the two is the hardware—the Spyder2PRO colorimeter actually reads your monitor to create a custom profile for your real monitor (not a hypothetical monitor).

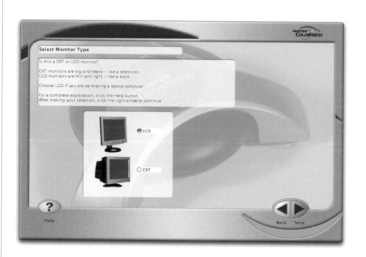

Step Two:

Once you've answered all their questions (including a series of probing personal questions about your arrest record, previous marriages, etc.), it then instructs you to position the Spyder2PRO sensor directly over the actual-size image of the Spyder2PRO that appears onscreen. Drape the sensor over the top of your monitor so it sits flat against your screen (there's a counterweight attached to the cable so you can set it to any length you want).

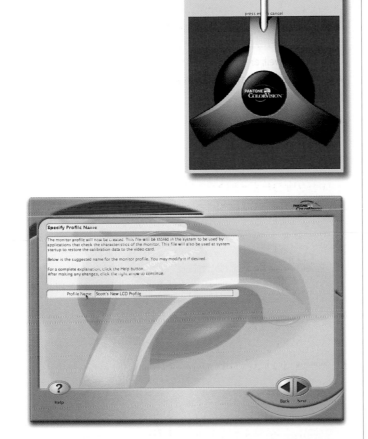

Step Three:

Once the colorimeter sensor is aligned with the one onscreen, click Continue, and it will conduct a series of tests, starting with reading your monitor's black point. It will continue by reading samples of red, green, and blue. The window onscreen (directly under the sensor) will start measuring each color while appearing nearly black, but then slowly each color will get brighter and more saturated until each reaches its full intensity. Once it reads the gray point, the process is done.

Step Four:

When all the measurements are done, you'll be asked to remove the hardware sensor and give your new profile a name (it suggests a name, but the name it suggests is too close to my existing canned profiles, so I usually rename it so it will be easier to find). Now click the Next button in the bottom right-hand corner of the screen.

Step Five:

The final screen is important in that you get to see how your monitor looked before calibration and how it looks now after being hardware calibrated. Click the Switch button at the bottom of the window to toggle between the before-and-after view. Chances are you'll gasp when you see how "off" your monitor was before calibration. You don't have to do anything else at this point—it will automatically tell Photoshop about your new monitor profile.

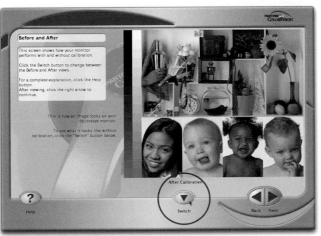

Getting (or Creating) a Custom Profile for Your Printer

When you buy a color inkjet printer and install the printer driver that comes with it, you get what's known as a "standard" profile. It basically lets Photoshop know what kind of printer is being used, and that's about it. But to get pro results, you need a profile that includes the printer and the exact paper you'll be printing on (basically, a custom profile). Most inkjet paper manufacturers now create custom profiles for their papers, and you can download them free from their websites. You can also create your own custom printer profiles, but it requires buying printer-profiling hardware (more on this later).

Step One:

When you first install your printer, it installs a standard printer profile, which is chosen from within Photoshop CS2's Print with Preview dialog (found under the File menu). But that profile doesn't take into account the type of paper you're using, meaning you won't get the pro results you're looking for. You need a profile that describes both the printer and the exact paper you're printing to. So where do you get those? That's next.

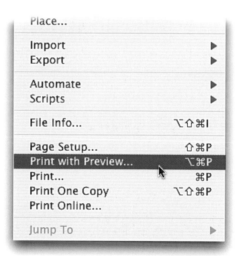

Step Two:

I personally use an Epson Stylus Photo 2200 color inkjet (which is one of the most popular 13x19" color inkjets for pros), and I often use Epson papers with it. But, since I don't know which printer you have, we'll have to go with mine for our example. To get the best results, we'll have to go to Epson's website and download a free, custom-made profile for the exact paper we're using. Start by going to Epson.com, select your country, and click on the Drivers & Support link. *Note:* Websites change their look and navigation fairly often, so if you go to Epson's site and it doesn't look just like this, don't be surprised.

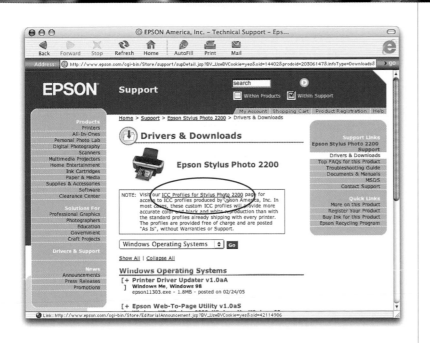

Step Three:
When you get to the Drivers & Support area, click on the Printers link and navigate to the color inkjet printer section. Once you find the inkjets, click on the Drivers & Downloads link, then find your particular printer in the list of printer models (in my case, it's an Epson Stylus Photo 2200). Find your printer in the list, click on it, and you'll arrive at the page where the standard drivers are found. But you don't want the standard drivers, so click on the link for the professional, custom ICC profiles page (just below the printer's name, in this case).

Step Four:
When you click on that link, a page appears with a list of Mac and PC ICC profiles for Epson's papers and printers. This is the Holy Grail—the pot of gold at the end of the rainbow—and best of all, it's free. Now, is it really worth this treasure hunt? Well, here's what Epson says right on their website about these free profiles: "In most cases, these custom ICC profiles will provide more accurate color and black-and-white print quality than with the standard profiles already shipping with every printer." So in short, if you want more accurate color and black-and-white prints, download these profiles. Download one for every paper you're using (I've been using the Velvet Fine Art, Premium Luster, and the Enhanced Matte, so I downloaded all three). Now, once you download them, then what?

Continued

Step Five:

When you download a profile from Epson's website, it comes with a built-in installer (shown here on the left in the window), so just double-click on it to install it automatically. If you download a profile like the one on the right side of the window, you'll have to install it manually (don't worry—it's easy). On a Windows PC, just Right-click on it and choose Install Profile. Easy enough. On a Mac, it takes a few more steps: First go to your hard disk, open your Library folder, and open your ColorSync folder, where you'll see a folder named Profiles. Just drag the file in there (you may need to restart your machine).

Step Six:

When you relaunch Photoshop CS2 (after your restart), choose Print with Preview from the File menu. In the resulting dialog, under the Options section, change the Color Handling pop-up menu to Let Photoshop Determine Colors. Then, click on the Printer Profile pop-up menu, and now all the new printer/paper profiles will appear—you just have to choose the one for the paper you're getting ready to print to (in this example, I'm printing to my 2200 using Epson's Velvet Fine Art paper at 2880 dpi, so that's what I'm choosing as my printer profile). More on when to actually make this choice later in this chapter, but for now, we're mostly concerned with just getting these custom profiles installed.

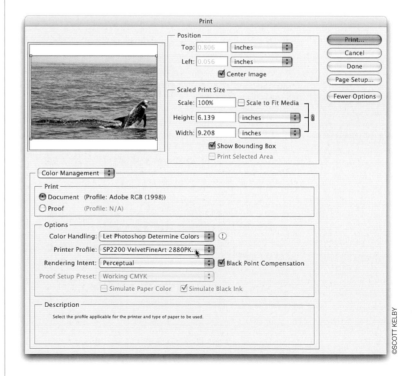

Step Seven:

Moab also has some beautiful papers that work wonderfully on the 2200 (I just printed an entire wedding album using Moab's Kayenta Photo Matte), so when it was time to do the actual printing, I went to www.moabpaper.com and clicked on the ICC Profiles link. I downloaded and installed their custom profile (and after restarting), it appeared in the Print with Preview dialog in the Printer Profile pop-up menu. If you decide to try a new color inkjet paper, before you do any printing you'll need to go to the paper manufacturer's website and see if free custom profiles are provided.

Step Eight:

Crane's Museo Fine Art Papers website (www.crane.com and click on Printer Settings and Profiles) provides custom profiles for their paper for use with most Epson printers. The inset here shows their Epson 2200 profile installed in Photoshop. *Note:* You can also pay an outside service to create a custom profile for your printer. You just have to print a test sheet (which they provide), overnight it to them, and they'll use an expensive colorimeter to measure your test print and create a custom profile. The catch: It's only good for that printer, on that paper, with that ink. If anything changes, your custom profile is about worthless. So, if you want to go that route, you should probably do your own personal printer profiling (using something like ColorVision's SpectroPRO) so you can re-profile each time you change paper or inks. Otherwise, just keep updating the profiles from the paper manufacturers.

Printing (This Is Where It All Comes Together)

Okay, you've set your camera to Adobe RGB (1998); you've calibrated your monitor; you've set up Photoshop to use Adobe RGB (1998); and you've set it up so any photos you bring in that are not in Adobe RGB (1998) will automatically be converted to Adobe RGB (1998). You've even downloaded a printer profile for the exact printer model and style of paper you're printing on. In short—you're there. You're just a few clicks away from grabbing the brass ring, baby! Let's do it!

Step One:
Go under Photoshop's File menu and choose Print with Preview. You can't just choose Print anymore. That's for wusses. That's for non-calibrated, color management-less wusses—not you, my friend.

Step Two:
In the resulting dialog, click on the Page Setup button. In the Page Setup dialog, choose which printer you're printing to from the Format For pop-up menu (in this case, an Epson Stylus Photo 2200), and then choose your Paper Size (in this case, a 13x19" sheet). You also choose your page Orientation. Leave the Scale at 100% (you can change that later), and click OK to return to the Print dialog. Now you'll need to access the Color Management controls (which should be at the bottom of the Print dialog by default). *Note:* If you don't see the options, click on the More Options button on the right in the dialog.

©DAVE MOSER

Step Three:

In the expanded Print dialog, under the Preview window, make sure Color Management is selected from the pop-up menu below the preview window (it should be by default). Then, in the Print section, make sure Document is selected (rather than Proof). However, it's down a little farther, in the Options section, where we have to make some very important changes (for what we're doing, using the default settings would be fairly tragic).

Step Four:

In the Options section near the bottom of the dialog, go under the Color Handling pop-up menu and choose Let Photoshop Determine Colors. That way, we're staying consistent by letting Photoshop do the color management all the way through the process. So far, so good, but don't click the Print button yet.

Continued

Step Five:

After you've selected Let Photoshop Determine Colors, the currently selected Printer Profile will appear in the pop-up menu directly below it. This is where you need to choose the profile for the printer you're using and paper you're printing to. I'm going to be printing to an Epson 2200 on Epson's Velvet Fine Art paper at 2880 dpi, so I choose the printer/paper profile that matches that (which I downloaded in the previous tutorial). Doing this optimizes the color to give the best possible color print on that printer using that paper at that dpi.

Options

Color Handling:
Printer Profile:
Rendering Intent:
Proof Setup Preset:

SP2200 Enhanced Matte_MK
SP2200 Prem.Luster 1440.icc
SP2200 Prem.Luster 2880.icc
SP2200 Standard_MK
SP2200 Velvet Fine Art_MK
SP2200 VelvetFineArt 1440MK.icc
SP2200 VelvetFineArt 1440PK.icc
SP2200 VelvetFineArt 2880MK.icc
SP2200 VelvetFineArt 2880PK.icc
SP2200 Watercolor – RW_MK

Step Six:

For the Rendering Intent pop-up menu, I recommend choosing Perceptual because it seems to give the most consistent results for printing photographic images to color inkjet printers. Now, before you click the Print button, just make sure the Black Point Compensation checkbox is turned on (it should be by default). When you're printing photographic images (like we are here), this option helps maintain more detail and color in the shadow areas of your photos.

Options

Color Handling: Let Photoshop Determine Colors
Printer Profile: Working RGB – sRGB IEC61966...
Rendering Intent: Perceptual ☑ Black Point Compensation
Proof Setup Preset: Working CMYK
☐ Simulate Paper Color ☑ Simulate Black Ink

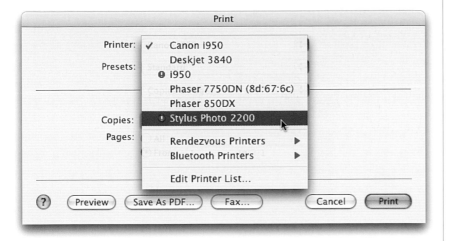

Step Seven:
Now you can click on the Print button, and when you do, another Print dialog will appear—your print driver's dialog. Choose your printer from the Printer pop-up menu, and below that, you'll see the Copies pop-up menu, where you choose options for your printer. (In the example shown here, I'm using a Macintosh computer running Mac OS X. However, on a Windows PC, choose your printer from the Name pop-up menu, and then click on the Properties button to choose from your printer's options.)

Step Eight:
Click on the Copies pop-up menu to reveal a list of all the printer options you can choose from. There are two critical changes we need to make here. First, choose Print Settings so we can configure the printer to give us the best quality prints.

WARNING: From this point on, what appears in the Copies pop-up menu is contingent on your printer's options. You may or may not be able to access these same settings, so you may need to view each option to find the settings you need to adjust. Also, if you're using a Windows PC, (after you click on the Properties button) click on the Advanced tab when your printer's options appear and you'll be able to choose from similar settings.

Continued

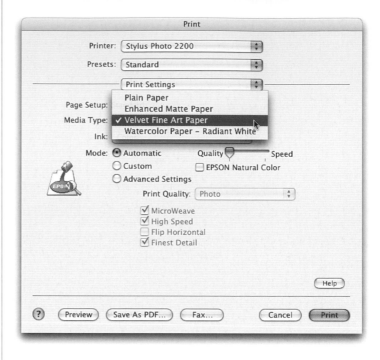

Step Nine:

Once you choose Print Settings, and those options appear, choose the type of paper you'll be printing to from the Media Type pop-up menu. Any ICC profiles you've downloaded for your chosen printer will appear in this menu.

Step Ten:

Under the Mode section, click on Advanced Settings. Choose your desired Print Quality from the pop-up menu. I choose SuperPhoto–2880 dpi to get the highest quality photo possible from this printer. If you don't mind sacrificing quality for speed, you can choose a lower print quality, and it won't take as long to print. However, I only choose a lower print quality when I'm doing testing or proofing—never for a final photo that will be framed or mounted.

Step Eleven:

The second important change you'll need to make in the printer driver software dialog is to turn the printer's own color management off. You do this by first choosing Color Management from the pop-up menu, to make the Color Management options visible. Now, this is a very tempting dialog, with a Gamma pop-up menu, a checkbox for Epson Natural Color, and lots of fun-looking sliders that are just begging you to mess with them—but don't do it. They are evil. So why did we come here in the first place? To turn this junk off—just click on the No Color Adjustment radio button.

Step Twelve:

When you select No Color Adjustment, all that tempting stuff is immediately hidden from view, because you just turned off the printer's color management features, which is precisely what you wanted to do. You want "no color adjustment" from that printer—you're doing it all in Photoshop. Now you're ready to hit the Print button to get prints that match your screen, as you've color managed this photo from beginning to end.

WARNING: If you're printing to a color inkjet printer, don't *ever* convert your photo to CMYK format (even though you may be tempted to because your printer uses cyan, magenta, yellow, and black inks). The conversion from RGB to CMYK inks happens within the printer itself, and if you do it first in Photoshop, your printer will attempt to convert it again in the printer, so the results will be way off.

Exposure: 0.4s

Focal Length: 78mm

Aperture Value: *f*/5.5

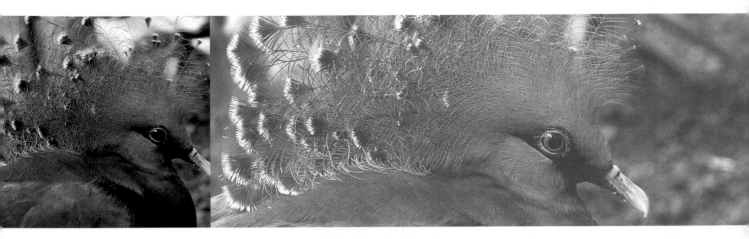

The Color of Money
color correction secrets

Okay, I went with a movie title for this chapter, even though I didn't actually like the movie. But that doesn't mean it's not a decent chapter title. In fact, I have two reasons why it's a good title: (1) Professionals charge money to color correct photos for their clients using the same techniques I'm going to show you, and (2) the title is so much better than the one I was going to use, which was "Color My World" (the song by the band Chicago). I've been avoiding "Color My World" since I first wrote about color correction. Any schmuck could come up with "Color My World," but I know you expect more from me than that. For example, when I wrote the Photoshop CS version of this book, I used the title "Color Me Badd," which isn't as obscure as you'd think—it was a hugely popular '80s band. Although you

might not remember them, they had a smash hit with the song "I Want to Sex You Up." (Ah, now you remember them.) By referencing that band in my previous book, I achieved a major marketing goal of my publisher, and that is to somehow work the word "sex" into my book at least once. They say it helps book sales. If I could only find a way to work it into this book, I could really "move some units" (that's book-publishing jargon), but it's hard to find a subtle way to work "sex" into a chapter intro about color correction. Hey, wait a minute—I just worked it in, not once, not twice, but three times, almost guaranteeing that this book will be a global best-seller. Now, back to the title "Color My World." I know it's lame, you know it's lame, and frankly, I only have one thing to say in my defense: Sex. (Cha-ching!)

Before You Color Correct Anything, Do This First!

Before we correct even a single photo, there are two quick little changes we need to make in Photoshop to get better, more accurate corrections. Although it's just two simple changes, don't underestimate their impact—this is critically important stuff.

Step One:

Go to the Toolbox and click on the Eyedropper tool (or just press the letter I). The default Sample Size setting for this tool (Point Sample) is fine for using the Eyedropper to steal a color from within a photo to make it your Foreground color. However, Point Sample doesn't work well when you're using it to read values in a particular area (like flesh tones) for color correction, because it gives you the reading from only one individual pixel, rather than a reading of the entire area under your cursor.

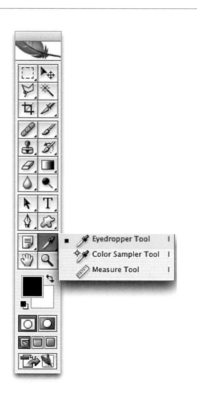

Step Two:

For example, flesh tone is actually composed of dozens of different-colored pixels (just open an image of a person, zoom way in using the Zoom tool [Z], and you'll see what I mean). If you're color correcting, you want a reading that is representative of the area under your Eyedropper, not just one of the pixels within that area, which could hurt your correction decision-making. That's why you need to go to the Options Bar, under the Sample Size pop-up menu, and choose 3 by 3 Average. This changes the Eyedropper to give you a 3-by-3-pixel average (so it's sampling more pixels) of the area you're reading.

Step Three:

The second part is setting up Photoshop visually for color correction. Although having a colorful desktop background is fine when we're doing just about anything else in Photoshop, you'll rarely find a professional doing color correction with a colorful desktop background. Why? Because that colorful background, which appears behind the image you're working on, changes how you perceive color. So much so, that it will influence how you color correct the photo. That's why the first thing pro photographers do when they're about to color correct an image is change their desktop background to a neutral gray.

Step Four:

To get the neutral gray correction background, click on the center button (the group of three buttons) at the bottom of the Toolbox, but honestly it's faster to press the letter F once on your keyboard. This immediately centers your photo onscreen and puts that neutral gray background around your photo. This view mode is technically called Full Screen Mode with Menu Bar, but unless you work at Adobe, you'll probably just call it "correction mode." To return to regular mode, just press the F key twice. (*Note:* If you're using a PC, you can also enlarge the Photoshop interface, which uses a gray background by default. Just click on the Maximize button in the top-right corner of the Photoshop window.) Now compare the captures on this page and ask yourself, "Which view would give me a better chance of a proper color correction?" I thought you'd ask that.

Color Correcting Digital Camera Images

As far as digital technology has come, there's still one thing that digital cameras won't do: give you perfect color every time. In fact, if they gave us perfect color 50% of the time, that would be incredible; but unfortunately, every digital camera (and every scanner) sneaks in some kind of color cast in your image. Generally, it's a red cast, but depending on the camera, it could be blue. Either way, you can be pretty sure—there's a cast. (Think of it this way: If there weren't, the term "color correction" wouldn't be used.) Here's how to get your color in line:

Step One:
Open the RGB photo you want to color correct. (The photo shown here doesn't look too bad, but as we go through the correction process, you'll see that, like most photos, it really needed a correction.)

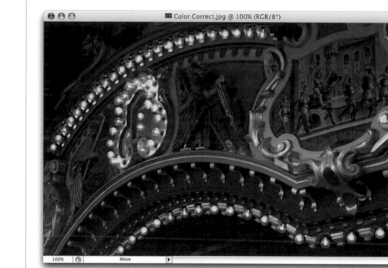

©SCOTT KELBY

Step Two:
Go under the Image menu, under Adjustments, and choose Curves. Curves is the hands-down choice of professionals for correcting color because it gives you a greater level of control than other tools, such as Levels (which we use for correcting black-and-white photos). The dialog may look intimidating at first, but the technique you're going to learn here requires no previous knowledge of Curves, and it's so easy, you'll be correcting photos using Curves immediately.

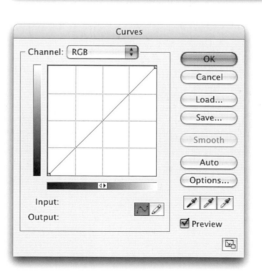

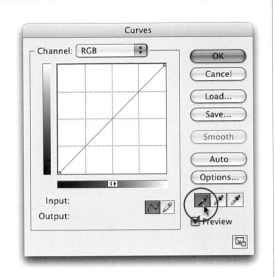

Step Three:

First, we need to set some preferences in the Curves dialog so we'll get the results we want when color correcting. We'll start by setting a target color for our shadow areas. To set this preference, in the Curves dialog, double-click on the black Eyedropper tool (it's on the lower right-hand side of the dialog, the first Eyedropper from the left). A Color Picker will appear asking you to Select Target Shadow Color. This is where we'll enter values that, when applied, will help remove any color casts your camera introduced in the shadow areas of your photo.

Step Four:

We're going to enter values in the R, G, and B (Red, Green, and Blue) fields of this dialog (the Red field is highlighted here):

For R, enter 20
For G, enter 20
For B, enter 20

Click OK. Because these figures are evenly balanced (neutral), they help ensure that your shadow area won't have too much of one color (which is exactly what causes a color cast—too much of one color). Additionally, using the numbers I'm giving you in this chapter will help your photos maintain enough shadow and highlight detail in case you decide to output them to a printing press (for a brochure, magazine cover, print ad, etc.).

Continued

Step Five:

Now we'll set a preference to make our highlight areas neutral. Double-click on the white Eyedropper (the third of the three Eyedroppers in the Curves dialog). The Color Picker will appear asking you to Select Target Highlight Color. Click in the R field, and then enter these values (*note:* To move from field to field, just press the Tab key):

For R, enter 244
For G, enter 244
For B, enter 244

Click OK to set those values as your highlight target.

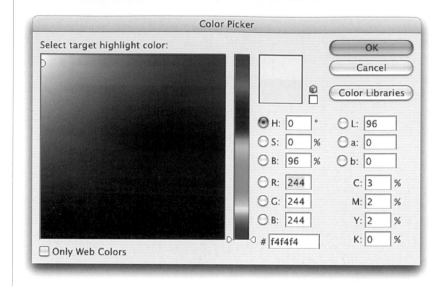

Step Six:

Now, set your midtone preference. You know the drill: Double-click on the midtone Eyedropper (the middle of the three Eyedroppers) so you can Select Target Midtone Color. Enter these values in the RGB fields:

For R, enter 133
For G, enter 133
For B, enter 133

Then click OK to set those values as your midtone target.

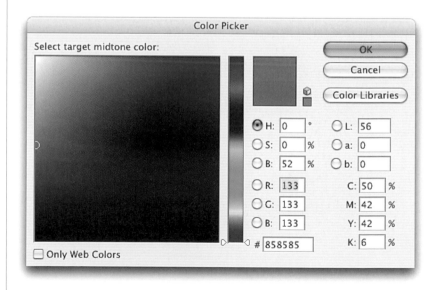

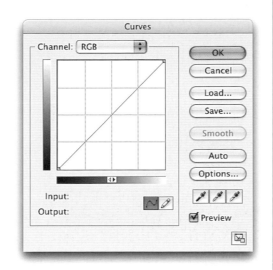

Step Seven:

Okay, now that you've entered your preferences (target colors) in the Curves dialog, you're going to use these Eyedropper tools that reside in the Curves dialog to do most of your correction work. Your job is to determine where the shadow, midtone, and highlight areas are, and then click the correct Eyedropper in the right place (you'll learn how to do that in just a moment). So remember your job: Find the shadow, midtone, and highlight areas, and click the correct Eyedropper in the right spot. Sounds easy, right? It is. You start by setting the shadows first, so you'll need to find an area in your photo that's supposed to be black. If you can't find something that's supposed to be the color black, then it gets a bit trickier—in the absence of something black, you have to determine which area in the image is the darkest. If you're not sure where the darkest part of the photo is, you can use a trick to have Photoshop tell you exactly where it is.

Step Eight:

If you still have the Curves dialog open, click OK to exit it for now. You'll get a warning dialog asking you if you want to "Save the new target colors as defaults." Click Yes, and from that point on, you won't have to enter these values each time you correct a photo, because they'll already be entered for you—they're now the default settings.

Continued

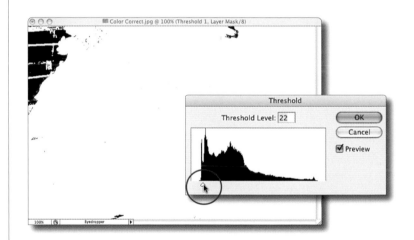

Step Nine:

Go to the Layers palette and click on the half-white/half-black circle icon to bring up the Create New Adjustment Layer pop-up menu (it's the fourth icon from the left at the bottom of the palette). Choose Threshold from this pop-up menu.

Step Ten:

When the Threshold dialog appears, drag the Threshold Level slider under the histogram all the way to the left. Your photo will turn completely white. Slowly drag the Threshold slider back to the right, and as you do, you'll start to see some of your photo reappear. The first area that appears is the darkest part of your image. That's it—that's Photoshop telling you exactly where the darkest part of the image is. Click OK to close the Threshold dialog. This adds an adjustment layer in your Layers palette.

Step Eleven:

Now that you know where your shadow area is, you can mark it. Click-and-hold on the Eyedropper tool in the Toolbox, and from the flyout menu that appears, choose the Color Sampler tool. Click this Color Sampler once on the area that is darkest and a target cursor will appear, marking that spot. When you do this, the Info palette automatically appears onscreen. You don't need this palette right now, so you can close it. Now to find a white area in your image....

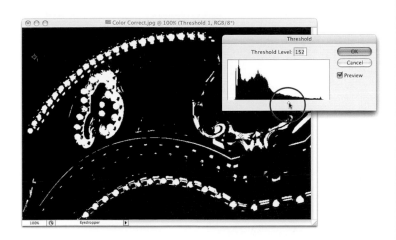

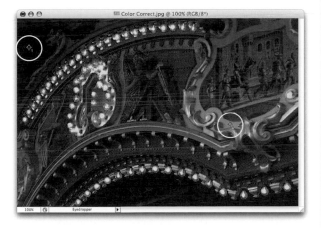

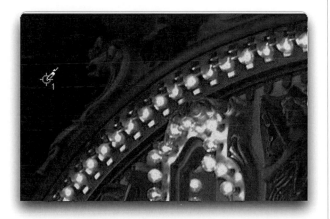

Step Twelve:

You can use the same Threshold technique to find the highlight areas. Go to the Layers palette and double-click on the adjustment layer thumbnail to bring up the Threshold dialog again, but this time drag the slider all the way to the right. Slowly drag the Threshold slider back toward the left, and as you do, the first area that appears in white is the lightest part of your image. Click OK, and then click the Color Sampler tool once on the brightest area to mark it as your highlight point.

Step Thirteen:

You're now done with your Threshold adjustment layer, so in the Layers palette, click-and-drag the adjustment layer onto the Trash icon to delete it. Click Yes in the warning dialog asking if you're sure you want to delete the layer. Your photo will look normal again, but now there are two target markers visible on your photo. Next, press Command-M (PC: Control-M) to bring up the Curves dialog.

Step Fourteen:

First, select the shadow Eyedropper (the one half filled with black) from the bottom right of the Curves dialog. Move your cursor outside the Curves dialog into your photo and click once directly on the center of the No. 1 target. When you click on the No. 1 target, the shadow areas will be corrected. (Basically, you just reassigned the shadow areas to your new neutral shadow color.)

Continued

TIP: If you click on the No. 1 target and your photo looks horrible, you either clicked in the wrong spot or what you thought was the shadow point actually wasn't. Undo the shadow setting by pressing Command-Z (PC: Control-Z) and try again. If that doesn't work, don't sweat it; just keep clicking in areas that look like the darkest part of your photo until it looks right. You can do this with the highlights and midtones, too.

Step Fifteen:
While still in the Curves dialog, switch to the highlight Eyedropper (the one filled with white). Move your cursor over your photo and click once directly on the center of the No. 2 target to assign that as your highlight. This will correct the highlight colors.

Step Sixteen:
Now that the shadows and highlights are set, you'll need to correct the midtones in the photo. Click the midtone Eyedropper (the middle of the three, half filled with gray) in an area within the photo that looks medium gray (in the photo shown here, you'll click the midtone Eyedropper in the gray moulding above the gold trim). Doing this corrects the midtones, and depending on the photo, this can either be a subtle or dramatic difference, but you'll never know until you try. Unfortunately, not every image contains an area that is gray, so you won't always be able to correct the midtones.

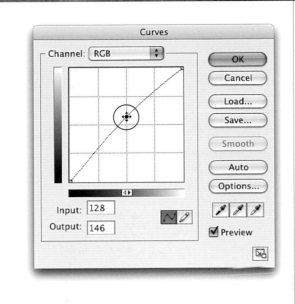

Step Seventeen:

There's one more important adjustment to make before you click OK in the Curves dialog to apply your correction. In the Curves grid, click on the center of the curve and drag it upward a bit to brighten the midtones of the image. This is a visual adjustment, so it's up to you to determine how much to adjust, but it should be subtle—just enough to brighten and bring out the midtone detail. When it looks right to you, click OK to apply your correction to the highlights, midtones, and shadows, removing any color casts and brightening the overall contrast.

Step Eighteen:

You can now remove the two Color Sampler targets on your photo by going up to the Options Bar and clicking on the Clear button to complete your RGB color correction. If you want to try this on a CMYK image, read on for more details.

Before

After

Continued

CMYK correction settings:

The values I gave you at the beginning of this correction technique were for photos that would be reproduced in RGB mode (i.e., your final output would be to a photo-quality color inkjet printer, a color laser printer, a dye-sub printer, etc.). However, if you're color correcting your photos for final output to a printing press (for a brochure, catalog, print ad, magazine, etc.), you need to use an entirely different set of values for your highlights, midtones, and shadows. Therefore, these numbers are entered into the CMYK fields, rather than the RGB fields. I've provided a set of values that are very common for prepress correction, because they enable significant details to be reproduced on press.

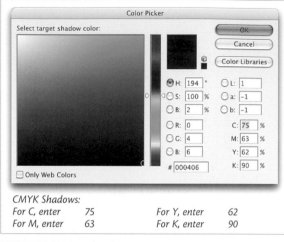

CMYK Shadows:
For C, enter	*75*	*For Y, enter*	*62*
For M, enter	*63*	*For K, enter*	*90*

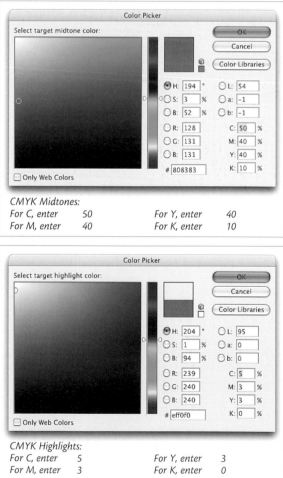

CMYK Midtones:
For C, enter	*50*	*For Y, enter*	*40*
For M, enter	*40*	*For K, enter*	*10*

CMYK Highlights:
For C, enter	*5*	*For Y, enter*	*3*
For M, enter	*3*	*For K, enter*	*0*

Drag-and-Drop Instant Color Correction

This is a wonderful timesaving trick for quickly correcting an entire group of photos that have similar lighting. It's ideal for studio shots, where the lighting conditions are controlled, but works equally well for outdoor shots, or really any situation where the lighting for your group of shots is fairly consistent. Once you try this, you'll use it again and again and again.

Step One:

First, here's a tip within a step: If you're opening a group of photos in the Adobe Bridge, you don't have to open them one by one. Just hold the Command key (PC: Control key) and click on all the photos you want to open. (If all your photos are consecutive, hold the Shift key and click on the first and last photo in the window to select them all.) Then, double-click on any one of your selected photos and the images will open in Photoshop. So now that you know that tip, go ahead and open at least four or five images, just to get started.

Step Two:

At the bottom of the Layers palette, there's a pop-up menu for adding adjustment layers (it's the half-white/half-black circle icon). Click on it and choose Curves. There are a number of advantages to having this correction applied as a layer, as you'll soon see, but the main advantage is that you can edit or delete this tonal adjustment at any time while you're working, plus you can save this adjustment with your file as a layer.

Continued

Step Three:

When you choose this adjustment layer, the regular Curves dialog appears, just like always. Go ahead and make your corrections to your topmost open image, just as you did in the previous tutorial (setting highlights, midtones, shadows, etc.). When your correction looks good, click OK.

Step Four:

In the Layers palette, you'll see that a new Curves 1 adjustment layer was created (if you can't read the Layers palette, expand its width by clicking-and-dragging on the very bottom-right corner of the palette). Because you applied this correction as an adjustment layer, you can treat this adjustment just like a regular layer, right? Right! So now we'll apply this Curves adjustment to your other open images.

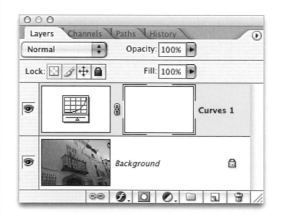

Step Five:

Since Photoshop lets you drag-and-drop layers between open documents, go to the Layers palette and simply drag this layer right onto one of your other open photos. That photo will instantly have the same correction applied to it. This technique works because you're correcting photos that share similar lighting conditions. Need to correct 12 photos? Just drag-and-drop it 12 times (making it the fastest correction in town!). In the example shown here, I've dragged-and-dropped that Curves adjustment layer onto one of the other open photos.

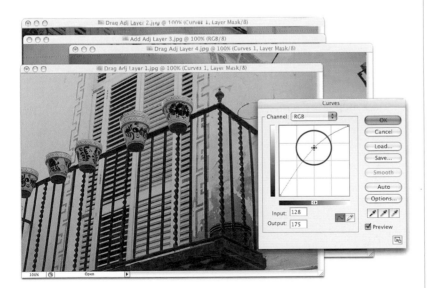

Step Six:

Okay, what if one of the "dragged corrections" doesn't look right? That's the beauty of adjustment layers; just double-click directly on the adjustment layer thumbnail for that photo and the Curves dialog will reappear with the last settings you applied still in place. You can then adjust this individual photo separately from the rest. Try this "dragging-and-dropping-adjustment-layers" trick once, and you'll use it again and again to save time when correcting a digital roll with similar lighting conditions.

FOR PROS ONLY!
ADVANCED TECHNIQUES

Studio Portrait Correction Made Simple

If you're shooting in a studio, whether it be portraits or products, there's a technique you can use that makes the color-correction process so easy that you'll be able to train laboratory test rats to correct photos for you. In the back of this book, I've included a color swatch card (it's perforated so you can easily tear it out). After you get your studio lighting set the way you want it, and you're ready to start shooting, just put this swatch card into your shot (just once) and take the shot. What does this do for you? You'll see.

Step One:
When you're ready to start shooting and the lighting is set the way you want it, tear out the swatch card from the back of this book and place it within your shot (if you're shooting a portrait, have the subject hold the card for you), and then take the shot. After you've got one shot with the swatch card, you can remove it and continue with the rest of your shoot.

Step Two:
When you open the first photo taken in your studio session, you'll see the swatch card in the photo. By having a card that's pure white, neutral gray, and pure black in your photo, you no longer have to try to determine which area of your photo is supposed to be black (to set the shadows), which area is supposed to be gray (to set the midtones), or which area is supposed to be white (to set the highlights). They're right there in the card.

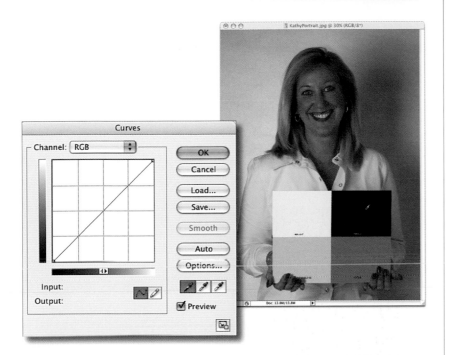

Step Three:

Press Command-M (PC: Control-M) to bring up the Curves dialog. Click the black Eyedropper on the black panel of the card (to set shadows), the middle Eyedropper on the gray (for midtones), and the white Eyedropper on the white panel (sets the highlights), and the photo will nearly correct itself. No guessing, no Threshold adjustment layers, no using the Info palette to determine the darkest areas of the image—now you know exactly which part of that image should be black and which should be white.

Step Four:

Now that you have the Curves setting for the first image, you can correct the rest of the photos using the exact same curve: Just open the next photo and press Option-Command-M (PC: Alt-Control-M) to apply the exact same curve to this photo that you did to the swatch card photo. Or, you can use the drag-and-drop color-correction method I showed in the previous tutorial.

TIP: If you want to take this process a step further, many professionals use a Macbeth color-swatch chart (from GretagMacbeth; www.gretagmacbeth .com), which also contains a host of other target colors. It's used exactly the same way: Just put the chart into your photo, take one shot, and then when you correct the photo, each color swatch will be in the photo, just begging to be clicked on.

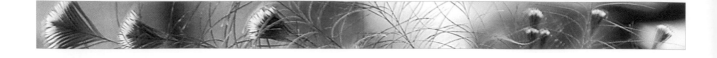

Taz's Target Two-Click Color Correction

One of the instructors who teaches with me at the Photoshop World Conference & Expo is Taz Tally. Taz is an incredibly talented teacher, writer, and general Photoshop whiz kid (well, for a Ph.D. anyway), and he's come up with his own color-correction method using a color-correction target he designed. Using his card (and his method), you can pretty much do your color correction in two clicks, and you can even use Levels (rather than Curves). Here's how it works:

Step One:

Here's the deal: You need to shoot a shot where Taz's color target actually appears in the shot. So if you're shooting portraits, just have your subject hold the card, then take the shot. If you're shooting products, put his card right by the product. It's only there for one shot (or unless you change the lighting setup significantly). By the way, if you don't already have Taz's target card, you can order his Calibration and Color Correction Target at www.tazseminars.com.

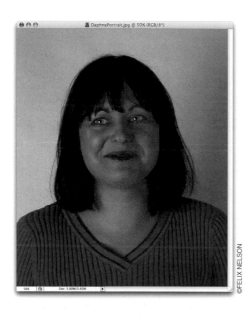

Step Two:

Open the photo that has Taz's target clearly in the scene (you'll use his target to do your correction). Press Command-L (PC: Control-L) to bring up Levels. Double-click on the white Eyedropper tool (in the bottom right-hand corner of the Levels dialog), and when the Color Picker appears, enter 245 for Red (R), 245 for Green (G), 245 for Blue (B), and click OK. This sets your highlights.

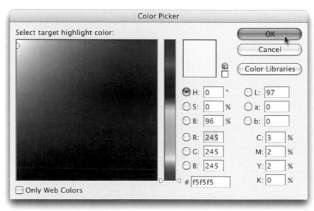

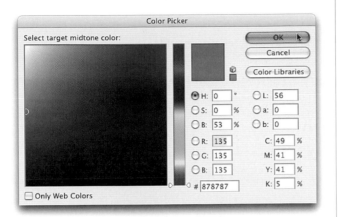

Step Three:
Now double-click on the gray Eyedropper (for midtones), and in the resulting Color Picker, enter 135 for Red (R), 135 for Green (G), 135 for Blue (B), and click OK. Then, click OK in the Levels dialog, and when a warning dialog appears asking if you want to save the target colors, click Yes.

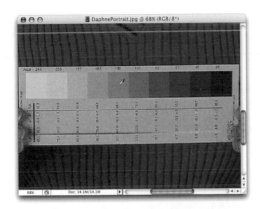

Step Four:
Press Z to get the Zoom tool and zoom in tight on Taz's target card within your photo. Next, bring up Levels again and click on the white Eyedropper tool to select it. Then, in your photo click directly on the white color chip on the left of the card. This removes the color cast in the highlight areas of your photo.

Step Five:
Now, click on the gray Eyedropper tool (for midtones) to select it, and then in your photo, click directly on the gray color chip in the center of the card. This removes the color cast in the midtone areas of your photo. Just these two clicks will pretty much correct most of the common color-correction situations you'll run into. Now press Command-0 (zero) (PC: Control-0) to fit your image onscreen and admire your corrected image

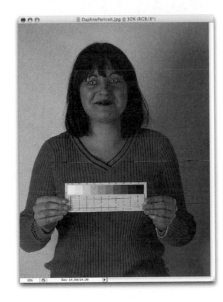

Dave's Amazing Trick for Finding a Neutral Gray

Finding a neutral midtone during color correcting has always been kind of tricky. Well, it was until Dave Cross, who works with me as Senior Developer of Education for the National Association of Photoshop Professionals (NAPP), came into my office one day to show me his amazing new trick for finding right where the midtones live in just about any image. When he showed me, I immediately blacked out. After I came to, I begged Dave to let me share his very slick trick in my book, and being the friendly Canadian he is, he obliged.

Step One:
Open any color photo, and click on the Create a New Layer icon at the bottom of the Layers palette to create a new blank layer. Then, go under the Edit menu and choose Fill. When the Fill dialog appears, in the Contents section, under the Use pop-up menu, choose 50% Gray, and then click OK to fill your new layer with (you guessed it) 50% gray.

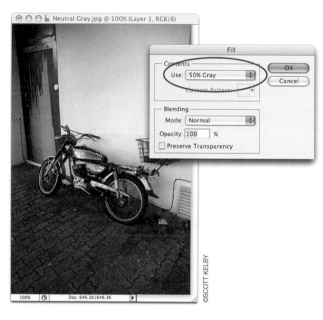

Step Two:
Now, go to the Layers palette and change the blend mode of this layer to Difference. Changing to Difference doesn't do much for the look of your photo (in fact, it rarely does), but just remember—it's only temporary.

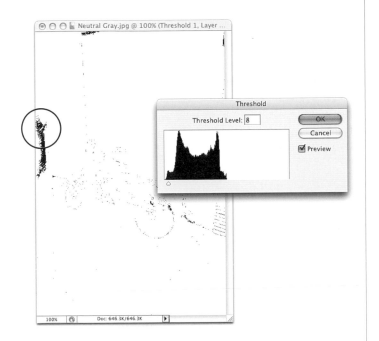

Step Three:
Choose Threshold from the Create New Adjustment Layer pop-up menu at the bottom of the Layers palette. When the dialog appears, drag the slider all the way to the left (your photo will turn completely white). Now, slowly drag the slider back to the right, and the first areas that appear in black are the neutral midtones. Click OK. Then press Shift-I until you get the Color Sampler tool (it's nested with the Eyedropper tool in the Toolbox) and click on one (or more) areas of neutral midtones (in the example shown here, the neutral midtones are on the far left and between the spokes of the back wheel of the motorcycle).

Step Four:
Now that your midtone point is marked, go back to the Layers palette and drag both the Threshold adjustment layer and the 50% gray layer onto the Trash icon to delete them (they already did their job, so you can get rid of them). You'll see your full-color photo again. Now, press Command-M (PC: Control-M) to open Curves, get the midtones Eyedropper (it's the middle Eyedropper), and click directly on one of the neutral Color Sampler points. That's it; you've found the neutral midtones and corrected any color within them. So, will this work every time? Almost. It works most of the time, but you will run across photos that just don't have a neutral midtone, so you'll have to either not correct the midtones or go back to what we used to do—guess.

Correcting Flesh Tones for Photos Going on Press

If the photos you're correcting are destined for a printing press, rather than just a color printer (i.e., they'll appear in a brochure, print ad, catalog, flyer, etc.), you have to compensate for how the inks react with one another on a printing press. Without compensating, you can almost guarantee that all the people in your photos will look slightly sunburned. Here's a technique that lets you correct flesh tone "by the numbers" to get perfect skin tones every time.

Step One:

When it comes to getting proper flesh tones on press, you're going to be concerned mainly with the relationship between the magenta and the yellow in the flesh-tone areas. Your goal will be to have at least 3% to 5% more yellow in your flesh-tone areas than magenta. The amount of yellow and magenta can be displayed in the Info palette, so start by going under the Window menu and choosing Info to bring up the palette. Then, convert your image to CMYK mode by going under the Image menu, under Mode, and choosing CMYK Color.

©SCOTT KELBY

Step Two:

First, you need to see what the current balance of yellow to magenta is, so press Command-M (PC: Control-M) to open Curves. Move your cursor outside the Curves dialog and into your photo over an area that contains flesh tones (we'll call this our "sample" area). While your cursor is there, look in your Info palette at the relationship of the magenta and the yellow.

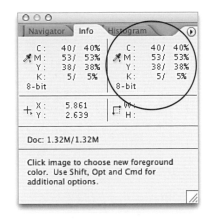

Step Three:
In the Info palette, look at the CMYK readout (on the right side of the palette). If the magenta reading is higher than the yellow reading, you'll have to adjust the balance of the magenta and the yellow. In the example shown here, the magenta reads 53% and the yellow is only 38%, so there's 15% more magenta, and that means instant sunburn; so you'll have to adjust this balance to get perfect flesh tones.

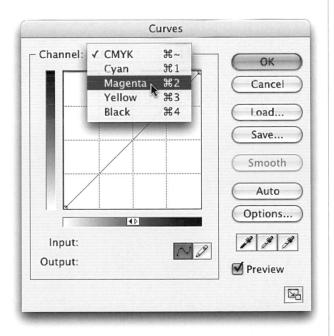

Step Four:
You might be tempted to just lower the amount of magenta, but to keep our adjustment from appearing too drastic, we'll do a balanced adjustment: Lower the magenta some, and then increase the yellow enough until we hit our goal of 3% to 5% more yellow. In the Curves dialog, choose Magenta from the Channel pop-up menu. To find out exactly where the magenta in your flesh-tone area resides on the curve, press-and-hold Shift-Command (PC: Shift-Control) and click once in the sample flesh-tone area. This adds a point to the Magenta channel curve right where the magenta in the flesh tone is located. (And because you added the Shift key, it also added a point to your yellow curve, which you'll see in a moment.)

Continued

Step Five:

In the Output field at the bottom of the Curves dialog, type in an amount that's 7% or 8% lower than the value shown. (Remember, the magenta reading was 15% more than the yellow, so you're going to reduce that difference by half.)

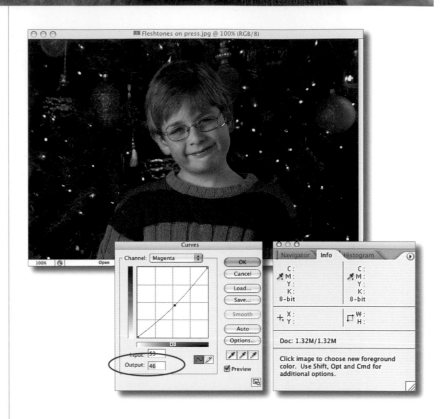

Step Six:

After you've lowered the magenta, switch to the Yellow channel by choosing it from the Channel pop-up menu at the top of the Curves dialog. You should already see a point on the curve. This is where the yellow resides in the sample flesh-tone area that you clicked on in Step 4. In the Output field at the bottom of the Curves dialog, type in a figure that's at least 3% higher than the number that you typed in the Output field for the magenta curve in Step 5. (The Info palette provides a before/after reading, with the before on the left and the reading after your adjustment on the right, so you can check your numbers in your sample area after you adjust the curve.) In our example, I lowered the magenta from 53% to 46%, and raised the yellow from 38% to 49%. This adds at least 3% more yellow than magenta in the flesh tones.

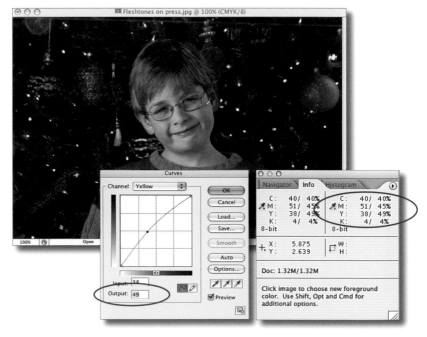

Before

After

Adjusting RGB Flesh Tones

So what do you do if you've used Curves to properly set the highlights, midtones, and shadows, but the flesh tones in your photo still look too red? You can't use the "getting-proper-flesh-tones-for-a-printing-press" trick, because that's only for CMYK images going to press. Instead, try this quick trick for getting your flesh tones in line by removing the excess red.

Step One:
Open a photo that you've corrected using the Curves technique shown earlier in this chapter. If the whole image appears too red, skip this step and go on to Step 3. However, if it's just the flesh-tone areas that appear too red, press L to get the Lasso tool and make a selection around all the flesh-tone areas in your photo. Press-and-hold the Shift key to add other flesh-tone areas to the selection, such as arms, hands, legs, etc., or press-and-hold the Option (PC: Alt) key to subtract from your selection. This can be a really loose selection like the one shown here (which includes strands of hair, sunglasses, etc.).

Step Two:
Go under the Select menu and choose Feather. Enter a Feather Radius of 3 pixels, and then click OK. By adding this feather, you're softening the edges of your selection, which will keep you from having a hard, visible edge show up where you made your adjustment.

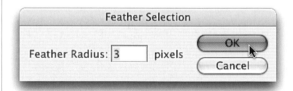

TIP: Once you've made a selection of the flesh-tone areas, you might find it easier if you hide the selection border from view (that makes it easier to see what you're correcting) by pressing Command-H (PC: Control-H).

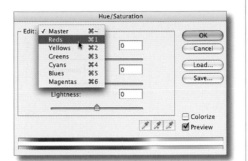

Step Three:
Go under the Image menu, under Adjustments, and choose Hue/Saturation. When the dialog appears, click-and-hold on the Edit pop-up menu and choose Reds, so you're only adjusting the reds in your photo in your selected areas (if you put a selection around just the flesh tones).

Step Four:
The rest is easy—you're simply going to reduce the amount of saturation so the flesh tones appear more natural. Drag the Saturation slider to the left to reduce the amount of red. You'll be able to see the effect of removing the red as you lower the Saturation slider. When it looks good to you, click OK in the dialog, and then press Command-D (PC: Control-D) to deselect, completing the technique.

Before

After

Getting Better Automated Color Correction

Photoshop has had two automated color-correction tools for some time now: Auto Levels and Auto Contrast. They're both pretty lame. And back in Photoshop 7, Adobe introduced Auto Color, which is much better than either Auto Levels or Auto Contrast; but here we'll show you how to tweak Auto Color to get even better results, all with just one click.

Step One:
Open a photo that needs correcting, but not so much that it warrants taking the time to do a full, manual color correction using Curves.

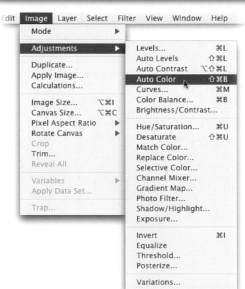

Step Two:
Go under the Image menu, under Adjustments, and choose Auto Color to apply an auto correction to your photo. When you apply Auto Color, it just does its thing. It doesn't ask you to input numbers or make decisions—basically, it's a one-trick pony that tries to neutralize the highlight, midtone, and shadow areas of your photo. In some cases, it does a pretty darn decent job, in others, well…let's just say it falls a bit short. But in this tutorial, you'll learn how to supercharge Auto Color to get dramatically better results, and transform it from a "toy" into a real color-correction tool.

Step Three:

After you've applied Auto Color, one way you can tweak its effect on your photo is by going under the Edit menu and choosing Fade Auto Color. (*Note:* This is only available *immediately* after you apply Auto Color.) When the Fade dialog appears, drag the Opacity slider to the left to reduce the effect of the Auto Color. Move the slider until the photo looks good to you. You can also change the blend mode (from the Mode pop-up menu) to further adjust your photo (Multiply makes it darker, Screen makes it lighter, etc.). When you click OK in the Fade dialog, your color is faded.

Step Four:

So now you know the "Apply-Auto-Color-and-Fade" technique, which is fine, but there's something better: tweaking Auto Color's options *before* you apply it. Believe it or not, there are hidden options for how Auto Color works. (They're not really hidden; they're just put some-place you'd probably never look.) To get to these Auto Color options, press Command-L (PC: Control-L) to bring up the Levels dialog. On the right side of the dialog, you'll see an Auto button. That's not it. Instead, click on the button just below it, named Options. This is where Adobe hid the Auto Color options (along with other options, as you'll soon see).

Continued

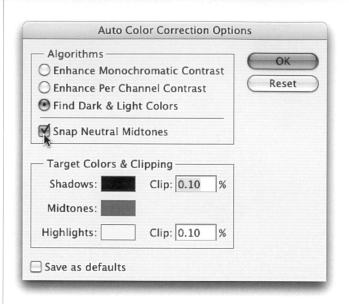

Step Five:

At the top of this dialog, under the Algorithms section, you can determine what happens when you click on the Auto button within the Levels or Curves dialog. If you click on the topmost choice, Enhance Monochromatic Contrast, clicking the Auto button will apply a somewhat lame Auto Levels auto correction. If you choose Enhance Per Channel Contrast, clicking the Auto button will apply the equally lame Auto Contrast auto correction. What you want instead is to choose both the Find Dark & Light Colors (which sets your highlight and shadow points) and Snap Neutral Midtones (which sets your midtones). With these settings, Auto Color (the most powerful of the auto-correction tools) will now be applied if you click the Auto button in either the Levels or Curves dialog.

Step Six:

In the Target Colors & Clipping section, you can click on each target color swatch (Shadows, Midtones, Highlights) and enter the RGB values you'd prefer Auto Color to use, rather than the defaults, which are...well, a bit yucky! I use the same settings that we entered in our manual Curves correction earlier in this chapter (Shadows: R: 20, G: 20, B: 20; Midtones: R: 133, G: 133, B: 133; and Highlights: R: 244, G: 244, B: 244).

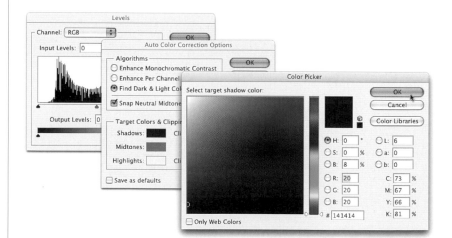

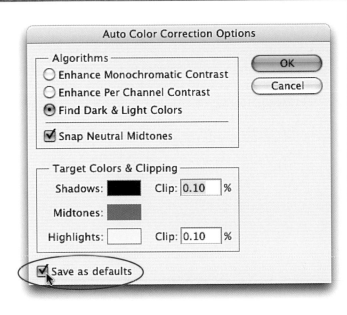

Auto Color Correction Options

Algorithms
- ○ Enhance Monochromatic Contrast
- ○ Enhance Per Channel Contrast
- ◉ Find Dark & Light Colors

☑ Snap Neutral Midtones

Target Colors & Clipping

Shadows: ■ Clip: 0.10 %

Midtones: ■

Highlights: □ Clip: 0.10 %

☑ Save as defaults

OK
Cancel

Step Seven:
To save these settings as your defaults, click on the Save as Defaults checkbox in the bottom-left side of the dialog. When you click OK to close the options dialog and save the settings, you've done three very important things:
(1) You've majorly tweaked Auto Color's settings to give you better results every time you use it.
(2) You've assigned Auto Color as the default auto correction when you click on the Auto button in the Curves or Levels dialog.
(3) You've turned Auto Color into a useful tool that you'll use way more than you'd think.

Before

After (tweaking the Auto Color options)

Color Correcting One Problem Area Fast!

This particular technique really comes in handy when shooting outdoor scenes, because it lets you enhance the color in one particular area of the photo (like the sky or water), while leaving the rest of the photo untouched. Real estate photographers often use this trick when shooting home exteriors to make it look like the sky was bright and sunny when they took the shot (even though the weather doesn't always cooperate). Here you'll use the technique to make the grayish sky look blue.

Step One:

Open an image containing an area of color that you would like to enhance. In this example, we want to make the sky blue (rather than gray). Go to the Layers palette and choose Color Balance from the Create New Adjustment Layer pop-up menu at the bottom of the Layers palette (it's the half-white/half-black circle icon, fourth from the left). A new adjustment layer named Color Balance 1 will be added to your Layers palette, but the name will probably be cut off by default. If you want to see the layer's name, you'll have to widen your Layers palette by clicking-and-dragging its bottom-right corner.

Step Two:

When the Color Balance dialog appears, drag the top slider to the left toward Cyan to add some bright blue into your sky, and then drag the bottom slider to the right toward Blue until the sky looks as blue as you'd like it. When the sky looks good to you, click OK. When you do this, the entire photo (building and all) will have a heavy blue cast to it.

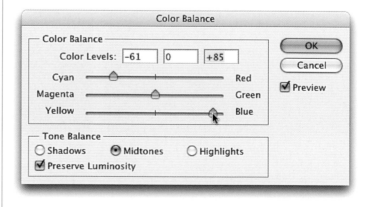

Step Three:
Press the letter X to set your Foreground color to black. Then press Option-Delete (PC: Alt-Backspace) to fill your adjustment layer's mask with black, which hides the blue layer.

Step Four:
Now you'll reveal parts of the blue layer using the Brush tool. Press the letter X to toggle your Foreground color to white. Press B to switch to the Brush tool, and then in the Options Bar, click on the thumbnail to the right of the word "Brush" and choose a large, soft-edged brush from the Brush Picker. Begin painting over the sky and the blue is revealed. If you accidentally paint over the building, press the X key to toggle your Foreground to black, and the original color will reappear. (*Note:* You may need to change the Opacity of your Brush to about 50% in the Options Bar when painting around detailed areas.)

TIP: If you feel the blue needs to be tweaked, try changing the blend mode of this adjustment layer to Screen (or Overlay) in the Layers palette, and then lower the Opacity a bit.

Before

After (making the sky bluer in Normal blend mode)

Removing Color Casts with One Click

This is kind of a weird trick, because the tool we're going to use was designed to match the overall tone of one photo to another photo (so if you shot one photo at dusk, and one just after lunch, you could have the afternoon shot match the warm tones of the sunset shot, or vice versa). However, in this case, we're only going to use one photo (so we're not matching it to anything), but we're going to use it to remove our color cast anyway. I know. It's weird. But it works.

Step One:

Start by opening a photo that has a strong color cast. In the example shown here, the motorcycle was shot through a store window at night, on a tripod, with no flash, so the color cast is created by the in-store lighting, which gives the photo its strong yellowish-reddish cast.

Step Two:

Go under the Image menu, under Adjustments, and choose Match Color.

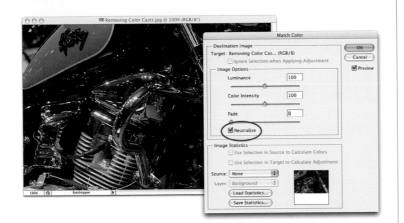

Step Three:

Are you ready for your "one click?" Just turn on the checkbox for Neutralize, and the color cast is gone (basically, you neutralized the color cast). Now, the only bad thing you may encounter here is that it does "too good of a job." By that, I mean when it removes the color cast, it really removes it, and on some photos it seems like it took a little too much cast out, leaving the photo feeling a bit cold. If that's the case with your photo, go on to the next step.

Step Four:

If Color Match took too much color out, drag the Fade slider slowly to the right until some of the color comes back (think of this Fade slider as "undo on a slider"—the farther you drag it to the right, the more it "undoes"). If your colors still look washed out, then drag the Color Intensity slider to the right a little to quickly bring them back. When it looks good to you, click OK.

Before

After

Exposure: 1/250s   Focal Length: 220mm   Aperture Value: $f/4.9$

Black & White
photoshop in
black and white

I know, I know, the title for this chapter is too obvious—Black & White for a chapter on black and white. Or is it? That's right, baby, I pulled a fast one on you—and don't think I stooped to the obvious choice, Michael Jackson's "Black or White." Too easy. Instead, I went with Three Dog Night's "Black & White" (which features the deep, thought-provoking lyrics: "A child is black. A child is white. Together they grow to see the light"). See, Eminem's lyrics suddenly don't seem so bad now, do they? In fact, Hanson's lyrics almost seem deep by comparison. Anyway, because the chapter title is so descriptive, it doesn't even really need a subhead (or me to explain what this chapter is about), right? So, whaddaya say we just spend some quality time together? Just you and me—one on one. Sound good? No? Rats!

I really didn't have a "Plan B" if you weren't up for the quality time thing, so now I'm kinda stuck. I guess this chapter intro will kind of be left just hanging there, like when one person puts up a high-five, but the person they're with doesn't high-five back. Maybe they're looking the other way, or preoccupied with something else, and you're just standing there with your hand up in the air. You're too embarrassed to pull your hand back down, because then it kind of brands you with the "high five loser" label, so you just leave your hand up there, hoping, praying, that the person will suddenly see it and complete "the five," before the stench of failure begins to permeate the air. But they never do, so your hand just stays up there, with no place to go, a lot like this chapter intro…(see, you should've taken my quality time offer).

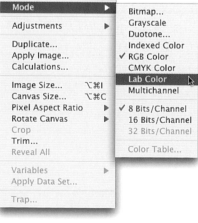

Using the Lightness Channel

This is one of the most popular methods for converting from color to grayscale, as it lets you isolate just the luminosity in the photo, separating out the color; and by doing so, you often end up with a pretty good grayscale image. However, since this uses the Lightness channel, we also add one little twist that lets you "dial in" a perfect grayscale photo almost every time. The most important thing for you to do in this chapter is to try all the different grayscale methods to decide which one you like best.

Step One:
Open the color RGB photo that you want to convert to grayscale using the Lightness channel method.

©DAVE MOSER

Step Two:
Go under the Image menu, under Mode, and choose Lab Color to convert your RGB photo into Lab Color mode. You won't see a visual difference between the RGB photo and the Lab Color photo—the difference is in the channels that make up your color photo (as you'll see in a moment).

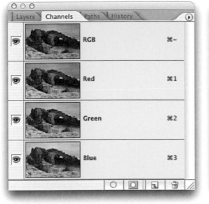

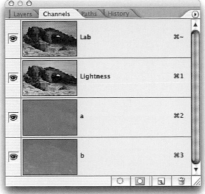

Regular RGB image   *Converted to Lab Color*

Step Three:
Go to the Channels palette (found under the Window menu), and you'll see that your photo is no longer made up of a Red, a Green, and a Blue channel. Instead, the luminosity (the Lightness channel) has been separated from the color data, which now resides in two channels named "a" and "b."

Step Four:
We're interested in the grayscale image that appears in the Lightness channel, so click on the Lightness channel in the Channels palette to make it active. Your photo will now look grayscale onscreen too, as it displays the currently active channel.

Continued

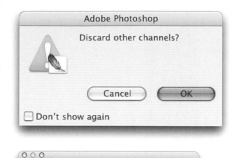

Step Five:
Now, go under the Image menu, under Mode, and choose Grayscale. Photoshop will ask if you want to discard the other channels. Click OK. If you look in the Channels palette, you'll now see only a Gray channel.

Step Six:
Go to the Layers palette, click on the Background layer, and then press Command-J (PC: Control-J) to duplicate the Background layer. Take a look at your image now. If it looks a little too dark, switch the layer blend mode of this duplicated layer from Normal to Screen, and you'll see the photo become much lighter. If the photo looks too light, choose Multiply as your blend mode instead. In the example shown here, changing the top layer to Screen made the photo too light, but don't sweat it—that's just a starting point.

Step Seven:

This is where you get to "dial in" your ideal tone (and fix that "too-light" look from the Screen layer). Just lower the Opacity of your layer in the Layers palette until you have the tonal balance you've been looking for. Using the Lab Color method gives you much more control and depth than just choosing the Grayscale mode from the Image menu's Mode submenu.

Standard grayscale conversion

Lab Lightness channel conversion

Better Black and Whites Using Channel Mixer

This has become the favorite of many professionals (and some will argue this is the absolute *best* way to create grayscale photos from color photos) because it lets you blend all three RGB channels to create a custom grayscale image. It's easier to use (and more intuitive) than applying the Calculations feature (that I'll show you later in this chapter). Here's how it works:

Step One:

Open the color photo you want to convert to grayscale. Choose Channel Mixer from the Create New Adjustment Layer pop-up menu at the bottom of the Layers palette (it's the half black/half white circle icon). Channel Mixer is also found under the Image menu, under Adjustments; however, by applying it as an adjustment layer, you have the added flexibility of being able to edit your grayscale conversion later in your creative process, or to change your mind altogether and instantly return to a full-color photo.

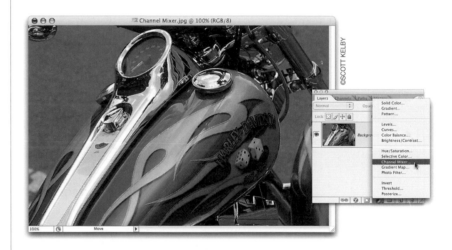

Step Two:

By default, the Channel Mixer is set to blend color RGB channels. When you're using this tool to create a gray-scale image, you have to turn on the Monochrome checkbox at the bottom of the dialog to enable the blending of these channels as grayscale. You can then use the three color sliders to combine percentages of each channel to create your grayscale (black-and-white) photo.

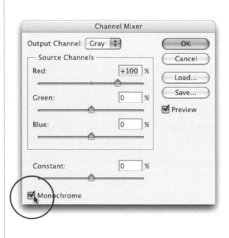

Step Three:
There was an old rule of thumb that your numbers had to equal 100%, but we've pretty much abandoned that (especially for printing to an ink printer). Now we just focus on how the print looks (not the numbers in the dialog), so feel free to push the numbers to create some nice contrast (I usually lower the Red setting, so I have some room to increase the Greens and Blues). When you click OK, the Channel Mixer is applied to your photo to create a black-and-white image.

TIP: If you decide you want to edit your settings, just double-click on the Channel Mixer thumbnail (to the left of the layer mask) in the Layers palette. The Channel Mixer dialog will appear with the last settings you applied to your photo.

Regular grayscale conversion

Channel Mixer black-and-white conversion

Scott's High-Contrast Black-and-White Technique

ADVANCED TECHNIQUES
FOR PROS ONLY!

Some of the best techniques unfold when you least expect it, and this technique is a perfect example. I was working on a completely different technique when I stumbled upon this. It's about the easiest, fastest, most reliable way to create stunning high-contrast black-and-white images that have incredible depth. Plus, at the end I show you how you can get three different variations to choose from with just a few clicks each. Not bad, eh matey?

Step One:

Open the color photo you want to convert into a high-contrast black-and-white image. Press the letter D to set your Foreground color to black, and then from the Create New Adjustment Layer pop-up menu at the bottom of the Layers palette, choose Gradient Map.

©SCOTT KELBY

Step Two:

When the Gradient Map dialog appears, it shows the Foreground to Background gradient by default (and because you chose black and white as your Foreground/Background colors, the gradient will be black and white). You don't have to do anything here, just click OK to apply this gradient map to your photo.

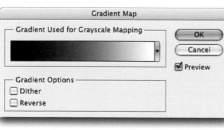

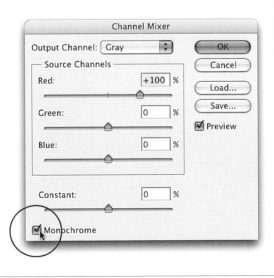

Step Three:

Believe it or not, just the simple act of applying this black-to-white gradient map will usually give you a much better gray-scale conversion than the standard method of choosing Grayscale from the Image menu's Mode submenu. But there's one drawback—if it doesn't look great, there's nothing you can do to the gradient map because there's really nothing to adjust. So, in the next step, we add the ability to adjust our black-and-white conversion.

Step Four:

Go to the Layers palette, and from the Create New Adjustment Layer pop-up menu, choose Channel Mixer. As you learned earlier in this chapter, you can use Channel Mixer to adjust the individual color channels of an image to create a better grayscale. Well, we're going to use it to adjust our image that's already grayscale, giving it the extreme contrast it so richly deserves.

Step Five:

Click on the Monochrome checkbox in the bottom left-hand corner of the dialog (otherwise, when you move the sliders, you'll get color tints instead of grayscale tweaks).

Continued

Step Six:

Here's where the fun begins. The technique starts with two predetermined steps: (1) Lower the Constant slider (at the bottom) to -8 to darken the entire photo, and (2) lower the Red channel to around 75% (I do this on every image). Now, you're going to increase the Green and Blue channels to create the extreme contrast. How much do you move them? For this image, I moved the Green to 26% and the Blue to 34%, but I came up with those numbers using a tried-and-true method, which I will disclose (for the first time ever) in the next step.

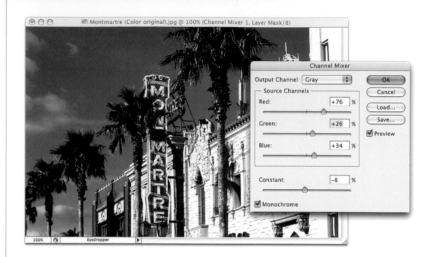

Step Seven:

I started dragging the Green slider to the right, and I kept dragging it as long as the photo continued to look better. As soon as it started to look bad, I stopped. Then, I did the exact same thing with the Blue slider. It sounds silly, but think about it—how can that not work? If it makes the photo look better—keep doing it. If it stops looking better, stop. Once I clicked OK, I went to the Layers palette's flyout menu and chose Flatten Image (don't do this just yet if you want to try out the other methods). Then I went to the Filter menu, under Sharpen, and I added an Unsharp Mask filter with the settings: Amount 85%, Radius 1 pixel, and Threshold 4 levels.

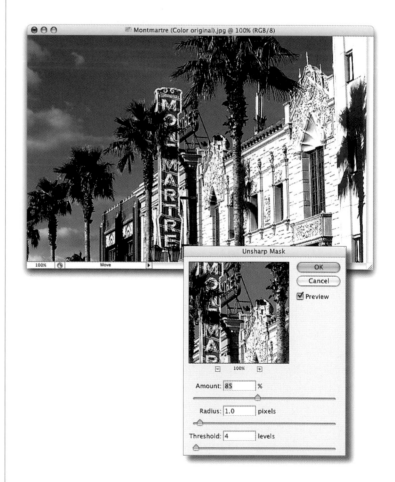

Alternate Version One:

I mentioned that I would give you two alternate versions you can achieve with just one click, so in total you can choose from three different high-contrast versions (because three choices are better than one, right?). For this version, go to the Layers palette and drag the Channel Mixer adjustment layer below the Gradient Map adjustment layer. Now take a look at the photo. It's a slightly different version. Do you like it better or not (it's totally up to you)?

Alternate Version Two:

Here's another great version to try: Click on the Background layer in the Layers palette, then go under the Image menu, under Adjustments, and choose Desaturate. This removes the color from the Background layer. Now, just choose the black-and-white version you like best from those three, and then make that one your high-contrast black-and-white conversion.

Regular grayscale conversion

Scott's high-contrast black-and-white conversion

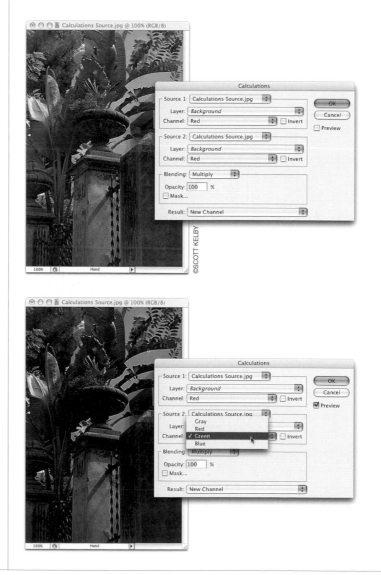

Calculations Method

FOR PROS ONLY!
ADVANCED TECHNIQUES

If there's one dialog in Photoshop that scares the living daylights out of people, it's the Calculations dialog. It's got an awfully intimidating layout for a dialog that simply lets you combine two channels, but that's part of the beauty of it—once you learn this technique, you can "name drop" it to impress other Photoshop users. So the next time you're at a Photoshop party and Deke McClelland strolls by, just casually mention something like: "I was converting this grayscale image using Calculations the other day…" and then see if he offers to buy you a Heineken.

Step One:

Open the color photo that you want to convert to grayscale using Calculations. Go under the Image menu and choose Calculations to bring up the Calculations dialog. Basically, what you're going to do here is choose two channels from your color photo that look great when blended together, then you'll use them to create an entirely new photo. For example, if you have one channel that looks too dark and one that looks too light, you can combine the two to create a black-and-white image with lots of depth (at least, that's the theory).

Step Two:

By default, Calculations tries to combine the Red channel (under Source 1) with another copy of the same Red channel (under Source 2). So your job is to experiment to find out which two channels from your color photo look best together, and then find out which blend mode looks best for blending them together. This is easier than it sounds, because you do this by simply choosing channels and blend modes from the pop-up menus. Start by leaving Source 1's Channel pop-up menu set to Red, but change Source 2's Channel pop-up menu to Green and see how that looks.

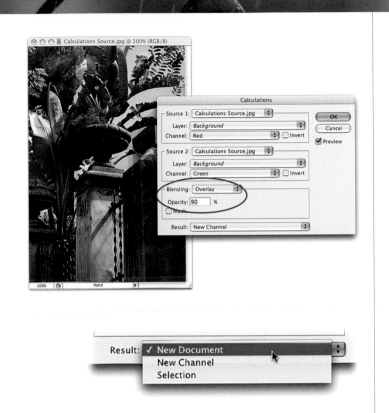

Step Three:
The default blend mode for Calculations is Multiply, which makes the combination of channels look darker, and that's fine in some situations, but here it makes the photo look too dark. So, change the Blending pop-up menu from Multiply to Overlay. If the tone looks more balanced, but it's too intense, you can lower the Opacity setting (I lowered it to 90% here). Now, just experiment by trying different combinations of channels and blend modes to see what looks best.

Step Four:
When you've come up with a combination that looks good to you, go to the Result pop-up menu at the bottom of the dialog and choose New Document. Click OK in the dialog and a new document will appear with your custom-calculated channel as the Background layer. One last thing: In this new document, go under the Image menu, under Mode, and choose Grayscale.

Regular grayscale conversion

Black-and-white conversion using Calculations

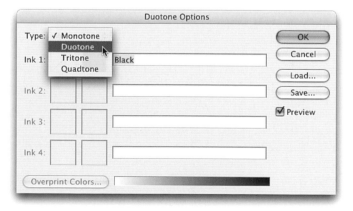

Creating Duotones

For some reason, creating a duotone (a photo that uses just two colors) in Photoshop is immeasurably more complex than creating one with four colors (as in CMYK). You definitely have to jump through a few hoops to get your duotones to look good and separate properly; but the depth added by combining a second, third, or fourth color with a grayscale photo is awfully hard to beat.

Step One:

Open the photo that you want to convert to a duotone. If you're starting with a color photo, you'll have to convert to grayscale first by going under the Image menu, under Mode, and choosing Grayscale. You'll get a warning dialog asking if you're sure you want to discard the colors, so just click OK.

Step Two:

Once your photo is grayscale, you can go under the Image menu, under Mode, and choose Duotone. This may seem weird, but the first time you open the Duotone Options dialog, for some reason Adobe set the default Type of Duotone to Monotone (I know, it doesn't make sense). So, to actually get a duotone, you'll first have to select Duotone from the Type pop-up menu in the top left of the dialog.

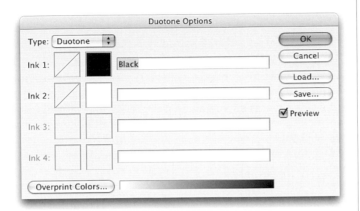

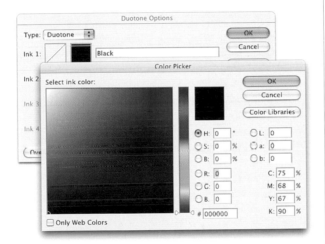

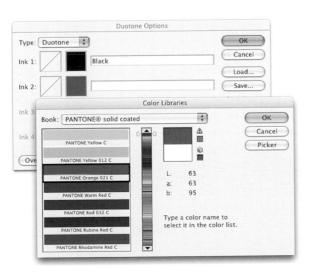

Step Three:

Now that Duotone is your selected Type, you have to choose which two inks you want to use. First, we'll look at Ink 1. The first box (the one with the diagonal line through it) is called the Curve Box, and this is where you determine how the color you choose will be distributed within your photo's highlights, midtones, and shadows. You determine this distribution using a curve. (Now don't stop reading if you don't know how to use Curves—you don't need to know Curves to create a duotone, as you'll soon see.)

Step Four:

The black box to the right of the Curve Box is the Color Box, in which you choose the color of Ink 1. By default, Ink 1 is set to black (that's actually pretty handy, because most duotones are made up of black and one other color). If you decide you don't want black as your Ink 1 color, just click on the Color Box and Photoshop's Color Picker will appear so you can choose a different color (but we're using black in this case).

Step Five:

You'll notice that Ink 2's Color Box is white. That's because it's waiting for you to choose your second ink color. To do so, click on the box to bring up Photoshop's Color Libraries, in which you can choose the color you'd like from the list of PANTONE® colors. (Photoshop assumes you're going to print this duotone on a printing press, and that's why it displays the PANTONE colors as the default. If you want to choose a custom color, just click on the Picker button to use the Color Picker.)

Continued

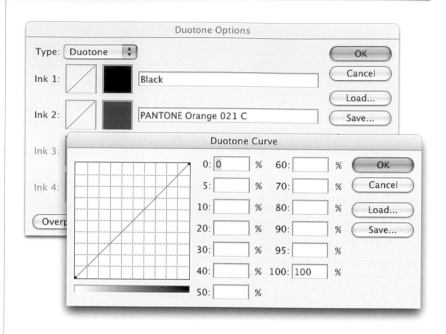

Step Six:

When you click OK in the Color Libraries dialog, the name of your Ink 2 color will appear beside the Color Box. Now that you've selected the two colors that will make up your duotone, it's time to determine the balance between them. Do you want more black in the shadows than your spot color? Should Ink 2 be stronger in the highlights? These decisions are determined in the Duotone Curve dialog for each ink, so click once on the Curves Box next to Ink 2 to bring up the dialog.

Step Seven:

If you look at the fields in the middle of the dialog, the default curve is flat. It mimics your black color, in that equal amounts of orange (Ink 2) will appear in the highlights, midtones, and shadows. For example, the field marked 100% indicates that 100% of the shadow areas will get 100% orange ink. However, if you want less orange in the shadows, type in a lower number in the 100% field. In this example, I entered 80% for the 100% shadow areas, so the darkest shadow areas will get 20% less orange (and will appear blacker). For 70% ink density areas, I lowered it to 60%, and for the 50% midtone, I entered 35%. When you enter these numbers manually like this, you'll see that Photoshop builds the curve for you. Vice versa, if you click-and-drag in the curve— Photoshop fills in the amounts in the corresponding fields.

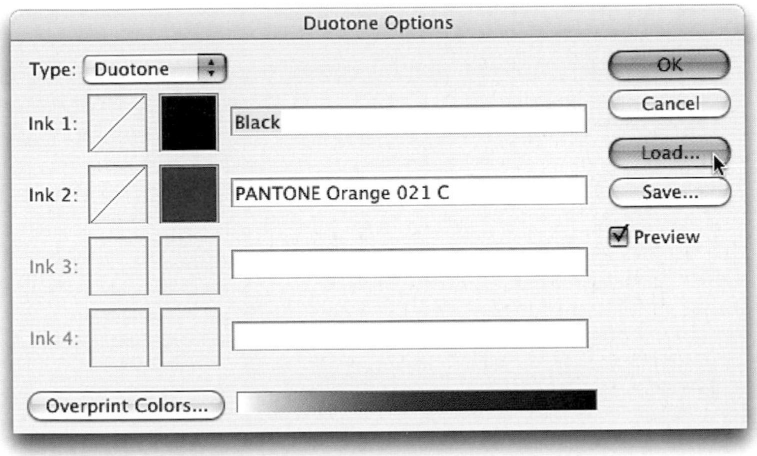

Step Eight:

If the idea of creating your own curve freaks you out, all is not lost. Adobe figured that first-time Duotoners might get the "willies," so they included a bunch of presets using popular colors and pre-built duotone curves. These duotone presets were loaded on your computer when you first installed Photoshop. To load them into Photoshop's Duotone Options dialog, first click on the Cancel button in the Duotone Curve dialog we've been working in, and then click on the Load button in the Duotone Options dialog.

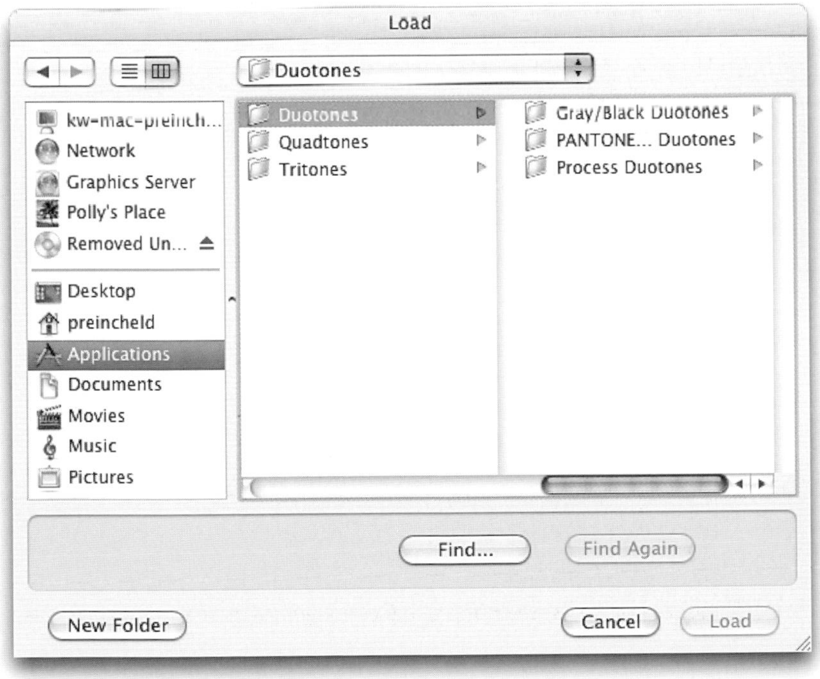

Step Nine:

The Load dialog will appear, and by default Photoshop targets the Duotones folder on your drive. If for some reason it doesn't (it's been changed or you don't see the Duotones folder), then the search is on—in this Load dialog, navigate to your Photoshop application folder. Then look for the Presets folder; inside you'll find a folder called Duotones. Within that folder, you'll find another folder named Duotones (you'll also see a folder called Tritones for mixing three colors and Quadtones for mixing four).

Continued

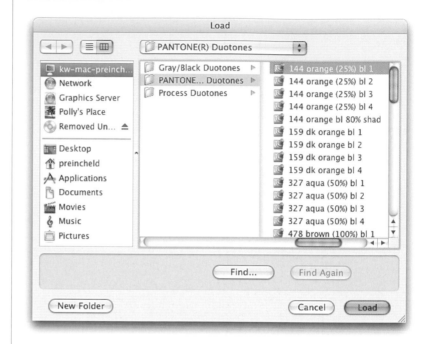

Step Ten:

In the Load dialog, click on this Duo-tones folder, and inside that folder is (believe it or not) yet another folder called PANTONE Duotones. This is where Adobe carefully buried the indi-vidual presets for you to choose from. Each color listed gives you four choices. The first color choice includes a duo-tone curve that gives you the strongest amount of spot-color ink, progressing to the least amount with the fourth choice. Try a couple out by double-clicking on the duotone color that you want to load. You'll get an instant onscreen preview, so you can decide if the color (and amount) of Ink 2 are right. If they aren't, click Load again and pick another from the list to try.

Step Eleven:

When you've got the combination that looks right to you, click OK in the Duotone Options dialog and the duotone will be applied to your photo. (*Note:* In the example shown here, I chose preset "144 orange 25% bl 1.")

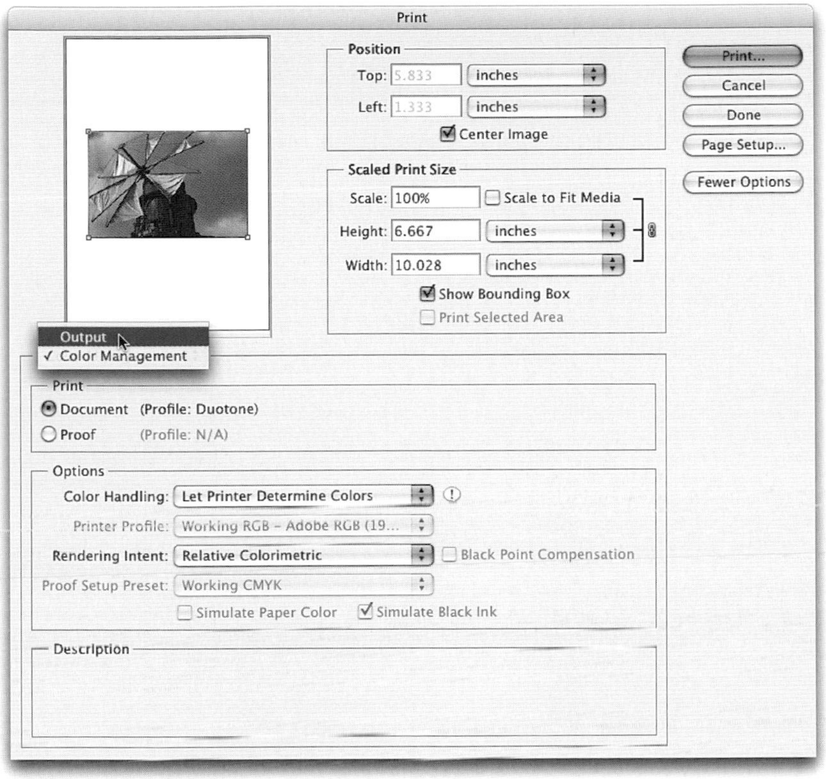

Step Twelve:

Okay, you've got what looks like a perfect duotone (onscreen anyway), but if it's going to press, before you save your file, you have to do a couple of simple but absolutely critical steps to ensure your duotone separates properly. Go under the File menu and choose Print with Preview. When the Print dialog appears, set the pop-up menu just below the preview to Output (it shows Color Management by default).

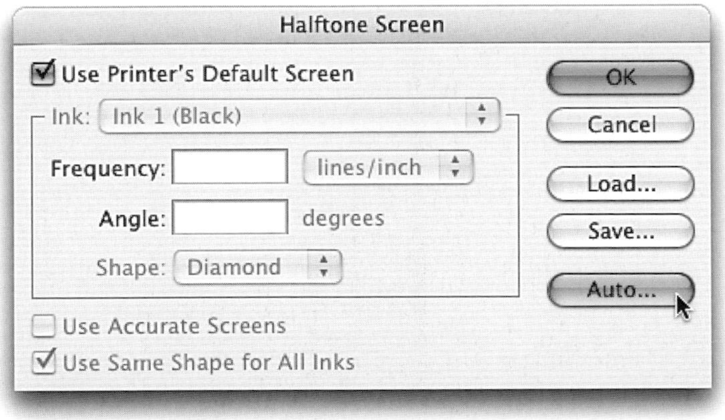

Step Thirteen:

As your duotone is set right now, both colors have the same screen angle. This will likely cause a distracting pattern (called a moiré pattern) to appear across your entire photo when outputting to a printing press. To avoid this, have Photoshop assign separate screen angles for your duotone by clicking on the Screen button in the Print dialog, which brings up the Halftone Screen dialog. Then, click the Auto button to bring up the Auto Screens dialog.

Continued

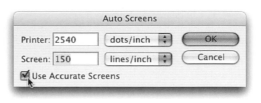

Step Fourteen:

In the Printer field of the Auto Screens dialog, enter the dots-per-inch (dpi) amount of the device your duotone will be output to. (In this case, I entered 2540, the resolution of the imagesetter that the prepress department of our print shop uses.) Then call the print shop that's printing your duotone, and ask them at what line screen your job will be printed. Enter that number in the Screen field. Also, turn on Use Accurate Screens (it could help, depending on the imagesetter that's used; otherwise, it will be ignored. Either way, no harm done).

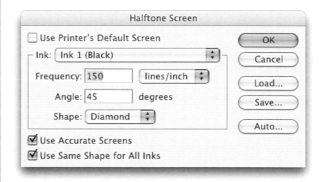

Step Fifteen:

Click OK to close the Auto Screens dialog with your new settings. You'll see in the Halftone Screen dialog that the screen frequencies have now been set for you. Don't change these settings or you'll undo the Auto Screens function you just applied (and risk ruining your print job).

Step Sixteen:

Click OK in the Halftone Screen dialog, click Done in the Print dialog, and then those settings are saved. Now, the trick is to embed that information into your duotone so it separates and prints properly. Easy—from the File menu, save your duotone as an EPS (choose Photoshop EPS from the Format pop-up menu in the Save As dialog). This will enable you to embed the screen info into your file to make sure it separates properly on press.

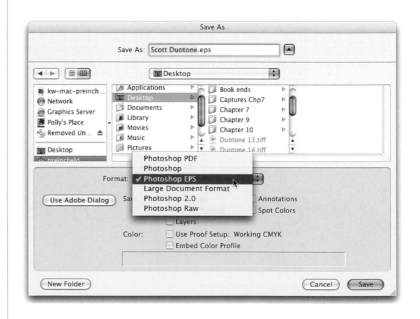

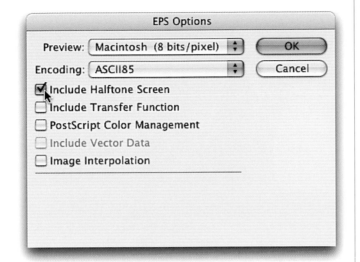

Step Seventeen:

Once you click Save in the Save As dialog, you'll be presented with the EPS Options dialog. You only have to choose one option—Include Halftone Screen. The screen angles that you set earlier will now be included with your file. Click OK to save your file, and your duotone is ready to be imported into your page-layout application. *Note:* When creating duotones, I recommend always printing a test to your color inkjet to make sure it separates correctly (giving you just two plates—one black and one with your color tint). *Another Note:* Again, if you're printing straight from Photoshop to a color inkjet printer or some other desktop printer, you can skip all this setting screens, halftone dialogs, etc., and just hit Print. These extra steps are only necessary if you're going to output your duotone for reproduction on a printing press.

Original color image   *Final duotone*

Exposure: 1/125s   Focal Length: 28mm   Aperture Value: f/18

Modern Problems
dealing with image problems

I'll admit it. I was totally stuck for a name for this chapter. I got so desperate I asked my wife and son if they could think of any song titles or TV or movie titles that had the words "image," "dealing," or "problems" in them. They had as much success as I did. My wife got so desperate that she actually called my mother-in-law (she calls her "Mom," go figure) to ask her for ideas (this falls under the category of "book research," and therefore becomes billable hours to my publisher). Anyway, my mother-in-law came up with the movie *Modern Problems*, which at first she said starred Queen Latifah and Chevy Chase. So I said, "Does she mean Queen Latifah and Steve Martin?" She said, "No, it's Chevy Chase." But when she told us the basic plot, we soon realized that there was no way Queen Latifah was in that movie. Although her expla-

nation of the plot sounded somewhat familiar, we still aren't sure who played opposite Chevy Chase, but she swears the name of the movie was either *Modern Problems* or *Caddyshack*. Anyway, this chapter on dealing with image problems is about how to deal with image problems. See, this chapter didn't even need a chapter intro, but I know some of you have stuck it out with me, through mindless intro after mindless intro, and if you thought I'd take the easy way out and just leave two blank pages here, well, you just don't know me. I care, dammit. I care so deeply that when every ounce of care is drained out of me, I somehow reach down deep inside myself and pull out just a little more care. Why? Because I care. Why do I care? Because I'm a Care Bear. (Can you tell it's 1:45 a.m. when I'm writing this?)

Dealing with Digital Noise

If you shoot in low-lighting situations, you're bound to encounter digital noise. Is there anything worse than these large red, green, and blue dots that appear all over your photo? Okay, besides that "crazy music" those teenagers play, like Limp Bizkit or…well…Limp Bizkit, is there anything worse? This digital noise (often called "Blue channel noise," "high ISO noise," "color aliasing," or just "those annoying red, green, and blue dots") can be reduced. Here's how:

Step One:

Open a photo that contains visible digital noise. Go ahead and do your color correction, and other adjustments first (like any Shadow/Highlight adjustments, Curves, etc.), because these will sometimes bring out noise in the image too. (In this case, the shot was taken at night with a point-and-shoot camera, and those red, green, and blue dots appear throughout the photo, but are especially visible in the sky. I know, it's kind of hard to see the noise in the small photo shown here, so in the next step we'll zoom in tighter so you can see the noise.)

Step Two:

Go under the Filter menu, under Noise, and choose Reduce Noise. When the Reduce Noise dialog appears, click on the Plus (+) sign (that's directly below the preview window) about four or five times to zoom into the sky area. To actually see the red, green, and blue noise pixels, click-and-hold within the preview area. This shows you the original image (before the filter is applied). Release the mouse button, and you'll see how the Reduce Noise filter reduces the noise. This is a quick way to get a before and after: click to see the before, release to see the after.

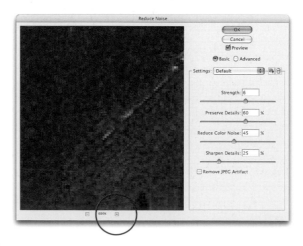

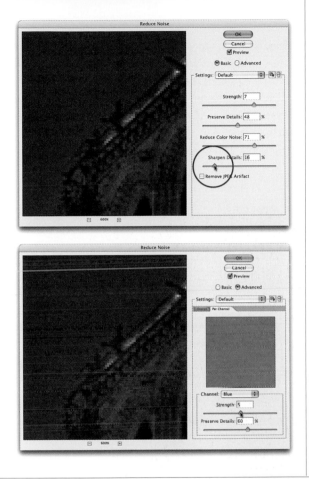

Step Three:

This filter seems to work best if you crank up the Strength fairly high (try 7 or 8). You want to find a sweet spot for keeping as much detail as possible, while still getting decent noise reduction, so try setting the Preserve Details slider between 40% and 50%. You want to really work the Reduce Color Noise slider (start between 60% to 70%, and then drag to the right for more reduction but without making the photo noticeably blurry). For Sharpen Details, keep that at no more than 15% to 20% (you'll probably get better results if you use the Smart Sharpen filter next, rather than applying the sharpening here). Click OK to reduce the color noise.

TIP: Some digital cameras produce what's called "Blue channel noise," because that's the channel where most of the noise winds up. To reduce that, click on the Advanced option, which lets you reduce noise in individual channels. Click on the Per Channel tab, and then from the Channel pop-up menu, choose Blue. Then, use the Strength slider to reduce noise in just the Blue channel.

Before

After (with color noise greatly reduced using the Reduce Noise filter)

Opening Up Shadow Areas (Digital Fill Flash)

Back in Photoshop CS, Adobe introduced a very slick new way to open up shadow areas (or pull back highlight areas) called—aptly enough—Shadow/Highlight. This lighting correction command can be as simple as moving a slider or you can tweak each little nuance of your photo's shadow and highlight areas by revealing its many options. It's ideal to use in situations where you wish you had used a fill flash (think of it as a highly flexible digital fill flash) and need to bring out detail lost in the shadows or to reduce your highlights.

Step One:

Open a photo containing shadow or highlight areas that need adjusting (in this case, it's a photo of part of the Chrysler Building in New York). In this example, the light is coming from the side and slightly behind our subject, so ideally we'd like to open up the shadows on this side. Needless to say, I couldn't get my flash to reach up 30 or 40 stories, but hey—that's why they invented Photoshop, right?

©SCOTT KELBY

Step Two:

Go under the Image menu, under Adjustments, and choose Shadow/Highlight.

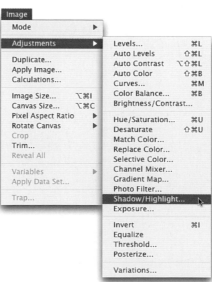

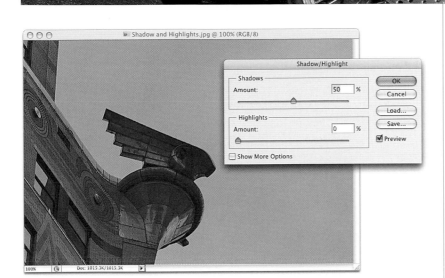

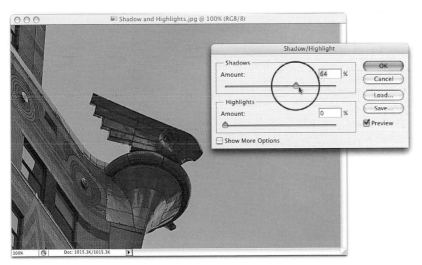

Step Three:
When the Shadow/Highlight dialog appears, by default the shadow areas are lightened by 50%. You can increase the amount for additional lightening, or you can decrease the amount if the shadows appear too light. (We're adjusting shadows in this image, but if you were adjusting highlights, you'd increase the Highlights Amount to decrease the highlights in the photo.)

Step Four:
In this example, the 50% default setting for shadows wasn't quite enough, so I dragged the Shadows Amount slider to the right to open up the shadow areas even more. When you click OK, your shadow lightening correction is applied to your photo.

Step Five:
If you want more control than these two sliders offer, click on the Show More Options checkbox in the bottom left-hand corner of the dialog. Once you click the checkbox, you get the "full monty" (as shown in Step 6). Don't let all those sliders intimidate you, because chances are you'll be tweaking either the shadows or the highlights—not both—so you can ignore half the sliders altogether.

Continued

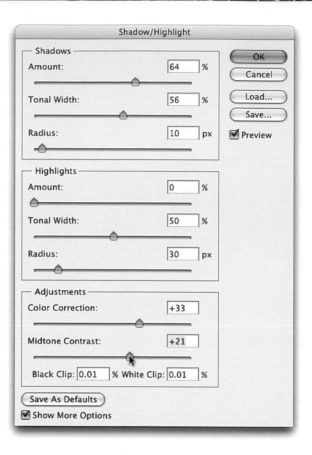

Step Six:

I generally use these expanded options if I tried to open the shadow areas on a photo and the adjustment looked too artificial or "milky," which the Shadows Amount slider tends to do, especially on people. In that particular case, try lowering the Shadows Amount to around 25%, then increasing the Shadows Tonal Width and Radius sliders (by dragging them to the right) to get a more realistic look. This is what the sliders here do: If you're tweaking shadows, lowering the Tonal Width lets you affect only the darkest shadow areas; increasing it affects a wider range of shadows. Increase it a bunch, and it'll start to affect the midtones as well. It works similarly for the Highlights. The Radius amount determines how many pixels each adjustment affects, so to affect a wider range of pixels, increase the amount. If you increase the shadow detail, the colors may become too saturated. If that's the case, reduce the Color Correction amount (which basically only affects the area you're adjusting). You can also adjust the contrast in the midtones using the Midtone Contrast slider.

Before

After (opening up the shadows with Shadow/Highlight)

Step Seven:

Okay, so we've opened up shadows, but what about pulling back highlights? Well, in the photo we just worked on, there's not much of a shadow problem, but the photo here has plenty. So go under the Image menu, under Adjustments, and pull up Shadow/Highlight again. Lower the Shadow amount to 0%.

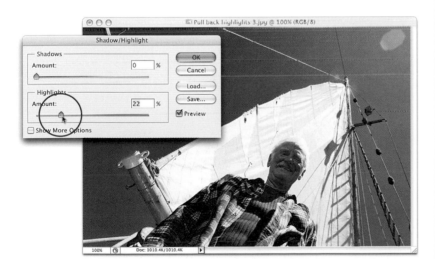

Step Eight:

Now drag the Highlights Amount slider to the right, and as you do, the highlights are pulled back. This is pretty much the opposite of the way every other dialog in Photoshop works. Usually if you drag a slider to the right, you get more of something—but in this case, increasing the Highlights Amount gives you less highlights.

Compensating for "Too Much Flash"

Don't ya hate it when you open a photo and realize that: (a) the flash fired when it shouldn't have; (b) you were too close to the subjects to use the flash and they're totally "blown out"; or (c) you're simply not qualified to use a flash at all, and your flash unit should be forcibly taken from you, even if that means ripping it from the camera body? Here's a quick fix to get your photo back from the "flash graveyard," while keeping your reputation—and camera—intact.

Step One:
Open the photo that is suffering from "flashaphobia." In the example shown here, the flash, which was mounted on the camera body, washed out the entire subject (although the background behind her looks okay).

Step Two:
Make a copy of the photo layer by dragging it to the Create a New Layer icon at the bottom of the Layers palette. Then, change the layer blend mode of this duplicate layer from Normal to Multiply, which has a "multiplier" effect, bringing back a lot of the original foreground detail the flash "blew out." She's still a little bit "blown out," so you'll probably need to repeat this process at least once more to get additional detail and tone back.

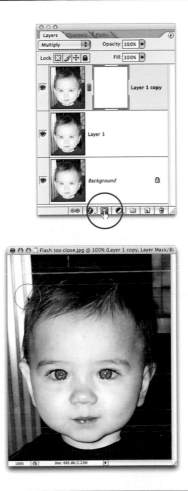

Step Three:

Press Command-J (PC: Control-J) to duplicate this Multiply layer again. This does a nice job of bringing back more detail and balancing the tone in her face, but now her hair and the background behind her head are a little too dark. Here's how to deal with that: Click on the Add Layer Mask icon at the bottom of the Layers palette.

Step Four:

Press the letter X to toggle your Foreground color to black, press B to get the Brush tool, and in the Options Bar, click on the Brush thumbnail and choose a soft-edged brush from the Brush Picker. Start painting over her hair and the background behind her head. As you paint, it will reveal the lighter version of her hair from the layer beneath it. You might want to lighten up her shirt as well. When you're done, the amount of flash is properly balanced. *Note:* If you make a mistake while you're painting, you can press X to switch your Foreground color to white, paint over those areas, and they'll return to how they looked before you started painting—that's the beauty of layer masks.

Before   *After*

Fixing Photos Where You Wish You Hadn't Used Flash

There's a natural tendency for people to react to their immediate surroundings, rather than what they see through the lens. For example, if you're shooting an indoor concert, there are often hundreds of lights illuminating the stage. However, some photographers think it's one light short—their flash—because it's dark where they're sitting. So when you look at your photos later, you see that your flash lit everyone in front of you, ruining an otherwise great shot. Here's a quick fix to make it look as if your flash never fired at all:

Step One:

Open a photo where shooting with the flash ruined part of the image (like the image shown here taken at Walt Disney World in Florida. The castle is beautifully lit, and that's all we want to see, not the tourists, although I'm sure they're perfectly nice people). Press L to get the Lasso tool and click-and-drag a selection around the part of shot ruined by the flash (in this case, the crowd on the street, who got lit by an inadvertent firing of the flash).

Step Two:

Now we're going to darken this selected area, but we don't want our adjustment to appear obvious. We'll need to soften the edges of our selection quite a bit so our adjustment blends in smoothly with the rest of the photo. To do this, go under the Select menu and choose Feather. When the Feather Selection dialog appears, enter 25 pixels to soften the selection edge. (By the way, 25 pixels is just my guess for how much this particular selection might need. The rule of thumb is the higher the resolution of the image, the more feathering you'll need.)

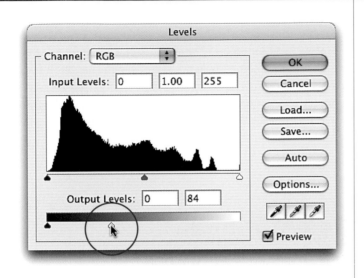

Step Three:
It will help you make a better adjustment if you hide the selection border (we call it "the marching ants") from view. We don't want to deselect—we want our selection to remain intact but without the annoying border, so press Command-H (PC: Control-H) to hide the selection border. Now, press Command-L (PC: Control-L) to bring up the Levels dialog. At the bottom of the dialog, drag the highlight Output Levels slider to the left to darken your selected area. Because you've hidden the selection border, it should be very easy to match the surroundings of your photo by just dragging this slider to the left. Now you can press Command-D (PC: Control-D) to deselect, and then admire the final image.

Before: The flash is obviously a couple hundred yards short of reaching the castle.

After: The effect of the flash is hidden, saving the shot!

Fixing Underexposed Photos the Easy Way

This is a tonal correction for people who don't like making tonal corrections (more than 60 million Americans suffer from the paralyzing fear of MTC [Making Tonal Corrections]). Since this technique requires no knowledge of Levels or Curves, it's very popular, and even though it's incredibly simple to perform, it does a pretty incredible job of fixing underexposed photos.

Step One:
Open an underexposed photo. The photo shown here could've used either a fill flash or a better exposure setting or both.

Step Two:
Press Command-J (PC: Control-J) to duplicate the Background layer (this duplicate will be named Layer 1 by default). On this new layer, change the blend mode in the Layers palette from Normal to Screen to lighten the entire photo.

Step Three:
If the photo still isn't properly exposed, just press Command-J (PC: Control-J) and duplicate this Screen layer until the exposure looks about right (this may take a few layers, but don't be shy about it—keep copying layers until it looks right).

Step Four:
There's a good chance that at some point your photo will still look a bit underexposed, meaning you duplicated the layer again, but now it looks overexposed. What you need is "half a layer." (Half as much lightening.) Here's what to do: Lower the Opacity of your top layer to "dial in" the perfect amount of light, giving you something between the full intensity of the layer (at 100%) and no layer at all (at 0%). For half the intensity, try 50% (did I really even have to say that? Didn't think so). Once the photo looks properly exposed, choose Flatten Image from the Layers palette's flyout menu.

TIP: To fix an overexposed photo, try this same technique, but instead of using Screen (in Step 2), choose Multiply instead.

Before   *After (using multiple Screen blend mode layers)*

Adjusting Exposure in CS2

One of the greatest advantages of shooting in RAW format is that you can go into Photoshop's Camera Raw and adjust your Exposure setting after the fact. But if you weren't shooting in RAW, you were pretty much out of luck (you'd have to try to fix exposure problems using Curves or Levels). But in CS2, there's a dedicated Exposure control that you can use on JPEGs, but it works a little differently than the one in Camera Raw (since it was actually designed for use on High Dynamic Range images, but it still works with regular 8-bit photos).

Step One:

Open an underexposed photo (we're continuing our tribute to German cars that I don't own with the photo shown here). Go under the Image menu, under Adjustments, and choose Exposure to bring up the Exposure dialog (seen in the capture in Step 2. While you're there, take a look at the three Eyedroppers—they work nothing like the ones in Levels and Curves—they only affect the photo's luminance, so don't get any cute ideas).

Step Two:

The Exposure slider acts like the exposure adjustment on your camera. Dragging the Exposure slider to the right (as we're doing here) mostly increases the photo's highlights, but also opens up some of the midtones as well (kind of like dragging the highlight Input slider in Levels to the left—it moves the midtones slider, too). This Exposure slider will generally do most of the work in fixing your image.

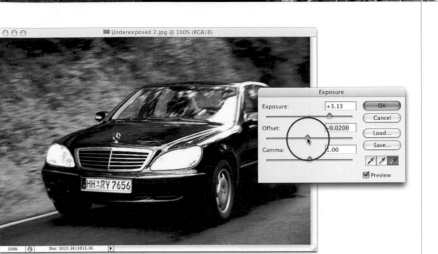

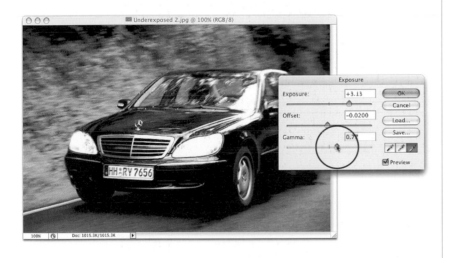

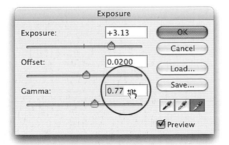

Step Three:

If you drag the Offset slider to the right (above 0), it kind of works like the Levels shadow Output slider (the one on the bottom-left of the Levels dialog) in that it lightens the overall image. However, if you drag the Offset slider to the left (below 0), it increases the shadow areas without really affecting the highlights (kind of like what the Levels shadow Input slider would do if you dragged it to the right). I know, it's freaky.

Step Four:

The Gamma slider mostly affects the midtones and some highlights (kind of like the midtones slider in Levels). Dragging to the right opens up the midtone areas; dragging to the left darkens the midtones.

TIP: Moving these sliders just a little can create a big adjustment, so here's a trick to make smaller adjustments: Hold the Command key (PC: Control key) and move your cursor over the number field you want to adjust. Your cursor will change into a scrubby slider, and now you can click-and-drag within that field to adjust in smaller increments.

Continued

Step Five:

When I adjusted the Exposure in Step 2, it blew out the detail in the headlights. Here's how I got around it—I started over. First I duplicated the Background layer by dragging it to the Create a New Layer icon, and then I clicked on its Eye icon to hide it from view. Then, I ran Exposure (set to +1.40) on the Background layer, made the duplicate layer visible again and did Steps 2-4. Then, I clicked on the Add Layer Mask icon with the duplicate layer active, and using the Brush tool (B), painted over the headlights (in black) to reveal the +1.40 Exposure headlights on the Background layer. Give that a try.

Before

After (using the Exposure feature and adding a layer mask for the headlights)

Dodging and Burning Done Right

If you've ever used Photoshop's Dodge and Burn tools, you already know how lame they are. That's why the pros choose this method instead—it gives them a level of control that the Dodge and Burn tools just don't offer, and best of all, it doesn't "bruise the pixels." (Photoshop-speak for "it doesn't mess up your original image data while you're editing.")

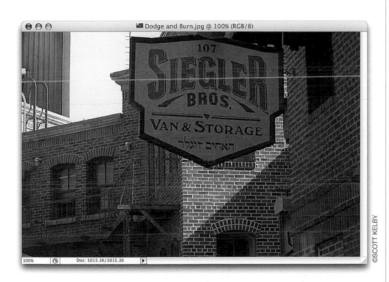

©SCOTT KELBY

Step One:

In this photo the light simply didn't fall where you wish it had. Here, we're going to dodge (lighten) an area that we wish had more light (like the hanging sign, the left side of the building, and the wall on the right), and then we're going to burn (darken) the harsh light falling on the building just below the hanging sign and the tin door at the top-left corner of the photo.

Step Two:

Go to the Layers palette, and from the palette's flyout menu, choose New Layer. The reason you need to do this (rather than just clicking on the Create New Layer icon) is that you need to access the New Layer dialog for this technique to work. But, if you're a flyout menu hater or shortcut freak (you know who you are), you can Option-click (PC: Alt-click) on the Create a New Layer icon instead to bring up the dialog. When the New Layer dialog appears, change the Mode to Overlay; then, right below it, choose "Fill with Overlay-neutral color (50% gray)." This is normally grayed out, but when you switch to Overlay mode, this choice becomes available. Click OK.

Continued

Step Three:

This creates a new layer (filled with 50% gray) above your Background layer. (When you fill a layer with 50% gray and change the Mode to Overlay, Photoshop ignores the color. You'll see a gray thumbnail in the Layers palette, but the layer will appear transparent in your image window.)

Step Four:

Press B to switch to the Brush tool, and in the Options Bar, click on the thumbnail to the right of the word "Brush" and choose a medium soft-edged brush from the Brush Picker. Now, lower the Brush tool's Opacity to approximately 30%.

Step Five:

Press the letter D then X to set your Foreground color to white. Begin painting over the areas that you want to lighten (in this example, click-and-hold the mouse button and paint over the sign). As you paint, in the Layers palette you'll see white strokes appear in the thumbnail of your gray transparent layer, and on the hanging sign you'll see soft lighting appear.

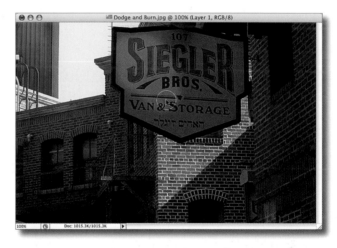

Step Six:

If the dodging isn't as intense as you'd like, just release the mouse button, click, and paint right over the same area again. Because you're dodging at a low Brush Opacity setting, the light areas will "build up" as you paint multiple strokes. (I painted over the windows about three times while lightening the second story of the building on the left.) *Note:* If the light areas appear too intense, try lowering the Opacity in the Layers palette.

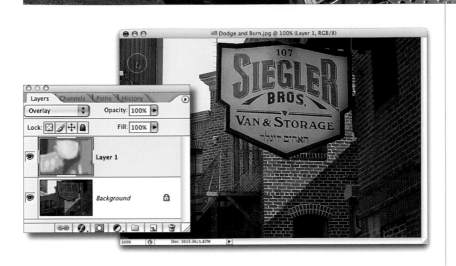

Step Seven:

Now press the letter D to set your Foreground color to black, and paint over that harsh area of light directly beneath the hanging sign. Then, paint over the tin door in the top left of the photo a couple of times to darken it. Now press X to set white as your Foreground color and paint over the wall on the far right of the photo, just to bring it out of the shadows a little bit. If you look in the Layers palette, you'll see that your Overlay layer has all sorts of white, gray, and black strokes over it.

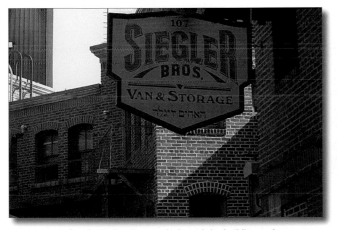

Before (with the sign too dark, and the building and windows on the left buried in shadows)

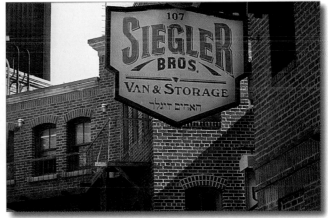

After (with the sign and left side of the building dodged, and the tin door and direct sunlight burned just a bit)

Instant Red-Eye Removal

When I see a digital camera with the flash mounted directly above the lens, I think, "Hey, there's an automated red-eye machine." If you're a pro, you probably don't have to deal with this as much, because your flash probably isn't mounted directly above your lens—you're using bounce flash, holding the flash separately, using studio lights, or one of a dozen other techniques. But even when the pros pick up a "point-and-shoot," red eye can find them. Here's the quick "I-just-want-it-gone" technique for getting rid of red eye fast.

Step One:

Open a photo where the subject has red eye (this is a photo of my buddy Dave's little boy, Eric).

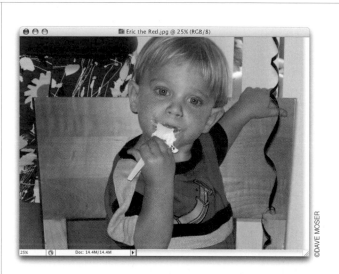

Step Two:

Press Z to get the Zoom tool and zoom in on the eyes by dragging a rectangle around them. Now get the Red Eye tool from the Toolbox (it's nested under the Spot Healing Brush, or you can press Shift-J until you get the tool).

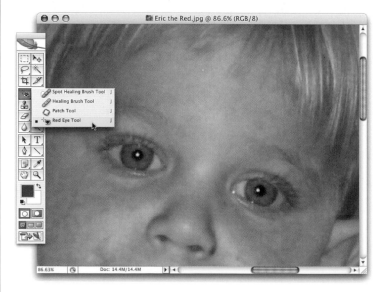

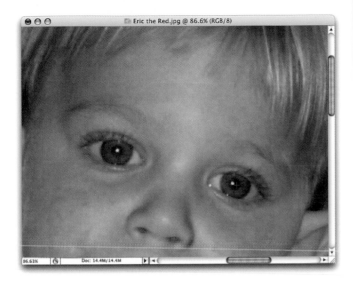

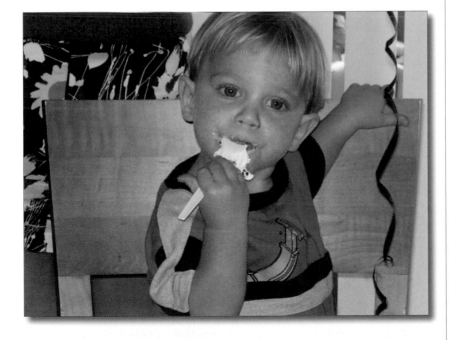

Step Three:

Tools don't get much easier to use than this—just click it once on the red area of the eye, and in just a second or two—the red is gone (as shown here, where I just clicked it in the red area of his left eye). Think of it as a "Red Eye Magic Wand" because it automatically selects all the red area with just one click. Now, what do you do if you click in the red, and you don't like the results? Well, there are two controls that can help you tweak the performance of the Red Eye tool: Pupil Size and Darken Amount (you find both of these in the Options Bar).

Step Four:

Think of the Pupil Size control like you would the Threshold setting for the Magic Wand tool (W)—the higher the amount, the more colors it will select, so if your first try doesn't select all the red, increase the Pupil Size. The Darken Amount basically determines how dark the color is that replaces the red eye. The default setting of 50% gives you a very dark gray pupil. If you want a pure black pupil, just increase the amount.

Step Five:

To complete the retouch, just click the Red Eye tool once in the right eye (you did the left eye earlier). Press Command-0 (zero) (PC: Conrol-0) to fit your image onscreen, and you'll have the red-eye retouched photo you see here.

Repairing Problems Caused by the Lens

In Photoshop CS2, Adobe introduced a new filter that is pretty much a "one-stop-shop" for repairing the most common problems caused by the camera's lens, including pincushion and barrel distortion, horizontal and vertical perspective problems, chromatic aberrations, and vignetting. Before CS2, you could only fix chromatic aberrations and vignetting if you were shooting RAW, because the fixes only appear in Camera Raw, but now you can apply these quick fixes on JPEG images as well.

Problem One: Perspective Distortion
Step One:
The first problem we're going to tackle is some perspective distortion. In the example shown here, the bases of the buildings look smaller than the tops (especially the building on the left), which gives the photo an almost cartoon-like perspective (but believe me, your client won't think it's funny).

Step Two:
To fix this problem (caused by the lens), go under the Filter menu, under Distort, and choose Lens Correction. When the dialog appears, turn off the Show Grid checkbox (it's on by default), then go to the Transform section (near the bottom-right side of the dialog) and drag the Vertical Perspective slider to the right until the buildings start to look straight and not so top-heavy. When you make this correction, the filter pinches the top third of your photo inward, which leaves transparent gaps along the top and upper-side edges of your photo (you can see the checkerboard in these areas).

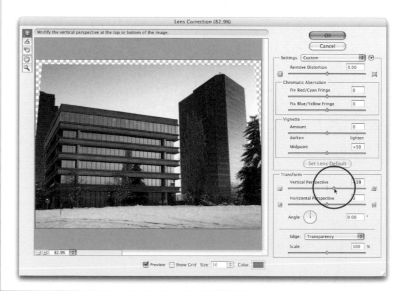

Step Three:
The Edge pop-up menu at the bottom of the Transform section lets you decide how to deal with these edge "gaps" caused by the perspective repair. From the pop-up menu, choose Edge Extension, which extends the edge areas of your photo to cover those gaps, and click OK to apply the fix. *Note:* You'll still need to do some clean-up to hide some of the stretched areas created by the Edge Extension, so just use the Clone Stamp tool (S) or the Healing Brush (J).

Before: The bases of the buildings are smaller than the tops.

After: The perspective distortion is corrected.

Continued

Problem Two: Barrel Distortion
Step One:

Another common lens correction problem is called barrel distortion, which makes your photo look bloated or rounded. So, open the Lens Correction filter again, but this time you're going to drag the Remove Distortion slider (in the top right of the dialog) slowly to the right to "pucker" the photo inward from the center, removing the rounded, bloated look. If you want a more visual way to do this correction, try the Remove Distortion tool (it's at the top in the Toolbox on the left). Click-and-drag it toward the center of your photo to remove barrel distortion (or toward an edge to remove pincushion distortion, in which the sides of your photo appear to curve inward). It's hard to make minor adjustments using the tool, so you'll probably wind up using the slider most of the time.

Step Two:

When you click OK, the correction will leave gaps around the edges, so get the Crop tool (C) and re-crop the image to hide the missing edges. It's hard to see the difference in the small images below, but try this technique, and you'll see the difference.

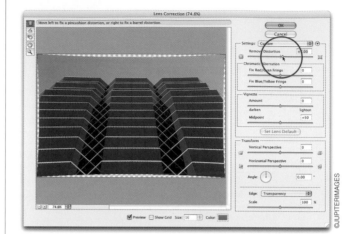

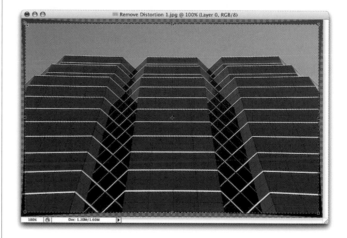

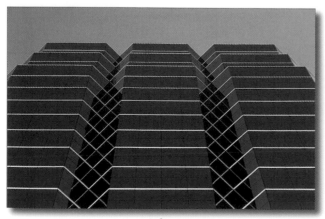

Before

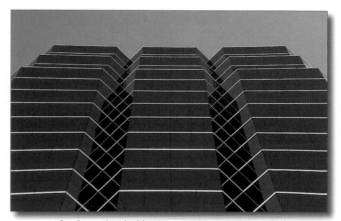

After (removing the bloating caused by barrel distortion)

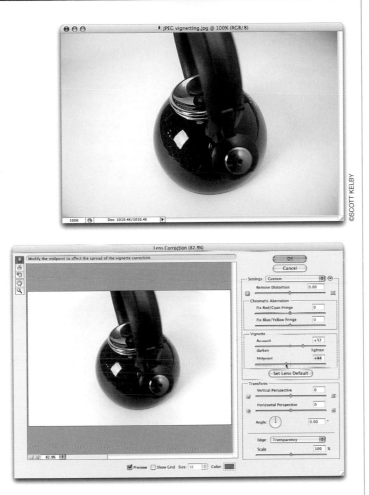

©SCOTT KELBY

Problem Three: Lens Vignetting
Step One:
Vignetting is a lens problem where the corners of your photo appear darkened. To remove this problem, go back to the Lens Correction filter.

Step Two:
In the Vignette section of the dialog, drag the Amount slider to the right, and as you do you'll see the edges brighten. Keep dragging the slider until the edges match the brightness of the rest of the photo. The Midpoint slider (just below the Amount slider) determines how far into the photo your corner brightening will extend. In this case, you have to extend it just a little bit by dragging the slider to the left (as shown here), then click OK. *Note:* You can also fix chromatic aberrations (colored-edge fringing). To see what that is and how to fix it using this filter (which works similarly to Camera Raw), check out the "Fixing Chromatic Aberrations" tutorial in Chapter 3.

Before: You can see the dark vignetted areas in the corners.

After: The vignetting is completely removed.

Saving Blurry Photos

This is a simple technique I came up with that enables you to save a blurry photo from the trash, but you have to know up front—there are limitations. First, it produces a photo that is really only suitable for emailing to friends and family, using in slide shows, or creating a 4x6" print. If you're okay with that, it works wonders. It's based on the premise that everything looks in focus when it's small (for proof of that, see the LCD monitor on the back of your camera, where every photo looks in focus, but when you open the full-size photo in Photoshop, you find out the truth).

Step One:
Open your blurred digital image. In the example shown here, I used a blurry high-res image imported directly from my digital camera and opened in Photoshop.

Step Two:
Go under the Image menu and choose Image Size (by the way, in CS2 there's now a keyboard shortcut for Image Size: Command-Option-I [PC Control-Alt-I]). When the dialog appears, you're going to leave the physical size alone (so it will still be 10" wide), but you're going to lower the Resolution from 300 ppi to 72 ppi, and then click OK. *Note:* If you're already working with a low-res image, you won't need to lower your Resolution setting (sorry, just in case you didn't know that already).

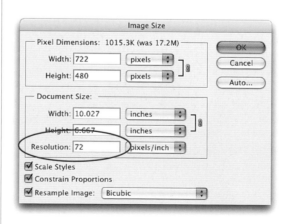

Step Three:
To get the resolution high enough to print to a color inkjet printer, go back to the Image Size dialog again. Turn off Resample Image and lower the Width to 6" (giving you a 6x4" finished size at 120 ppi in this case).

Step Four:
This is where CS2's Smart Sharpen filter really works wonders. Go under the Filter menu, under Sharpen, and choose Smart Sharpen. When the dialog appears, set the Amount at 58%, leave the Radius Set to 1 pixel, ensure the Remove pop-up menu is set to Gaussian Blur, turn on the More Accurate checkbox, and click OK to apply this first level of sharpening. Now, press Command-F (PC: Control-F) to run Smart Sharpen again, using the same settings. This second pass of sharpening really does the trick.

Before: This was one you'd simply delete.

After: Thanks to Smart Sharpen, she doesn't look oversharpened.

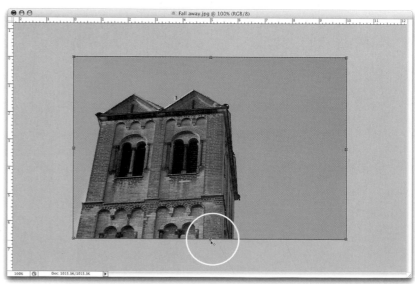

Repairing Keystoning

Keystoning is often found in photos with buildings or tall objects, where the buildings look as if they're falling away from the viewer (giving the impression that the tops of these buildings are narrower than their bases). The Crop tool has a Perspective function that can be used to fix these distortions, but actually I'm going to recommend that you don't use it, because it doesn't offer a preview of any kind—you're left guessing—so use this technique instead.

Step One:

Open an image that has a keystoning problem (such as the photo shown here, taken with a wide-angle lens, where the towers of this old church seem to be leaning away from the viewer).

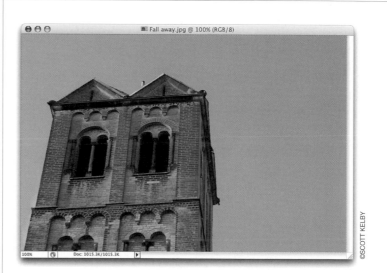

Step Two:

Press Command-R (PC: Control-R) to make Photoshop's rulers visible. Grab the bottom-right corner of your image window and drag outward to reveal the gray canvas background. Press Command-A (PC: Control-A) to select your entire image, and then press Command-T (PC: Control-T) to bring up the Free Transform function. Grab the center point of the bounding box and drag it straight downward until it touches the bottom-center point.

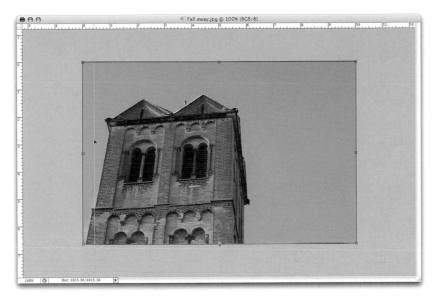

Step Three:

Click-and-drag out a guide from the left ruler into your photo (we'll use this straight guide to help us align our building). In this example, I lined up the guide with the left side of the building. Once you add this guide, you can really see how far back the building seems to be leaning and why a keystoning repair is so necessary.

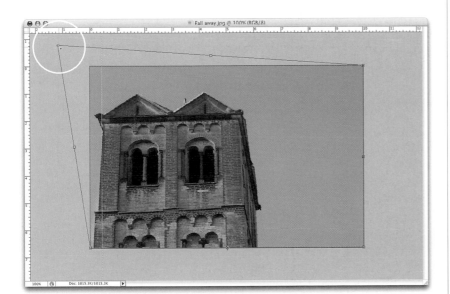

Step Four:

Once your guide is in place, hold the Command key (PC: Control key) and drag the top-left corner point of the bounding box upward and to the left until the left side of the tower touches your guide. It already looks better, but if you look at the line that separates the different levels (under the windows), you can see it's still tilted upward, so you'll have to fix that next.

Continued

Step Five:

To make that edge straighter, drag the bottom-right corner point down a bit (don't forget—keep holding down the Command/Control key). You might also have to drag the top-right corner point upward, just to get the building looking a little more flat.

Step Six:

Making all these corrections can sometimes make your building look a bit "smushed" and "squatty" (my official technical terms), so you can release the Command/Control key, grab the top-center point, and drag upward to stretch the photo back out and fix the "squattiness" (again, technically speaking).

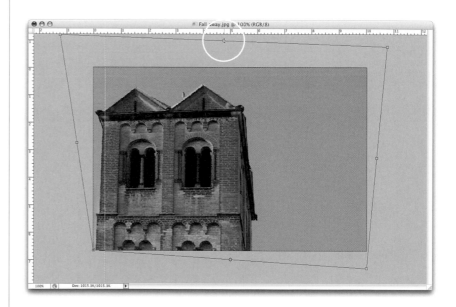

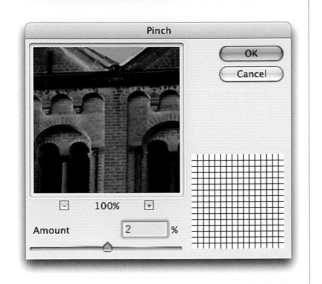

Step Seven:

When the photo looks right, press Return (PC: Enter) to lock in your transformation. (*Note:* By repairing this problem with Free Transform, you saw an onscreen preview of what you were doing, which the Crop tool's Perspective feature doesn't offer.) Now, if after making this adjustment, the building looks a bit "round" and "bloated," you can repair that problem by going under the Filter menu, under Distort, and choosing Pinch. Drag the Amount slider to 0% (toward the center of the slider), and then slowly drag it to the right to increase the amount of Pinch, while looking at the preview in the filter dialog, until you see the roundness and bloating go away. (In this case, I used 2% for my Amount setting.) When it looks right, click OK to complete your keystoning repair.

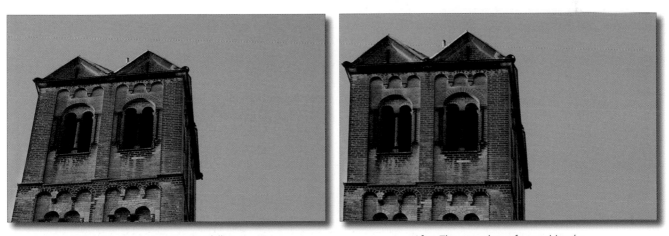

Before: The tower appears to be "falling away."

After: The same photo after repairing the perspective distortion (known as keystoning).

Take Me Away
removing unwanted objects

Is "Take Me Away" a perfect title for a chapter about removing unwanted objects from your photos or what? I've heard the song (by Christina Vidal from Disney's *Freaky Friday* soundtrack) a couple of thousand times now, because my 8-year-old likes to listen to it (over and over again) on the way to school each morning. Not only have I unconsciously memorized the words, I've actually begun to like the song. It happened around the 13-hundredth time I heard it. By my 14-hundredth listen, I started developing my own background harmonies, and by the 15-hundredth time, I went out and bought the sheet music. This is highly embarrassing stuff (unless you're a preteen), so don't tell anyone. Besides, I'm actually way older than a preteen. I'm more like a "ween." Wait a minute—I don't like the sound of that. I am not a ween. Anyway, this chapter shows you how to remove things that ruin otherwise beautiful photos. For example, let's say you get married, and you've got some great photos from your wedding, but then a year or so later, you get divorced. You looked really great in your wedding dress, so you want to keep the photos, but you hate seeing your ex in there. Well, this chapter will show you how to remove him. Well, it doesn't show you exactly that—how to remove your ex from your wedding photos—but it does show you how to remove any annoying thing, so technically you could apply these techniques to your wedding photos. But I gotta tell ya, if you spend your time removing your ex from your wedding photos, perhaps learning new Photoshop techniques shouldn't be your biggest concern.

Cloning Away Unwanted Objects

The Clone Stamp tool has been the tool of choice for removing distracting or other unwanted objects in photos for years now. Although the Healing Brush and Patch tool in many ways offer a better and more realistic alternative, there are certain situations where the Clone Stamp tool is still the best tool for the job. Here's an example of how this workhorse removes unwanted objects:

Step One:

A photo of a palm tree on a tropical island near a shutter window is usually not a bad thing. But then when you see that palm, it's usually not as ratty-looking as the one shown here. In fact, it looks so ratty (and the light is so unflattering on it), I think it would look better if it weren't there at all (and what luck—this is a chapter about removing unwanted objects). So our project, in short, is to cut down that palm tree. Digitally.

Step Two:

Press S to get the Clone Stamp tool. In the Options Bar, click on the thumbnail to the right of the word "Brush" and choose a medium, soft-edged brush in the Picker. Now, Option-click (PC: Alt-click) in an area of ocean just to the left of the palm. This is called "sampling." You just sampled some ocean, and in the next step, you're going to clone that ocean area over the part of the palm tree to the immediate right. (By the way, when you sample, that little "target" cursor appears, letting you know you're sampling.)

Step Three:

Now move directly to your right and begin painting with the Clone Stamp tool. As you paint over the palm frond on the left side of the tree, the ocean you sampled is cloned right over it, so it looks like the palm has disappeared. Paint a little in this area to get a feel for how the Clone Stamp works (at least, if it's your first time cloning; if it's not, then you know what to do—start cloning over that palm).

Step Four:

The key technique to remember here is to sample just to the left of the palm (sampling in the sky and ocean), then move straight over to the palm. Now, in the captures shown here, the little "plus-sign" cursor (the area where you sampled) is just to the immediate left of the target cursor (where you're painting now). By keeping them side-by-side like that, you're making sure you don't pick up patterns or colors from other parts of the photo that would make your cloning look obvious. In the next step, I'll intentionally sample from the middle-left side of the photo, and then move to the top and start painting. Then, you'll see how obvious it looks when you don't sample near the area you're trying to cover.

TIP: There's a trick to cloning that horizon line and keeping it straight. See the next tutorial called "Removing Things in a Straight Line."

Continued

Step Five:

Look at the plus-sign cursor (near the middle left of the palm). That's where I sampled, but instead of moving directly to the right to clone a nearby area, I moved my brush to the top (just under the horizon on the right of the palm) and started painting. Look how much darker (and obvious) the cloning looks. That's why you have to paint *very* close to where you sample. If not, it's a dead giveaway.

TIP: Sample often (by Option/Alt-clicking) in different but nearby areas so that your cloning appears random, therefore avoiding repeating patterns in the waves, for example.

Step Six:

Use this same technique of sampling to the left of the palm, painting over the trunk and palm fronds to the right of where you sampled, until the trunk and fronds are gone, except the tricky part at the top where the fronds meet the roof.

Step Seven:

To keep from cloning over the roof, you'll need to put a selection (a barrier) around the remaining palm fronds in the sky area. Since you can only paint inside the selected area, you don't have to worry about cloning away the roof. First, press Z to get the Zoom tool and zoom into the palm and roof area. Now press Shift-L until you have the Polygonal Lasso tool. Click along the straight edges of the roof to draw a straight-lined selection (like the one shown here) that traces around the roof edge, around the palm fronds, and returns to where you first clicked on the roof.

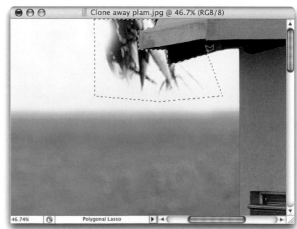

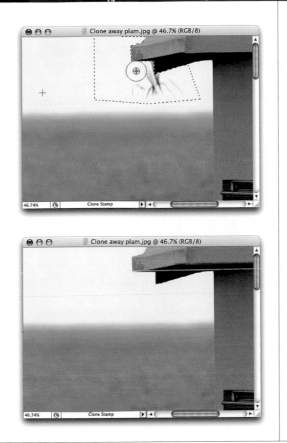

Step Eight:
Now, get the Clone Stamp tool again, sample the sky to the left of your selection, move over to the right inside your selection, and start cloning away the fronds. You can clone right up to the edge of the roof without worry, because you can't paint "outside the lines" thanks to that selection you created in the previous step. *Note:* The sample point will be outside the selected area, and that's fine—you can sample from anywhere.

Step Nine:
Keep painting (cloning) until the rest of the palm fronds around the roof are gone. Then, you can deselect by pressing Command-D (PC: Control-D). Now, after all that, I hope you like the image better without the palm, as it took less than five minutes to remove it. If not, just go under the File menu, choose Revert, and that butt-ugly palm will come crashing back into your photo, ruining an otherwise uninspired image.

Before   *After*

Removing Things in a Straight Line

This is an incredibly handy little trick I learned from Rich Harris, who contributes some great tutorials to our magazine, *Photoshop User* (www.photoshopuser.com), and I've found no better way to clone away objects that need to be straight (like horizons, walls, etc.). Thanks to Rich for sharing this technique with us.

Step One:

Press S to get the Clone Stamp tool, and then press-and-hold the Option (PC: Alt) key. Take a look at your cursor (shown here enlarged in the white box). See the horizontal line in the center of the circle? That's the key. You must position the cursor's center "target" line on the straight edge that you want to clone in your image (in this case, the top edge of a car's front bumper). With the Option/Alt key held down, click once when the target (called the "sample cursor") is aligned on the edge in your image.

Step Two:

Now drag directly to the right while pressing-and-holding the Option/Alt key, but don't click. With this key held down, align the sample cursor's horizontal center line with the bumper's edge.

Step Three:

With the horizontal line positioned along the edge in your photo, release the Option/Alt key and start cloning. As you clone, paint along the same straight line. It's all about making sure that the cursor's horizontal line is aligned with the edge in your image *before* you start painting.

Covering Unwanted Elements

If there are just one or two annoying things that are messing up your otherwise lovely photo, here's a quick way to get rid of them, while maintaining maximum texture and authenticity. (Because you're using another part of the photo to cover what you don't want visible, the grain, texture, and well—everything—is right on the money.)

©SCOTT KELBY

Step One:

In this example, we have a charming "old-world" door, but the plastic "16" house number pulls the charming "old-world" feel right out of the photo. So… the plastic numbers have to go. I could use the Patch tool (it's isolated, right?) or the Clone Stamp tool, but this method makes the removal perfect because you're actually going to cover the "16" with a chunk of the wall above it, which is an even more realistic fix and is as fast as, if not faster than, the alternatives.

Step Two:

Press Z to get the Zoom tool and zoom in on the area with the offensive plastic numbers. (I bet they got those at Euro-Home Depot.)

Continued

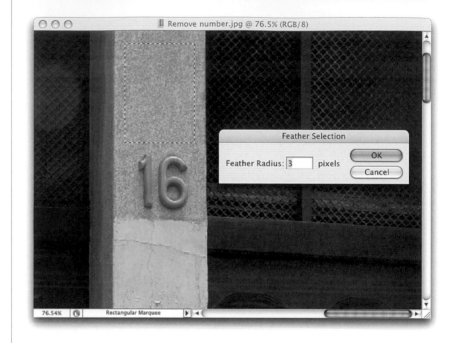

Step Three:

Press M to get the Rectangular Marquee tool, and drag out a selection around the "16." Then, click in the selection and drag it straight above the number, sliding right up the wall. Now, you'll need to put a feather on your selection so the edges will be soft and blend in perfectly, hiding the fact that you did anything to the photo at all. So, go under the Select menu and choose Feather. When the Feather Selection dialog appears, enter 1-3 pixels (depending on your percentage of zoom) for the Feather Radius and click OK.

Step Four:

Now, holding the Option and Command (PC: Alt and Control) keys, drag the selected area straight down. This makes a copy of the selected area, so you're really dragging along a copy of the rectangular chunk of the wall. That area fits perfectly over the plastic numbers (it fits perfectly because you first created that selection by dragging it over the numbers, remember?). By the way, you won't see any harsh edges to give you away because you feathered those edges in the previous step.

Before   After

Step Five:

Now, when you press Command-D (PC: Control-D) to deselect, the numbers will be gone, and your removal will be right on the money. Here's a before and after. You can see what a difference removing that one little area made. I probably would go one step further and zoom in on the center of the red door. Then, using the same technique, I'd remove the letter "A" and peephole from the top center of the door. (That way, I'm removing any hint of the possibility of "old-world" crime that peepholes suggest.)

Step Six:

Here's another application of the same technique. On the left side of the photo there's a distracting doorjamb, and the easiest fix (without re-cropping and shrinking the width of the photo) is to extend the wall to cover the doorjamb. Get the Rectangular Marquee tool, and draw a tall, thin rectangular selection from the top to the bottom, and then feather your selection (under the Select menu).

Step Seven:

Hold Option-Command (PC: Alt-Control) and the Shift key (to keep it perfectly in line as you drag), and drag the selected area of the wall to the left. You'll have to drag several copies of the thin wall selection to cover the doorjamb. Also, if you see any repeating pattern when you're done, just get the Patch tool (Shift-J), draw a selection around that area, drag the selection into a clean area, and then press Command-D (PC: Control-D) to deselect.

Removing Spots and Other Artifacts

In Photoshop CS2, Adobe added the Spot Healing Brush tool, which is just about *the* perfect tool for getting rid of spots and other artifacts. (By the way, the term "artifacts" is a fancy "ten-dollar" word for spots and other junk that wind up in your photos.) Believe it or not, it's even faster and easier to use than the regular Healing Brush, because it's pretty much a one-trick pony—it fixes spots.

Step One:

Open a photo that either has spots or other artifacts (whether they're in the scene itself or are courtesy of specs or dust on either your lens or your camera's sensors). In the photo shown here (featuring my son Jordan, posing with a Slik Carbon Fiber tripod with a Slik AF2100 trigger-style ball head; you have to admit, he has great taste in tripods), there are all sorts of distracting little white spots on the pavement.

Step Two:

Press Z to get the Zoom tool and zoom in on an area with lots of spots (in this case, I zoomed in on the lower left-hand corner of the image). Now get the Spot Healing Brush tool from the Toolbox (or just press the letter J).

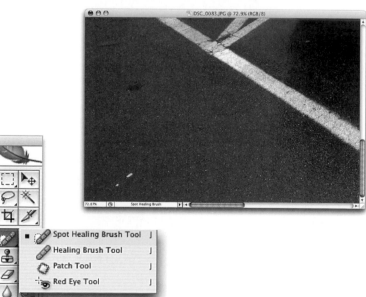

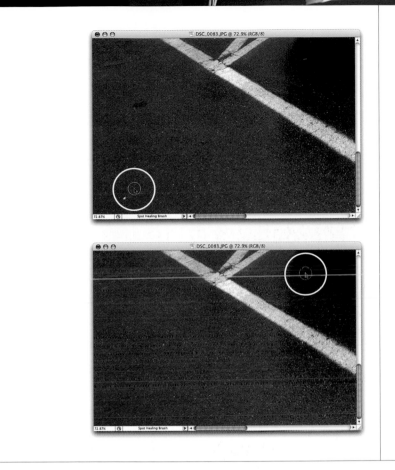

Step Three:
Position the Spot Healing Brush directly over the spot you want to remove and click once. That's it—you don't have to sample an area or Option/Alt-click anywhere first. You just move it over the spot and click—the spot is gone.

Step Four:
You remove other spots the same way—just position the Spot Healing Brush over them and click. I know it sounds too easy, but that's the way it works. So, just move around and start clicking away the spots. Now you can "de-spot" any photo, getting a "spotless" version in about 30 seconds, thanks to the Spot Healing Brush.

Before

After

Removing Distracting Objects (Patch Tool)

Okay, if the Clone Stamp tool is so great, why should you even use the Patch tool? Two reasons: (1) It's faster, and (2) it's better—much better—because it keeps more of the original texture and the fix looks more realistic. Okay, so why not use the Patch tool all the time? Because it has a major limitation: It only does a great job of removing things that are isolated all by themselves. When your object gets near the edge of another object (or the edge of your image area), it doesn't work worth a darn. So you'll see how it works, why it doesn't always work, and a great trick for making it work most of the time (with some help from the Clone Stamp tool).

Step One:

Here's a photo of the magnificent La Sagrada Familia church in Barcelona. There's quite a bit of construction going on (as you can see), and since I'm not a photojournalist, I don't want to see all those cranes that detract from Gaudi's amazing architecture. So, we're going to use a combination of the Patch tool (and a little bit of the Clone Stamp tool) to remove all those cranes from the skyline.

Step Two:

First we'll look at how the Patch tool works, and then you'll see what the limitation of the Patch tool is. Start by pressing Z to get the Zoom tool and zoom into an area you want to remove. Press Shift-J to get the Patch tool (or look under the Spot Healing Brush in the Toolbox), and draw a selection around something you want to remove. At this stage, the Patch tool works just like the regular Lasso tool, so click-and-drag to make a freeform selection like the one shown here.

TIP: If you need to add to your selection, press-and-hold the Shift key, or to subtract from your selection, press-and-hold the Option (PC: Alt) key.

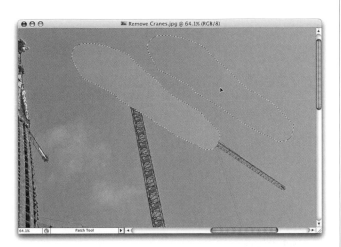

Step Three:
Once your selection is in place, click your cursor inside the selected area (the cursor will change to an arrow) and drag the entire selection into an area of the photo that has a similar texture and color (like I have here, where I dragged into some open sky).

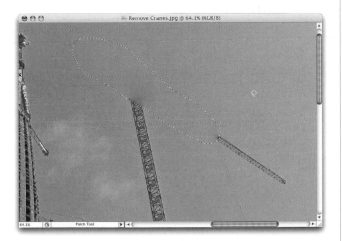

Step Four:
When you release the mouse, the Patch tool's selection snaps back to its original location (where you first drew it), and it erases what was there. Ahh, now you see the problem: Where the edges of the selection meet the rest of the crane, it's all smudged. As bad as it looks here, believe it or not, this is pretty mild compared to what often happens when the area you're patching isn't isolated. The Patch tool only gives you a clean patch-job if you can drag a selection around the entire object without hitting an edge.

Step Five:
Undo this patch-job by pressing Command-Z (PC: Control-Z), and then deselect by pressing Command-D (PC: Control-D). Now we'll try getting around that limitation: Press S to switch to the Clone Stamp tool, and Option-click (PC: Alt-click) to sample an area below the crane.

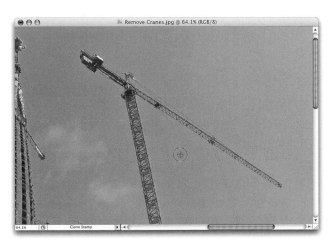

Continued

Step Six:
Move the Clone Stamp tool to the left (right over the center of the crane) and clone the blue sky you sampled, putting a break in the crane.

Step Seven:
Now do the same thing on the right side of the crane—sample a nearby area by Option/Alt-clicking, and then clone over a middle section of the crane. By doing this, you've isolated the top of the crane—it's no longer connected to the ends of the crane, which means now you can put a selection around the top of the crane using the Patch tool, totally encircling it without touching any edges.

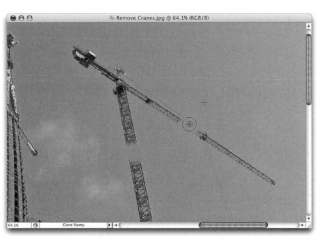

Step Eight:
So now it's time to repeat Steps 1–3: Get the Patch tool, put a selection around isolated parts of the crane, and then click in the center of your selection and drag to an open area of sky near the crane. *Note:* Use the Zoom tool to zoom out if needed.

Step Nine:

When you release the mouse button, it snaps back, creating a perfect patch—with perfect texture—and no smudged edges. It's a precise, seamless fix using this new trick! Just press Command-D (PC: Control-D) to deselect.

Step Ten:

Getting rid of the top-right side of the crane is simple because it's now isolated—just draw a Patch tool selection around it, drag the selection into a different area, let it snap back, and—BAM—it's gone!

Step Eleven:

Alright, are you ready for a little more of a challenge? Take a look at the crane on the left of the image. It's right up against one of the towers. Now what? You do the same thing; it just takes one extra step to ensure you don't accidentally clone over some of the church (I'll show you the trick for that in the next step).

Continued

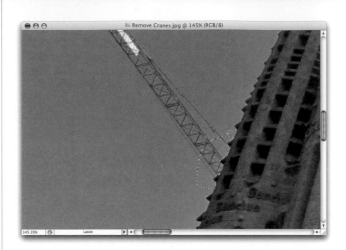

Step Twelve:

First, use the Zoom tool to zoom in tight on the area where the crane meets the church. Press L to switch to the regular Lasso tool and trace along the edge of the church where the crane comes out. It sounds harder than it is, but because you're only tracing for about an inch, it's actually pretty easy. Trace along the church edge, drag to the left to select part of the crane, and then click back to where you first started your edge selection, creating a selection like the one you see here.

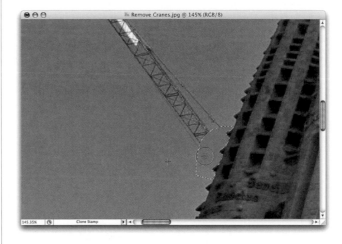

Step Thirteen:

When you make a selection like this, you're basically putting up a fence, because now any cloning you do with the Clone Stamp tool will appear only inside that "fence," so it's impossible to accidentally erase part of the church (in other words, you can't paint outside that selected area—only inside it). So, get the Clone Stamp tool, Option/Alt-click in the sky near the edge of the church, and clone in the sky over the end of the crane.

Step Fourteen:

Once you've pressed Command-D (PC: Control-D) to deselect, zoom out a bit with the zoom tool. Now, switch to the Patch tool and draw a selection around the crane (since there's now a break between the church and the crane). Then, click inside the selection and drag your Patch tool selection into an open area of sky.

Step Fifteen:

Release the mouse button, and once your selection snaps back to remove the crane cleanly, deselect by pressing Command-D (PC: Control-D). You're going to continue to use this same technique of isolating parts of the crane and drawing a Patch tool selection around them until all the cranes are gone. Again, could you have used the Clone Stamp tool for the whole process? Yes. Would it have taken you longer? Yes. Would it have looked blotchier and more obvious that things were removed? Probably. The Patch tool is just that much better, so if you can find a way to use it (like we did here), you're better off in more ways than one.

Before

After

Removing Things in Perspective

Until Photoshop CS2's introduction of the Vanishing Point filter, cloning away things in perspective was one of the hardest removal tasks of all. Luckily, this incredibly cool filter not only simplifies removing things in perspective, it actually makes it fun. In fact, this is one of those filters that's so amazing, you can wind up spending hours cloning away things that have no business being cloned away. Don't say I didn't warn you.

Step One:

Here's a photo of my buddy Dave Moser. We were shooting the International Car Show on press day (which is why you only see cleaning crew in the background), and Dave was lying on his back shooting a Hummer H2 that was positioned on an angle. Where's Dave's tripod, you might ask? I asked the same question, but apparently Dave doesn't mind camera shake (kidding). Anyway, since he didn't use a tripod, he should be cloned out of this photo to hide the evidence. Start by clicking on the Create a New Layer icon in the Layers palette so we can do our cloning work on a new blank layer.

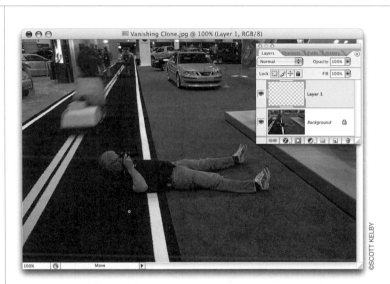

Step Two:

Go under the Filter menu and choose Vanishing Point (it's near the top). First, you have to define the angle of perspective by drawing with the Create Plane tool (C). (Don't let the fancy name throw you—you use it pretty much like you would the Polygonal Lasso tool.) Just click where you want to start, and keep clicking at angles to create your selection. (Here, I clicked halfway down the road along the carpet's edge, clicked at the end of the carpet at the bottom of the image, and then clicked again where I thought the road's yellow line would end.)

Step Three:

Use the tool to trace down the yellow line. You can pretty much see what's going on here—I'm simply tracing the area that has the perspective angle of the photo.

TIP: When you're placing these points far away (like I am here), you can temporarily zoom in to make sure you're aligning them correctly by pressing the letter X.

Step Four:

When you reach the original point you started with, a blue grid will appear. Well, hopefully it's a blue grid. If it's blue, it means you drew it correctly, and Vanishing Point is happy with you. If it's yellow, it means that you're close, and it may work, but you'd be better off switching to the Edit Plane tool (V) (it looks like an arrow) and adjusting your points until they turn blue. If your grid outline turns red, it's a bad grid (your perspective isn't right), and you'll need to tweak the points until it's right.

Step Five:

Once your blue grid is in place, you can stretch it to cover the object you want to remove. Just click on one of the center points using the Edit Plane tool, and drag in the direction you want the grid to spread. In the example shown here, I grabbed the right-center point and dragged it over to the right until Dave's legs and feet were covered.

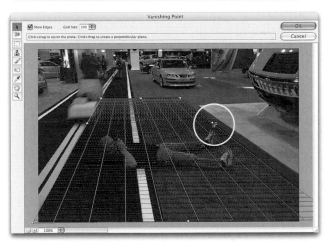

Continued

Step Six:

Press S to switch to the Stamp tool (it looks like the Clone Stamp tool), and the grid in the center will go away, leaving just the blue outline to show the boundaries of the grid. Option-click (PC: Alt-click) on a straight line in your image (if possible) to help you line things up. In this case, I Option/Alt-clicked on the line where the black and gray carpets meet.

Step Seven:

Now, just move up that line and click-and-drag to start painting. As you do, the unwanted object (Dave) is removed, and the cloning automatically adjusts for the perspective. In this example, you can see how the white line automatically shrinks as it moves away.

Step Eight:

Like the regular Clone Stamp tool, if you paint too far, it starts cloning over itself (meaning it's picking up other objects) so just paint a little bit (say ½" or so); then move to a different area, Option/Alt-click again, and this time clone over the legs. Again, just clone away a little of his legs at a time—don't try to remove them all at once, or you'll start cloning objects back in.

Step Nine:
Continue using this technique to clone away other unwanted areas. Remember to Option/Alt-click several times to keep the retouch looking random, and to keep from "repeat" cloning. When it looks good to you, click OK in the dialog. Since the cloning will appear on a separate layer, you can adjust it or easily erase any extra areas using the Eraser tool (E) (if you cloned too large an area, for example). With the perspective right on the money, Vanishing Point works wonders.

TIP: If you notice any repeating patterns in your cloning, just click on Layer 1, get the Patch tool (Shift-J), draw a selection around one of the repeating patterns, drag the selection into a new area on that layer, and the repeating pattern will be removed. Press Command-D (PC: Control-D) to deselect.

Before

After

Removing Backgrounds

I figured I'd include probably the most-requested masking task—removing someone from a background while keeping hair detail. We use Extract for this, and even if you've used Extract dozens of times, there's a trick near the end that is so simple, yet so incredibly effective, it will change the way you use Extract forever, or my name isn't Deke McClelland.

Step One:
Open the photo containing a person (or an object) that you want to extract from its background. Go under the Filter menu and choose Extract (it's the first filter from the top).

Step Two:
This brings up the Extract dialog. Press B to get the Edge Highlighter tool (it's the top tool in Extract's Toolbox and looks like a marker), and trace the edges of the object you want to remove. As you trace, leave half the marker border on the background and half on the edge of the object you want to extract.

TIP: Use a small brush size when tracing areas that are well defined (like along the shirt), and a very large brush for areas that are less defined (such as flyaway hair). You can change the brush size by holding down the Left Bracket key to make it smaller or the Right Bracket to make it larger.

Step Three:
After your Highlighter edge is in place, you now have to tell Photoshop what parts of the photo to retain when extracting. This is pretty simple—you just press G to switch to the Fill tool (it's the second tool from the top in Extract's Toolbox and looks like a paint bucket), and click it once inside the Highlighter edge border you drew earlier. This fills the inside of your highlighter border with a blue tint.

Step Four:
If the blue tint spills out into the rest of your photo when you click the Fill tool, that means your subject isn't completely enclosed by the edge border. If that happens, just press Command-Z (PC: Control-Z) to undo, then take the Edge Highlighter and make certain there are no gaps at the bottom or sides of your border. Now you can click on the Preview button to see how your extraction looks.

Step Five:
It's time to take a good look at the photo and see if Extract did what you really wanted it to. Namely, did it work on the hair, which is the hard-to-select area? If it worked, then click OK because fixing the rest of the photo is a breeze, as you'll see. Even if parts of his clothes are dropping out, or there are dropouts in his face, hands, etc., don't sweat it—as long as the edge of the hair looks good, go ahead and click OK to perform the extraction and your image will appear on an editable layer (Layer 0).

Continued

Step Six:

Now that the extraction is done, it's "fix-up" time. Here, you can see dropouts (slightly transparent areas) in his hair, a few little spots in his shirt, and a couple of little spots in other places. Start by simply duplicating the layer. That's right, just press Command-J (PC: Control-J). The mere act of duplicating the layer will fix about 90% of the dropouts in your photo. It sounds weird, but it works amazingly well, and when you try it, you'll be astounded. Press Command-E (PC: Control-E) to merge these two layers.

Step Seven:

For the rest of the dropouts, press Y to get the History Brush tool and simply paint over these areas. The History Brush will paint those missing pieces back in because it's really an "undo on a brush." So, if part of your subject drops out, use the History Brush to paint it right back in. You can usually fix the dropouts in about two minutes using this technique.

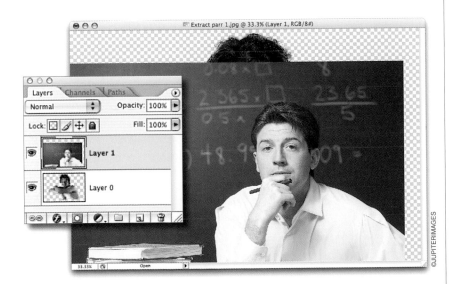

Step Eight:
During the fix-up stage, I'm painting over dropouts along the man's shoulder. As you see, using the History Brush paints the original image back in.

Step Nine:
Next, open the photo that you want to use as a background behind your extracted person. It's best to drag this background photo onto your extracted-person document, because as long as you work in the same document where you extracted, you'll have access to the History Brush for your extracted image. That way, if you see a dropout when you bring in the background, you can return to that layer and quickly touch it up with the History Brush. So press V to switch to the Move tool, and drag-and-drop this photo on top of your extracted image. The background will appear on top of your extracted image on a separate layer (Layer 1) in the Layers palette.

Continued

Step Ten:

In the Layers palette, drag the layer with your background photo (Layer 1) beneath the layer with your extracted photo, putting your extracted person in front of the background (as shown here, where the man in the background photo is partially covered by the extracted man). Using the Move tool, position this background layer until your extracted person appears where you want him. Then, you'll usually have to switch to the Eraser tool (E) to erase any leftover "junk" outside his hair, along his shirt, etc., but you can usually clean up these leftovers pretty easily once you see them over the background.

Step Eleven:

In this example, because I only want part of the background to appear, I'm stuck with a lot of empty space and unneeded areas. Press the letter C to get the Crop tool, drag a cropping border around the areas you want to keep, and then press Return (PC: Enter) to crop the photo down to size. Now that the photo is cropped, a new problem is visible—his skin tone looks too warm for the bluish background we've placed him on (and this is something you'll deal with often when combining photos—the tones have to match to look realistic).

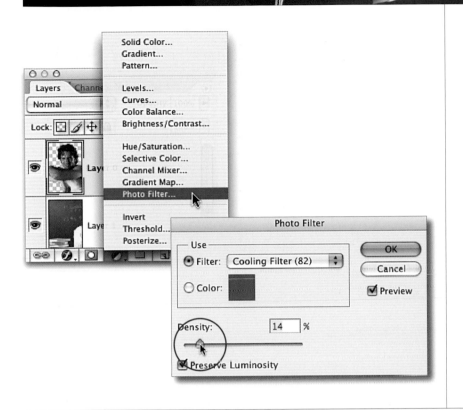

Step Twelve:

To cool down his warm skin tones, make sure the top layer is active in the Layers palette, and then go under the Create New Adjustment Layer pop-up menu at the bottom of the Layers palette and choose Photo Filter. These Photo Filters replicate the traditional screw-on lens filters used with film cameras to accommodate bad lighting situations.

Step Thirteen:

In the Photo Filter dialog, you can choose a filter from the Filter pop-up menu (like the Cooling Filter [82] I chose here), or choose to fill with a solid color. You can also control the Density of the effect using the Density slider (I lowered it to 14%). Click OK and the warm areas are cooled, so your subject's flesh tones now better fit the background image you dragged him onto.

The original photo

The subject extracted, placed onto a different background, re-cropped, and his tone cooled to match the new background.

Exposure: 1/60s   Focal Length: 120mm   Aperture Value: ƒ/5.7

Photograph
retouching portraits

Ah, finally, a decent song for a chapter title— Def Leppard's "Photograph." Hey, you weren't thinking about that wimpy Ringo Starr song "Photograph" that goes "all I've got is a photograph…" were you? Come on, you can tell me. I think we've built up enough trust, enough rapport, enough of a bond where we can be honest with each other, right? You were thinking of that Ringo Starr song at first, weren't you? I knew it! You loser! You spaz! You geek! I can't believe you like that song. There's no WAY we can be friends anymore. See, that's what we call "turning on you" in this business. Other authors would do that, but not me. That was just a simulation to show you how other authors, those no-caring, soulless, devil-wor-shipping authors, might treat you when they learned you thought the title "Photograph" was

tied to a wimpy song. But not me. I think you're gutsy to choose such a wuss song. A lot of people (especially some of those smug music critics) would laugh at you, but I'm not like that. In fact, I have more respect for you now than I ever did, and I'd be the first one to stand up next to you, and defend her still today. There ain't no doubt, I love that song (love that song), God Bless that Ringo Starr song! Just now, as I'm writing this, I started thinking about something. Previous versions of this book have been translated into a dozen different languages (including Russian, Chinese, Korean, French, German, Japanese, among others). Sometime soon, Chinese or Russian translators will be translating these "highly American" chapter intros into Chinese or Russian. Wouldn't you love to see the look on their faces….

Removing Blemishes

When it comes to removing blemishes, acne, or any other imperfections on the skin, our goal is to maintain as much of the original skin texture as possible. That way, our retouch doesn't look pasty and obvious. Here are three techniques that work pretty nicely, and when you have all of these methods in your retouching arsenal, if one doesn't carry out the repair the way you'd hoped, you can try the second, or even the third.

Method One: The Clone Stamp Tool
Step One:

Open a photo containing some skin imperfections you want to remove (in this example, we're going to remove the mole on her left cheek).

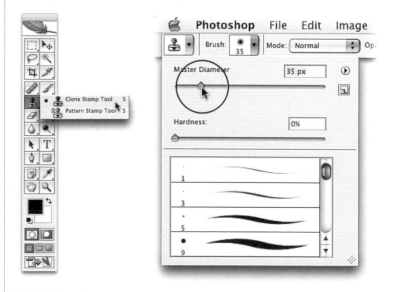

©JUPITERIMAGES

Step Two:

Press the letter S to get the Clone Stamp tool from the Toolbox. In the Options Bar, click on the thumbnail to the right of the word "Brush," and in the Brush Picker, choose a soft-edged brush that's slightly larger than the blemish you want to remove. You can use the Master Diameter slider at the top of the Brush Picker to dial in on the size you need. Once you're working, if you need to quickly adjust the brush size up or down, use the Bracket keys on your keyboard: The Left Bracket key makes your brush smaller; the Right Bracket makes it larger.

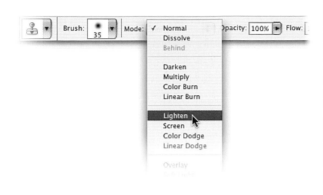

Step Three:

In the Options Bar, change the Mode pop-up menu for the Clone Stamp tool to Lighten. With its Mode set to Lighten, the Clone Stamp will affect only pixels that are darker than the sampled area. This means the lighter pixels (the regular flesh tone) will pretty much stay intact, while only the darker pixels (the blemish) will be affected.

Step Four:

Find an area right near the blemish that's pretty clean (no visible spots, blemishes, etc.), press-and-hold the Option (PC: Alt) key, and click once. This samples the skin from that area. Try to make sure this sample area is *very* near the blemish so the skin tones will match. If you move too far away, you risk having your results appear in a slightly different color, which is a dead giveaway you've done a repair.

Step Five:

Move your cursor directly over the blemish and click once. Don't paint! Just click. One click will do it—it will remove the blemish instantly, while leaving the skin texture intact. But what if the blemish is lighter than the skin, rather than darker? Simply change the Mode to Darken instead of Lighten—it's that easy. On to Method 2.

Continued

Method Two: The Spot Healing Brush
Step One:
You can also use the Spot Healing Brush tool to remove blemishes effectively and quickly. (Notice I said "Spot" Healing Brush. A tutorial is coming up soon about the regular Healing Brush, which works better on large areas.) So, press J to get the tool from the Toolbox.

Step Two:
Just like the Clone Stamp tool, the key thing to remember when using the Spot Healing Brush for repairing blemishes is to choose a brush size that's just slightly larger than the blemish you're trying to remove. In the Options Bar, click on the thumbnail to the right of the word "Brush," and choose the size you need using the Diameter slider. (*Note:* The default for the Spot Healing Brush is a hard edge, and that's fine—it works great that way.) However, unlike the Clone Stamp stool, you don't need to sample an area before clicking. You just click on a blemish and it's gone, so start clicking (here I clicked on all the visible moles on her face and neck). Now for Method 3....

Method Three: The Lasso Tool
Step One:
Press L to switch to the Lasso tool. Find a clean area (no blemishes, spots, etc.) near the blemish that you want to remove (in this case, it's a mole on her right cheek). In this clean area, use the Lasso tool to make a selection that is slightly larger than the blemish.

Step Two:
After your selection is in place, go under the Select menu and choose Feather. When the Feather Selection dialog appears, enter 1 pixel as your Feather Radius and click OK. Feathering blurs the edges of our selected area, which will help hide the traces of our retouch. Feathering (softening) the edges of a selection is a very important part of facial retouching, and you'll do this quite a bit to "hide your tracks," so to speak.

Continued

Step Three:

Now that you've softened the edges of the selection, hold Option-Command (PC: Alt-Control), and you'll see your cursor change into two arrowheads—a white one with a black one overlapping it. This is telling you that you're about to copy the selected area. Click within your selection and drag this clean skin area right over the blemish to completely cover it.

Step Four:

When the clean area covers the blemish, release the keys (and the mouse button, of course) and press Command-D (PC: Control-D) to deselect. As you can see, the blemish is gone. Best of all, because you dragged skin over from a nearby area, the full skin texture is perfectly intact, making your repair nearly impossible to detect.

Lessening Freckles or Acne

This technique is popular with senior-class portrait photographers who need to lessen or remove large areas of acne, pockmarks, or freckles. This is especially useful when you have a lot of photos to retouch (like a portrait retoucher) and don't have the time to use the methods shown previously, where you deal with each blemish individually.

Step One:
Open the photo that you need to retouch.

Step Two:
Go under the Filter menu, under Blur, and choose Gaussian Blur. When the Gaussian Blur dialog appears, drag the slider all the way to the left, and then drag it slowly to the right until you see the freckles (or acne) blurred away. The photo should look very blurry, but we'll fix that in just a minute, so don't let that throw you off. Make sure it's blurry enough that the freckles are no longer visible, and then click OK.

Continued

Step Three:

Go under the Window menu and choose History to bring up the History palette. This palette keeps track of the last 20 things you've done in Photoshop. If you look at the list of steps (called "History States"), you should see two States: The first will read "Open" (this is when you opened the document), and the second will read "Gaussian Blur" (this is where you added the blur).

Step Four:

Click on the Open State to return your photo to what it looked like when you originally opened it. The History palette also works in conjunction with a tool in the Toolbox called the History Brush, so press Y to get the brush. When you paint with it, by default it paints in what the photo looked like when you first opened it. It's like "undo on a brush." That can be very handy, but the real power of the History Brush is that you can have it paint from a different History State. You'll see what I mean in the next step.

Step Five:

In the History palette, click in the first column next to the Gaussian Blur State. If you painted with the History Brush now, it would paint in what the photo looked like after you blurred it (which would do us no good), but we're about to fix that.

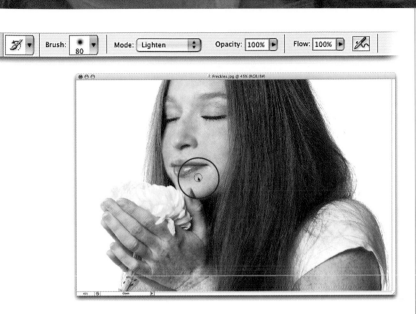

Step Six:

To keep from simply painting in a blurry version of our photo, go to the Options Bar and change the History Brush's Mode pop-up menu to Lighten. Now when you paint, the brush will affect only the pixels that are darker than the blurred state. Ahhh, do you see where this is going? So, click on the thumbnail to the right of the word "Brush" in the Options Bar and choose a medium, soft-edged brush in the Brush Picker. Now paint over the blemished areas with the History Brush, and as you paint, you'll see the freckles diminish quite a bit. If they diminish too much, and the person looks "too clean," press Command-Z (PC: Control-Z) to undo your History Brush strokes, then return to the Options Bar, lower the Opacity of the brush to 50%, and try again.

Before   *After*

Removing Dark Circles under Eyes

Here are two different techniques for removing the dark circles that sometimes appear under a person's eyes—especially after a hard night of drinking. At least, that's what I've been told.

Method One: The Clone Stamp Tool
Step One:

Open the photo that has the dark circles you want to lessen. (*Note:* If needed, press Z to get the Zoom tool and zoom in closer on your subject's eyes.) Press the letter S to select the Clone Stamp tool from the Toolbox. In the Options Bar, click on the thumbnail after the word "Brush," and in the resulting Brush Picker, choose a soft-edged brush that's half as wide as the area you want to repair.

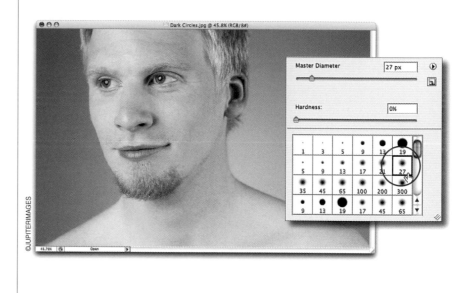

@JUPITERIMAGES

Step Two:

Go up to the Options Bar and lower the Opacity of the Clone Stamp tool to 50%. Then, change the Mode pop-up menu to Lighten (so you'll only affect areas that are darker than your sample).

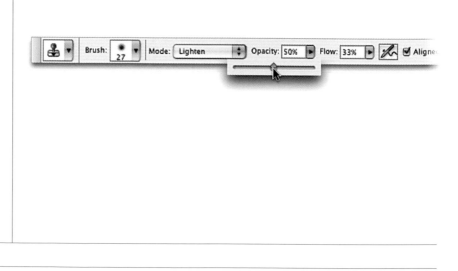

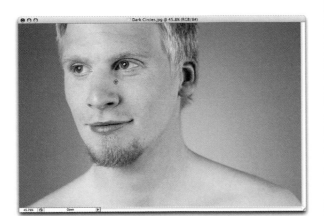

Step Three:
Hold the Option (PC: Alt) key and click once in an area near the eye that isn't affected by the dark circles. If the cheeks aren't too rosy, you can click there, but more likely you'll click on (sample) an area just below the dark circles under the eyes.

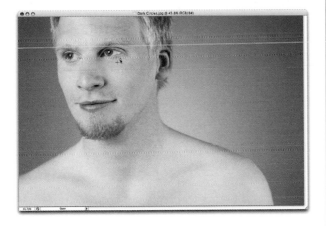

Step Four:
Take the Clone Stamp tool and paint over the dark circles to lessen or remove them. It may take two or more strokes for the dark circles to pretty much disappear, so don't be afraid to go back over the same spot if the first stroke didn't work.

Before

After

Continued

Method Two: The Patch Tool
Step One:
Go to the Toolbox and choose the Patch tool (click-and-hold on the Healing Brush until the flyout menu appears or just press Shift-J until you have the tool).

Step Two:
Make sure the Patch tool is set to Source in the Options Bar and draw a selection around one of the dark circles under the eye. The Patch tool operates much like the Lasso tool for drawing selections (meaning you simply click-and-drag to create a selection). Also, like the Lasso tool, once your selection is in place, if you need to add to it, just hold the Shift key and "lasso" in some more areas. If you need to subtract from your Patch tool selection, hold the Option (PC: Alt) key instead.

Step Three:
After your selection is in place, click directly within the selected area and drag it to a part of the face that's clean and doesn't have any edges. By that I mean you don't want your dragged selection to overlap the edge of any other facial features such as the nose, lips, eyebrows, edge of the face, and so on. You need a clean, uninterrupted area of skin. In Photoshop CS2, you'll see a preview of what your patch will look like (that's why you see two selections in the capture shown here).

Step Four:
After you've found that clean area, release the mouse button and the Patch tool will automatically sample it, snap back to the original selected area, and perform the retouch for you.

Continued

Step Five:

Press Command-D (PC: Control-D) to deselect, and you'll see the dark circle is completely gone. The Healing Brush can also be used to diminish or erase dark circles, but the Patch tool does it so quickly and effortlessly that I greatly prefer it for this retouch.

Before (dark circles under the eyes)

After (dark circles removed using the Patch tool)

Photoshop has two tools that are nothing short of miracle workers when it comes to removing wrinkles, crow's feet, and other facial signs of aging. We've touched on these tools slightly in previous techniques in this chapter, but here's a closer look at how to use these amazing tools to quickly take 10 or 20 years off a person's appearance.

Removing the Signs of Aging

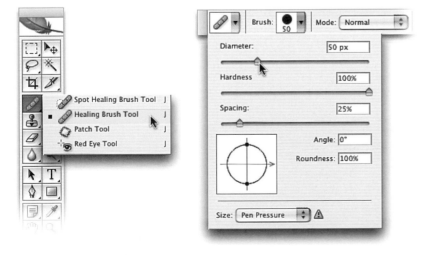

@JUPITERIMAGES

Method One: The Healing Brush
Step One:
Open the photo of the person whose signs of aging you want to remove.

Step Two:
Choose the Healing Brush from the Toolbox (or press Shift-J until you have the tool). In the Options Bar, click on the thumbnail to the right of the word "Brush" and choose a brush size that's wide enough to cover the wrinkles in your image. By default, the Healing Brush is set to have a hard edge, and that typically works fine for this technique.

Continued

Step Three:

Hold the Option (PC: Alt) key and click on an area of smooth skin near your wrinkles. This samples the texture of the area you're clicking on and uses it for the repair.

Step Four:

With the Healing Brush, paint a stroke over the wrinkles you want to remove (I painted over the wrinkles just below his left eye). When you first paint your stroke, for a moment the tones won't match and it'll look like an obvious retouch; but a second later, the Healing Brush does its calculations and presents you with its final "magic" that seamlessly blends in the original texture, removing the wrinkle. Continue this process of sampling a clean area and then painting over a wrinkled area until all the signs of aging are removed.

TIP: As amazing as the Healing Brush is, it sometimes gives you a mottled look, or you can see the texture repeated in your "healing." Well, NAPP member Stephanie Cole came up with a neat trick to change the shape of the brush, making those nasties go away. When you have the Healing Brush tool, go to the Options Bar and click on the thumbnail to the right of the word "Brush" to bring up the Brush Picker (it's set to a black, round, hard-edged brush by default). Leave the Hardness set to 100% and the Spacing to 25%, but the real trick comes in shaping the brush. You're going to make a tall, thin oval brush by setting the Angle to -49° and the Roundness to just 16%. Now as you paint, the brush creates what looks like a star pattern, and it's this pattern that makes the texture look so random and realistic.

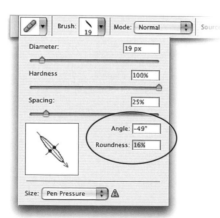

Before (visible wrinkles on forehead and under eyes)

After (removing wrinkles on forehead and under eyes)

Method Two: Pro Wrinkle Removal
Step One:

This is a simple trick fashion photographer Kevin Ames uses for more realistic healing: Open the photo you want to "heal." Duplicate the Background layer in the Layers palette by pressing Command-J (PC: Control-J). You'll perform your "healing" on this duplicate layer—just repeat Method One.

Continued

Step Two:

In the Layers palette, reduce the Opacity to bring back some of the original wrinkles. What you're really doing here is letting a small amount of the original photo (on the Background layer, with all its wrinkles still intact) show through. Keep lowering the Opacity until the wrinkles are visible but not nearly as prominent, so the photo looks much more realistic.

TIP: You can get a similar effect by choosing Fade (found under the Edit menu) *immediately* after painting a stroke with the Healing Brush. In the Fade dialog, you can lower the Opacity to bring back in some of the original wrinkles.

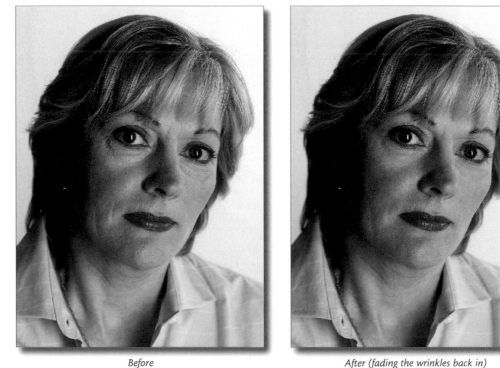

Before   *After (fading the wrinkles back in)*

@JUPITERIMAGES

Method Three: The Patch Tool
Step One:

You can achieve similar results using the Patch tool, and personally, I prefer this tool to the Healing Brush for most instances, because the Patch tool lets you correct larger areas faster. Press Shift-J until you have the Patch tool, make sure that it's set to Source in the Options Bar, and draw a selection around the wrinkled area. It works like the Lasso tool, so if you need to add to your selection, hold the Shift key; to subtract from it, hold Option (PC: Alt).

Step Two:

After your selection is in place, click-and-drag it onto an area on the person's face that has a clean texture (in Photoshop CS2, you'll see a preview of what your patch will look like—that's why you'll see two lasso selections). Make sure your selected area doesn't overlap any other facial features (such as the nose, lips, eyes, edge of the face, etc.), and then release the mouse button. When you do, the selection will snap back to the area that you originally selected, and the wrinkles are gone.

Step Three:

Press Command-D (PC: Control-D) to deselect, and view the amazing job the Patch tool did on his right eye.

Colorizing Hair

This technique (that I learned from Kevin Ames) gives you maximum control and flexibility while changing or adjusting hair color. Best of all, because you use layer masks and an adjustment layer, you're not "bruising the pixels"; instead, you're following the enlightened path of "nondestructive retouching."

Step One:
Open the photo you want to retouch. Choose Color Balance from the Create New Adjustment Layer pop-up menu (it's the half-black/half-white circle icon) at the bottom of the Layers palette.

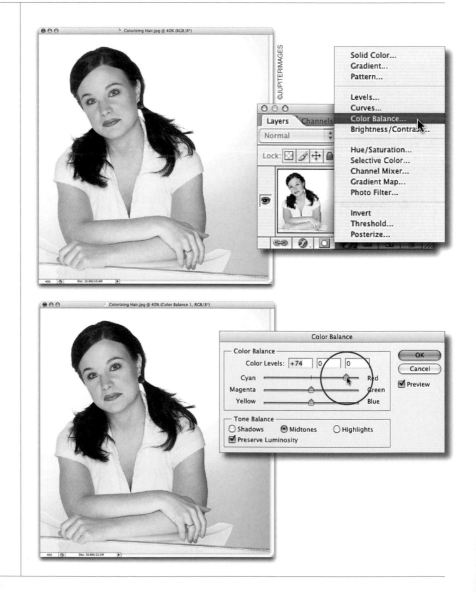

Step Two:
When the dialog appears, adjust the sliders until you have a color that you want as the hair color. You can adjust the Shadows, Midtones, and Highlights by selecting each in the Tone Balance section of the Color Balance dialog and then moving the color sliders. In this case, we want to make her hair red, so we'll move the top slider toward Red for the Shadows (to +16), then the Midtones (to +74), and then the Highlights (to +45). Now, click OK, and the entire photo will have a heavy red cast over it.

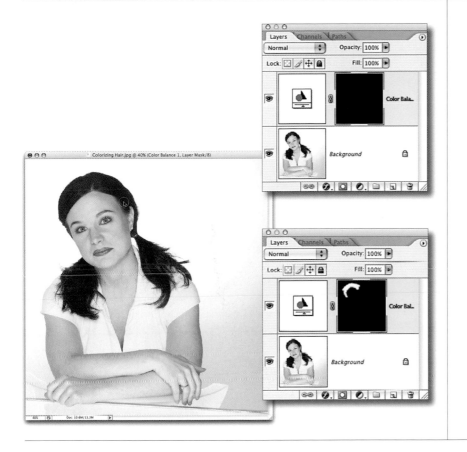

Step Three:
Press the letter X until your Foreground color is black, and press Option-Delete (PC: Alt-Backspace) to fill the Color Balance layer mask with black. Doing so removes the red tint from the photo.

Step Four:
Press B to get the Brush tool from the Toolbox, click on the thumbnail to the right of the word "Brush" in the Options Bar, and then choose a soft-edged brush in the Brush Picker. Press D to set your Foreground color to white, and then begin painting over her hair. As you paint, the red tint you added with Color Balance is added back in. Once the hair is fully tinted, go to the Layers palette and change the layer blend mode of your Color Balance adjustment layer from Normal to Color, and then lower the Opacity until the hair color looks natural (around 50%).

Before

After

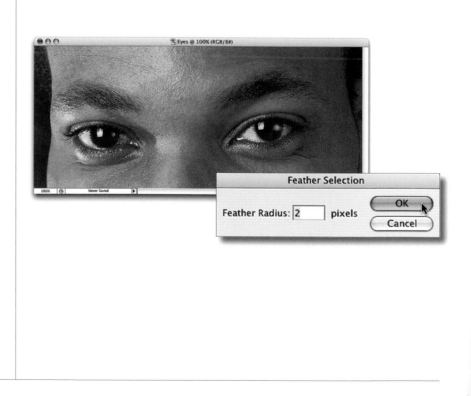

Whitening the Eyes (Quick Trick)

This is a great little technique for quickly whitening the whites of the eyes, and it has the added benefit of removing any redness in the eye along the way.

Step One:

Open the portrait you want to retouch. Press L to get the Lasso tool from the Toolbox and draw a selection around the whites of one of the eyes. Press-and-hold the Shift key and draw selections around the whites of the other eye, until the whites of both eyes are selected. *Note:* Press Z to get the Zoom tool and zoom in if needed.

Step Two:

Go under the Select menu and choose Feather, which will soften the edges of your selection so your retouch isn't obvious. In the Feather Selection dialog, enter 2 pixels and click OK.

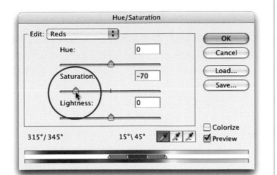

Step Three:

Go under the Image menu, under Adjustments, and choose Hue/Saturation. When the Hue/Saturation dialog appears, choose Reds from the Edit pop-up menu at the top (to edit just the reds in the photo). Now, drag the Saturation slider to the left to lower the amount of saturation in the Reds (which removes any bloodshot appearance in the whites of the eyes).

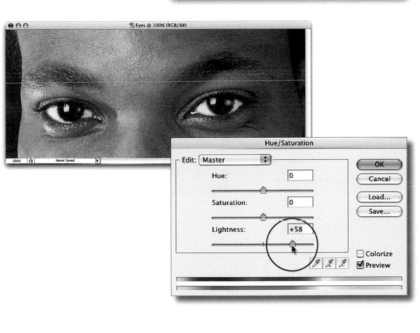

Step Four:

While you're still in the Hue/Saturation dialog, from the Edit menu switch back to Master. Drag the Lightness slider to the right to increase the lightness of the whites of the eyes. Click OK in the Hue/Saturation dialog to apply your adjustments, and then press Command-D (PC: Control-D) to deselect, completing the retouch. The enhancement appears fairly subtle in the capture shown here, but when you try it yourself at full size, the effect will appear much more pronounced.

Before

After (bloodshot lessened and whites brightened)

Whitening Eyes

Here's Kevin Ames's technique for brightening the whites of the eyes, and I have to say, even though it takes a little longer and has a few more steps, it really does a brilliant job, and offers the most realistic eye-whites brightening I've seen.

Step One:

Open the photo of the person whose eyes you want to whiten. Go to the Layers palette and choose Curves from the Create New Adjustment Layer pop-up menu at the bottom of the palette. When the Curves dialog appears, don't make any adjustments—just click OK.

©JUPITERIMAGES

Step Two:

When the Curves adjustment layer appears in your Layers palette, change the layer blend mode of this adjustment layer from Normal to Screen. This will lighten the entire photo. Press the letter X until your Foreground color is black, and then press Option-Delete (PC: Alt-Backspace) to fill the Curves adjustment layer mask with black. This hides the lightening effect brought on by changing the blend mode to Screen.

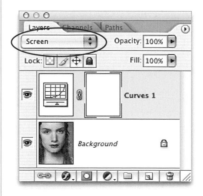

Step Three:
Press the letter D to switch your Foreground color to white, and then press B to get the Brush tool. In the Options Bar, click on the thumbnail after the word "Brush" and choose a very small, soft-edged brush from the Brush Picker. Now, begin painting over the whites of the eyes and along the bottom of the eyelid. As you paint, you're lightening the areas because you're bringing back the Screen effect you applied earlier. *Note:* To change your brush size, press the Left Bracket key to make it smaller or the Right Bracket key to make it larger.

Step Four:
The eyes will look too white (giving your subject a possessed look), so lower the Opacity of this Curves adjustment layer to make the whitening more subtle and natural (I lowered it to around 55%) to complete the effect.

Before

After

Making Eyes Sparkle

This is another one of those "30-second miracles" for brightening eyes, enhancing the catch lights, and generally drawing attention to the eyes by making them look sharp and crisp (crisp in the "sharp and clean" sense, not crisp in the "I burned my retina while looking at the sun" kind of crisp).

Step One:

Open the photo you want to retouch. Go under the Filter menu, under Sharpen, and choose Unsharp Mask. When the Unsharp Mask dialog appears, enter your settings (if you need some settings, check out Chapter 13); then click OK to sharpen the entire photo.

Step Two:

After you've applied the Unsharp Mask filter, apply it again using the same settings by pressing Command-F (PC: Control-F), and keep applying it using the same keyboard shortcut until the eyes stand out (here I applied it four times). Although the eyes probably look nice and crisp at this point, the rest of the person is severely oversharpened, and you'll probably see lots of noise and other unpleasant artifacts, but we'll fix that in the next step.

Step Three:

Go under the Window menu and choose History to bring up the History palette. This palette keeps track of your last 20 steps, and you'll see the five steps you've done thus far listed in the palette (an Open step, followed by your Unsharp Mask steps. By the way, these steps are actually called "History States"). Click on the Open State to return your photo to how it looked before you applied the Unsharp Mask filter.

Step Four:

In the History palette, click once in the first column beside the bottom Unsharp Mask State. Press Y to switch to the History Brush, and in the Options Bar, click on the Brush thumbnail to choose a soft-edged brush (about the size of the iris) from the Brush Picker. Click once right over the iris, and it will paint in the crisp, sharpened eye, leaving the rest of the face untouched. It does this because you clicked in that first column in the History palette, which tells Photoshop to "paint from what the photo looked like at this point." Pretty cool!

Before

After (with eyes that sparkle)

Changing Eye Color

Well, Kevin Ames did it to me again. He calls me up, and we're talking about how I have just about finished the update to this book, and he says, "You're going to hate me again." I let him know I never stopped hating him for all the extra work he made me do in the last version of the book, then he says, "No, you're *really* gonna hate me." Stupidly, I said, "Why?" and he said, "Have you tried the Color Replacement tool for changing eye color?" He's really getting on my nerves.

Step One:
Open the photo that contains an eye color you want to change. In this case, the subject has green eyes and we want to change them to blue (hey, it's not me—that's what the client wants).

Step Two:
Go to the Toolbox and choose the Color Replacement tool. (*Note:* It's hidden behind the Healing Brush.) In Photoshop CS, Adobe had this tool in mind for removing red eye, but since they added the Red Eye tool in CS2, you can just use that tool for red eye (and the Color Replacement tool actually works quite well for removing red eye, I might add, but we're going to do a more respectable job here).

Step Three:

You'll need to open a source photo, a photo that has the eye color you'd like. Take the Color Replacement tool and move it over the eye in your source photo. Hold the Option (PC: Alt) key over the eye and click once to sample that eye color.

Step Four:

Now switch back to the photo where you want to change the eye color, and begin painting over the eye. As you paint, the new color (from the blue eye you sampled earlier) replaces the green eye (as shown in the subject's left eye here). *Note:* If needed, press Z to switch to the Zoom tool and zoom into the subject's eyes while replacing the color.

Before

After

Enhancing Eyebrows and Eyelashes

After Kevin Ames showed me this technique for enhancing eyebrows and eyelashes, I completely abandoned the method I'd used for years and switched over to this method because it's faster, easier, and more powerful than any technique I've seen yet.

Step One:

Open the photo that you want to enhance. Press L to get the Lasso tool and draw a loose selection around one eyebrow. It isn't necessary to make a precise selection; make it loose like the one shown here. Your subject might be turned so that there's only one eyebrow showing; but if there are two (meaning the person doesn't have a unibrow), after you select one eyebrow, press-and-hold the Shift key while creating a selection around the other eyebrow.

©JUPITERIMAGES

Step Two:

Once your eyebrows are selected, press Command-J (PC: Control-J) to put the eyebrows on their own separate layer. Then, switch the layer blend mode of this eyebrow layer from Normal to Multiply in the Layers palette, which will darken the entire layer.

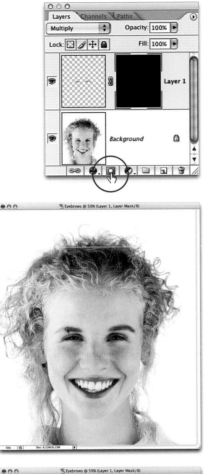

Step Three:

Press-and-hold the Option (PC: Alt) key and click on the Add Layer Mask icon at the bottom of the Layers palette. Holding down the Option/Alt key fills the layer mask with black, which hides the Multiply effect from view. The eyebrows will look normal again. Now, ensure your Foreground color is set to white (it should be by default), and then press B to switch to the Brush tool. In the Options Bar, click on the thumbnail to the right of the word "Brush," and choose a soft-edged brush from the Brush Picker that's about the size of the largest part of the eyebrow.

Step Four:

Begin painting over the eyebrows, going from right to left. As you paint, press-and-hold the Left Bracket key to make your brush smaller as you trace the eyebrow. Painting on the layer mask reveals the Multiply effect, darkening the eyebrows.

Step Five:

The final effect will probably be too intense, but you can fix that by lowering the Opacity of the Multiply layer in the Layers palette.

Continued

Step Six:

Now, on to the eyelashes: In the Layers palette, click on the Background layer. Get the Lasso tool again and draw a loose selection around the eyes, making sure your loose selection fully encompasses the eyelashes.

Step Seven:

For the lashes, you're going to repeat what you just did to the eyebrows, so once the eyes and lashes are selected, press Command-J (PC: Control-J) to copy them to their own layer. Change the blend mode of this layer from Normal to Multiply, which darkens the entire layer.

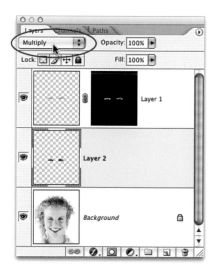

Step Eight:

Hold the Option (PC: Alt) key and click on the Add Layer Mask icon again to add a black-filled layer mask. Just like the eyebrows, doing this will hide the Multiply effect. With your Foreground color set to white, paint along the base of the eyelashes to darken that area using a very small, soft-edged brush. Also paint along the top eyelid at the base of the eyelashes. (Incidentally, we put the eyelashes and eyebrows on separate layers so you can control the Opacity of each individually.)

TIP: To enhance individual lashes, use the same technique. Just zoom in close on the eye using the Zoom tool (Z), and then with a very, very small brush, trace at the base of the eyelash, following its contours to darken it. You may have to use a 1- or 2-pixel brush. If the effect seems a bit too intense, just lower the layer's Opacity.

Before

After

Whitening Teeth

This really should be called "Removing Yellowing, *then* Whitening Teeth" because almost everyone has some yellowing, so we remove that first before we move on to the whitening process. This is a simple technique, but the results have a big impact on the overall look of the portrait, which is why I do this to every portrait where the subject is smiling.

Step One:

Open the photo you need to retouch. Press L to switch to the Lasso tool, and carefully draw a selection around the teeth, being careful not to select any of the gums or lips. *Note:* Press the Z key to switch to the Zoom tool and zoom in if needed.

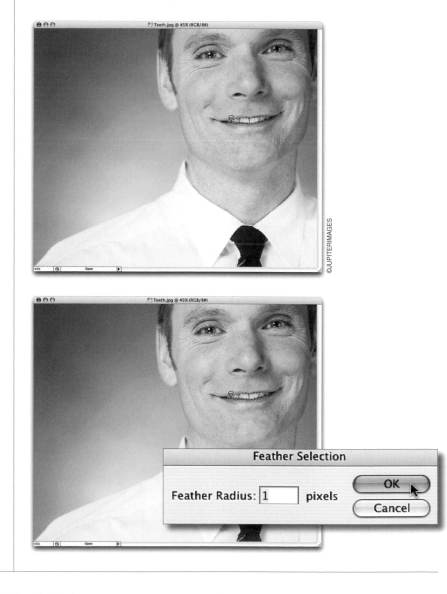

Step Two:

Go under the Select menu and choose Feather. When the Feather Selection dialog appears, enter 1 pixel and click OK to smooth the edges of your selection. That way, you won't see a hard edge along the area you selected after you've whitened the teeth.

Step Three:
Go under the Image menu, under Adjustments, and choose Hue/Saturation. When the dialog appears, choose Yellows from the Edit pop-up menu at the top. Then, drag the Saturation slider to the left to remove the yellowing from the teeth.

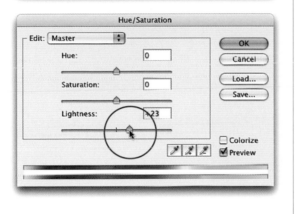

Step Four:
Now that the yellowing is removed, switch the Edit pop-up menu back to Master, and drag the Lightness slider to the right to whiten and brighten the teeth. Be careful not to drag it too far or the retouch will be obvious. Click OK in the Hue/Saturation dialog to apply your enhancements. Now press Command-D (PC: Control-D) to deselect and see your finished retouch.

Before

After

Removing Hot Spots

If you've ever had to deal with hot spots (shiny areas on your subject's face caused by uneven lighting or the flash reflecting off shiny surfaces, making your subject look as if he or she is sweating), you know they can be pretty tough to correct. That is, unless you know this trick.

Step One:
Open the photo that has hot spots that need to be toned down.

©JUPITERIMAGES

Step Two:
Press S to select the Clone Stamp tool from the Toolbox. In the Options Bar, change the Mode pop-up menu from Normal to Darken, and lower the Opacity to 50%. By changing the Mode to Darken, we'll only affect pixels that are lighter than the area we're sampling (those lighter pixels are the hot spots).

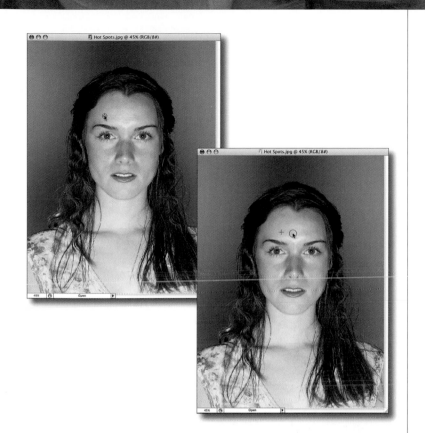

Step Three:
In the Options Bar, click on the thumbnail after the word "Brush" and choose a large, soft-edged brush from the Brush Picker. Then, press-and-hold the Option (PC: Alt) key and click once in a clean area of skin (an area with no hot spots). This will be your sample area (or reference point) so Photoshop knows to affect only pixels that are lighter than this.

Step Four:
Start gently painting over the hot-spot areas with the Clone Stamp tool, and as you do, the hot spots will fade away. As you work on different hot spots, you'll have to resample (Option/Alt-click) on nearby areas of skin so the skin tone matches. For example, when you work on the hot spots under her eyes, sample an area of skin from her cheeks (or even her forehead) where no hot spots exist. It's amazing what 60 seconds of hot-spot retouching can do for your image.

Before

After

Advanced Skin Softening

This technique, which I picked up from Kevin Ames, does an amazing job of simulating a Hasselblad Softar No. 2 filter in that it softens the skin tones, but at the same time introduces a little bit of soft flare and lowers the contrast of the image—perfect for fashion photography.

Step One:

Open the photo you want to soften. Press Command-J (PC: Control-J) twice to create two duplicates of your Background layer in the Layers palette. Hide the top copy (Layer 1 copy) by clicking on the Eye icon next to it in the Layers palette, and then click on the middle layer (Layer 1) to make it active and change its layer blend mode from Normal to Darken.

Step Two:

Go under the Filter menu, under Blur, and choose Gaussian Blur. Apply a 40-pixel blur to the photo.

Step Three:
In the Layers palette, hide the middle layer (Layer 1) from view by clicking on its Eye icon, and then click on the top layer (Layer 1 copy) and click in the empty box on the left to make it visible again (the Eye icon will reappear). Change the layer blend mode of this top layer to Lighten.

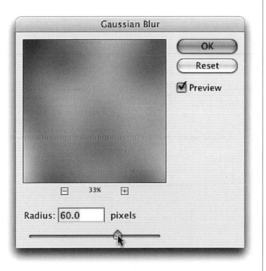

Step Four:
Now, go back to the Filter's Blur sub-menu and apply a 60-pixel Gaussian Blur to this top layer.

Step Five:
After you've applied the blur, click on the middle layer (Layer 1), click on the empty box to reveal its Eye icon, and then lower its Opacity to 40% in the Layers palette.

Continued

Step Six:

Hide the Background layer from view by clicking on its Eye icon, and then create a new layer by clicking on the Create a New Layer icon at the bottom of the Layers palette. Click-and-drag this layer to the top of your layer stack. Then, press-and-hold the Option (PC: Alt) key and choose Merge Visible from the Layers palette's flyout menu. This creates a flattened version of your document in your new layer.

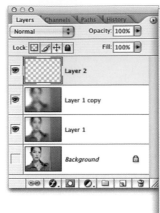

Step Seven:

In the Layers palette, make the Background layer visible again by clicking on the empty box on the left, but hide the two duplicate layers in the middle (Layer 1 and Layer 1 copy) by clicking on their Eye icons. Make sure the top layer in the stack (Layer 2) is still the active layer, and then lower its Opacity to 40%. Lowering the Opacity of that layer creates the overall softening effect (which is fine if you want an overall effect), but in most cases, you won't want to soften the detail areas (eyes, lips, etc.).

Step Eight:
Click on the Add Layer Mask icon at the bottom of the Layers palette to add a layer mask to your blurred layer. Press the letter X until your Foreground color is black, and then press B to get the Brush tool. In the Options Bar, click on the thumbnail after the word "Brush" and choose a medium, soft-edged brush from the Brush Picker. Now, paint over the areas that should have full detail (lips, eyes, eyebrows, eyelashes, hair, ears, clothing—pretty much everything but the skin). *Note:* Press the Left Bracket key to make your brush size smaller or press the Right Bracket to make it larger.

Before

After

Transforming a Frown into a Smile

This is a pretty slick technique for taking a photo where the subject is frowning (or is expressionless) and tweaking it just a bit to add a pleasant smile instead—which can often save a photo that otherwise would've been ignored.

Step One:
Open the photo that you want to retouch.

Step Two:
Go under the Filter menu and choose Liquify. When the Liquify dialog appears, choose the Zoom tool (it looks like a magnifying glass) from the Liquify Toolbox (found along the left side of the dialog). Click it once or twice within the preview window to zoom in closer on your subject's face. Then, choose the Warp tool (it's the top tool in Liquify's Toolbox).

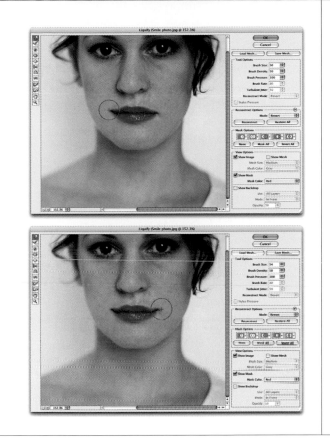

Step Three:
Press the Left/Right Bracket keys on your keyboard to adjust the brush size until it's about the size of the person's cheek. Place the brush near the corner of the mouth, click and "tug" slightly up. This tugging of the cheek makes the corner of the mouth turn up, creating a smile.

Step Four:
Repeat the "tug" on the opposite side of the mouth, using the already tugged side as a visual guide as to how far to tug. Be careful not to tug too far, or you'll turn your subject into the Joker from *Batman Returns*. Click OK in Liquify to apply the change, and the retouch is applied to your photo.

Before

After

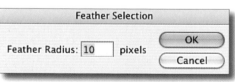

Digital Nose Job

This is a very simple technique for decreasing the size of your subject's nose by 15–20%. The actual shrinking of the nose is a breeze and only takes a minute or two. You may spend a little bit of time cloning away the sides of the original nose, but since the new nose winds up on its own layer, it makes this cloning a lot easier. Here's how it's done:

Step One:
Open the photo that you want to retouch. Press L to get the Lasso tool, and draw a loose selection around your subject's nose. Make sure you don't make this selection too close or too precise because you need to capture some flesh-tone area around the nose.

Step Two:
To soften the edges of your selection, go under the Select menu and choose Feather. When the Feather Selection dialog appears, for Feather Radius enter 10 pixels (for high-res, 300-ppi images, enter around 22 pixels), and then click OK.

Step Three:
Now, press Command-J (PC: Control-J) to copy your selected area onto its own layer in the Layers palette.

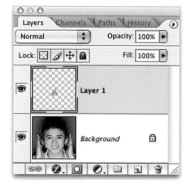

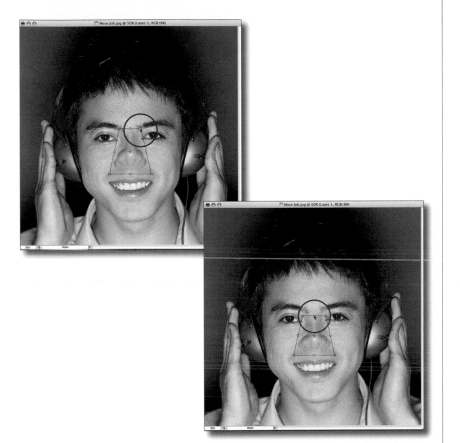

Step Four:

Press Command-T (PC: Control-T) to bring up the Free Transform bounding box. Hold Shift-Option-Command (PC: Shift-Alt-Control), then grab the upper-right corner point of the bounding box and drag inward to add a perspective effect to the nose. Doing this gives the person a pug nose, but you'll fix that in the next step.

Step Five:

To get rid of the "pug-nose" effect, release all the keys, then grab the top-center point and drag straight downward to make the nose look natural again, but now it's smaller. When the new size looks about right, press Return (PC: Enter) to lock in your changes. If any of the old nose peeks out from behind the new nose, click on the Background layer and use the Clone Stamp tool (S) to clone away those areas: Option-click (PC: Alt-click) an area next to the nose to sample it, and then paint (clone) right over it to complete the retouch.

Before

After

Slimming and Trimming

This is an incredibly popular technique because it consistently works so well, and because just about everyone would like to look about 10–15 pounds thinner. I've never applied this technique to a photo and (a) been caught, or (b) not had the clients absolutely love the way they look. The hardest part of this technique may be not telling your clients you used it.

Step One:
Open the photo of the person that you want to put on a quick diet. Press Command-A (PC: Control-A) to put a selection around the entire photo. Then press Command-T (PC: Control-T) to bring up the Free Transform function. The Free Transform handles might be a little hard to reach, so I recommend expanding your image window a little bit by clicking-and-dragging its bottom-right corner outward. This makes some of the gray canvas area visible and makes grabbing the Free Transform handles much easier.

©JUPITERIMAGES

Step Two:
Grab the left-center handle and drag it horizontally toward the right to slim the subject. The farther you drag, the slimmer the person becomes. How far is too far (in other words, how far can you drag before people start looking like they've been retouched)? Look at the Width field in the Options Bar for a guide—you're pretty safe to drag inward to around 95% (or even 94.7% as I did here) without getting caught.

Step Three:
When your person looks "naturally" slimmer, press Return (PC: Enter) to lock in your transformation. Doing this transformation leaves you with some excess white canvas area on the left side of the photo; so with your image's selection border still in place (from Step 1), go under the Image menu and choose Crop to remove the white space. Press Command-D (PC: Control-D) to deselect, and you're done!

Before

After

Removing Love Handles

This is a very handy body-sculpting technique, and you'll probably be surprised at how many times you'll wind up using it. It uses Liquify, which many people first dismiss as a "toy" for giving people "bug-eyes" and "huge lips," but it didn't take long for professional retouchers to see how powerful this tool can really be.

Step One:

Open the photo that has a love handle repair just waiting to happen. (I know this is probably the last person in the world to need a love handle removal, but when you're looking through stock photos, finding a person who doesn't have a perfect physique is nearly impossible.)

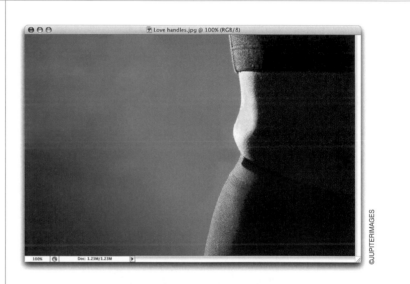

©JUPITERIMAGES

Step Two:

Go under the Filter menu and choose Liquify. When the Liquify dialog appears, click on the Zoom tool in the bottom of the Toolbox on the left-hand side of the dialog. Then, drag out a selection around the area you want to work on to give you a close-up view for greater accuracy.

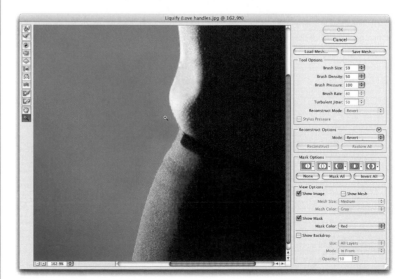

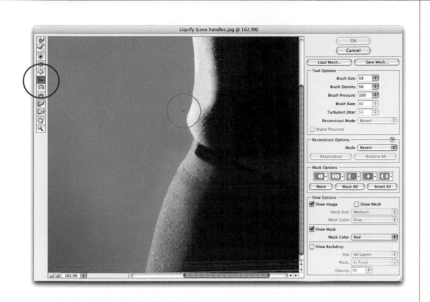

Step Three:

Get the Push Left tool from the Toolbox (it's the sixth one down from the top). It was called the Shift Pixels tool in Photoshop 6 and 7, but Adobe realized that you were getting used to the name, so they changed it, just to keep you on your toes. Then, choose a relatively small brush size using the Brush Size field near the top-right of the Liquify dialog. Now paint a downward stroke starting just above and outside the love handle and continuing downward. The pixels will shift back in toward the body, removing the love handle as you paint.

Step Four:

When you click OK, the love handle repair is complete. (*Note:* If you need to remove love handles on the left side of the body, paint upward rather than downward. Why? That's just the way it works.)

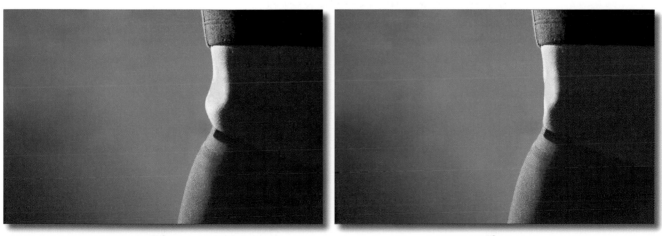

Before   *After*

38 Special
photographic special effects

Everything up to this point has been all "scientific" and "by the book." It hasn't been fun. It's been work. Okay, it's been fun work, but it's all been correcting and managing and balancing color and fixing blemishes and stuff like that. But you know, and I know, that's not why you bought Photoshop. You didn't buy your first copy of Photoshop because you wanted to create a tonal balance within your images. You did it to meet girls. Unless, of course, you're already a girl, in which case you might have bought it to meet girls, but girls aren't as impressed with Photoshop as guys are (we tend to like anything that runs on a computer or comes with a remote), so my guess is you bought it to meet boys. Okay, that's not why any of us really bought Photoshop, is it? It is? Wow, I didn't see that

coming. Anyway, if you didn't buy Photoshop to attract the opposite sex in some kind of weird mating ritual (sex and mating in the same sentence—I might as well order a Jag!), you probably bought it because of all the cool effects you can pull off. You probably thought, "I can't wait to create some flaming text, and then some ice text, and then I want to scan a photo of my friend Earl and put his head on my other friend Dean's body, and then...." That stuff wears off pretty fast, doesn't it? But now, you want to do real stuff. Effects that matter. Effects clients are willing to pay for. I'm here for you, to lead you away from the flaming text and toward the light—the light of a new tomorrow that's brimming with hope and glistening with the soft edges that only a well-placed drop shadow can bring.

Creating Drama with a Soft Spotlight

This is a great technique that lets you focus attention by using dramatic soft lighting. The technique I'm showing you here I learned from famous nature photographer Vincent Versace. I had been getting a similar look by filling a layer with black, making an oval selection, feathering the edges significantly, and then knocking a hole out of the layer, but Vincent's technique, using the Lighting Effects filter, is so much easier that it's just about all I use now.

Step One:
Open the RGB photo to which you want to apply the soft spotlight effect. In this example, I want to focus attention on the top center of the lily, and away from the background and vase the flower is sitting in.

Step Two:
Go under the Filter menu, under Render, and choose Lighting Effects. I have to tell you, if you haven't used this filter before, it's probably because its interface (with all its sliders) looks so complex, but luckily there are built-in presets (Adobe calls them "Styles") that you can choose from, so you can pretty much ignore all those sliders. Once you ignore the sliders, the filter is much less intimidating, and you can really have some fun here. The small preview window on the left side of the dialog shows you the default setting, which is a large oval light coming from the bottom right-hand corner.

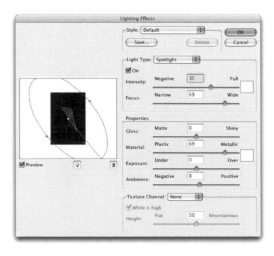

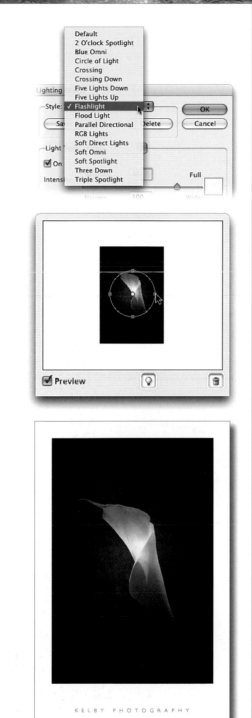

Step Three:
For this effect, we're going to use a very soft, narrow beam, so go under the Style pop-up menu at the top of the dialog (this is where the presets are) and choose Flashlight.

Step Four:
Once you choose Flashlight, look at the preview window and you'll see a small spotlight in the center of your image. Click on the center point (inside the circle) and drag the light into the position where you want it. If you want the circle of light a little bit larger, just click on one of the side points and drag outward.

Step Five:
When you click OK, the filter applies the effect, darkening the surrounding area and creating the soft spotlight effect you see here (the final photo is shown using the "Poster Presentation" technique from Chapter 14). If the Lighting Effect filter seems too intense, you can remedy it immediately after the fact by going under the Edit menu and choosing Fade Lighting Effects. Drag the Opacity slider to the left to reduce the effect of the filter. The farther you drag, the less the intensity of the effect. You can think of this Fade command as "undo on a slider."

Soft Focus Effect

This is a quick way to emulate the effect of a soft focus filter on your lens. Besides being quick and easy, what I like about this effect is the soft glow it gives your images. Try this technique on a sharp photo of some trees and you'll love what it does for the image.

Step One:
Open the photo to which you want to apply a soft focus effect. Duplicate the Background layer by pressing Command-J (PC: Control-J). By default, this duplicate layer is named Layer 1.

Step Two:
Go under the Filter menu, under Blur, and choose Gaussian Blur. For high-res images, enter about 20 pixels (for low-res images, try 6–10 pixels instead) and click OK.

Step Three:

That amount of Gaussian Blur will blur the entire image so much that it'll be hard to see any detail. So, to bring back the detail, go to the Layers palette and lower the Opacity setting of this blurred layer to 50%.

Step Four:

Lowering the Opacity setting allows the detail to come back, but along with it comes a soft glow that gives the image a dreamy, almost painted look, which completes the effect.

Burned-In Edge Effect (Vignetting)

In the Camera Raw chapter, I showed you how to add vignetting (burned-in edges) using the Vignette option in the Camera Raw dialog, but to use Photoshop's Camera Raw plug-in, you have to be shooting in RAW mode on your camera. However, if you want to apply a similar technique (a very wide vignette that acts more like a soft light) to your regular photos (JPEG, TIFF, etc.), here's how to do just that:

Step One:

Open the photo to which you want to apply a burned-in edge effect. Just so you know, what we're doing here is focusing attention through the use of light—we're burning in all the edges of the photo (not just the corners, like lens vignetting, which I usually try to avoid), which leaves the visual focus in the center of the image.

Step Two:

Go to the Layers palette and add a new layer by clicking on the Create a New Layer icon at the bottom of the palette. Press the letter D to set your Foreground color to black, and then fill your new layer with black by pressing Option-Delete (PC: Alt-Backspace).

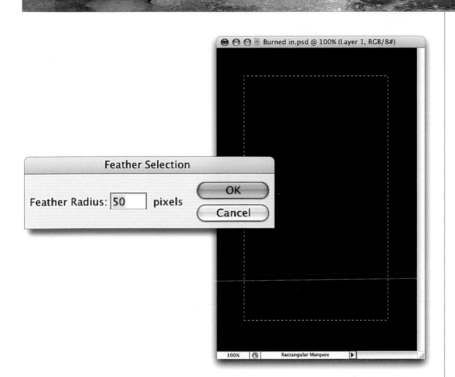

Feather Selection

Feather Radius: 50 pixels

OK

Cancel

Step Three:
Press M to get the Rectangular Marquee tool and drag a selection about 1" inside the edges of your photo. Then, to greatly soften the edges of your selection, go under the Select menu and choose Feather. When the dialog appears, enter 50 pixels for a low-res photo (or 170 pixels for a high-res, 300-ppi photo), and click OK.

Step Four:
Now that your edges have been softened, all you have to do is press Delete (PC: Backspace), and you'll knock a soft hole out of your black layer, revealing the photo on the Background layer beneath it. Now press Command-D (PC: Control-D) to deselect. *Note:* If the edges seem too dark, you can go to the Layers palette and lower the Opacity of your black layer (in the example shown here, I lowered the Opacity to around 80%).

Creating Realistic Shadows

If you're doing most any type of product photography, chances are the product will wind up being used on a white background. So what if we (and many of us do) shoot the product, put a selection around it, copy the product to its own layer, delete the old background (which is usually kind of a grayish background), and then we add a drop shadow in Photoshop? Well, the problem is that the shadow always looks so "added-later-in-Photoshop." But here's a pro-trick that lets you get the most realistic shadow—the real shadow.

Step One:

Open the photo to which you want to apply the "real shadow" technique. In this example, the product (a Bose SoundDock for the iPod) is shot against a seamless white background, which looks kind of grayish (which is pretty typical unless the background is well lit). To get the product off this background, you'll have to put a selection around it first, so get the selection tool of your choice and go to it. (In this example, I used the Pen tool [P] set to Path in the Options Bar to trace a path around the dock and speakers, and then I converted my path into a selection by pressing Command-Return [PC: Control-Enter].) Once you've got a selection around your product, press Command-J (PC: Control-J) to put the product on its own layer. Then, go to the Layers palette and click on the Background layer to make it active.

Step Two:

Press Command-A (PC: Control-A) to put a selection around the entire background, and then press Delete (PC: Backspace) to delete the gray background, leaving just your product on its own layer, with a completely white background layer below it. Deselect by pressing Command-D (PC: Control-D).

©DAVE GALES

Step Three:

Press Y to get the History Brush tool (it's right above the Gradient tool in the Toolbox). In the Options Bar, click on the thumbnail to the right of the word "Brush," and choose a medium-sized, soft-edged brush from the Brush Picker. Now, start painting along the bottom edge of your product where the original shadow used to be. The trick is to paint mostly over your product and have just about a third of the brush extending outside your product. So, as you paint, the original shadow will be painted in.

Step Four:

Continue painting along the bottom edge, and remember not to let your brush tip extend too far into the white space—you really want to hug the bottom edge of your product, so only the original shadow is painted in and not too much of the old gray background. The complete shot is shown here, with the original shadow back in place, minus the ugly gray background. Sweet!

Mapping One Image onto Another (Image Warp)

If you've been using either Photoshop 7 or CS, you're probably familiar with the Warp Text feature, which lets you bend type in a number of preset shapes. Well, in CS2 Adobe found a way to apply basically the same technique to photos, and it's one of the most amazing things in all of CS2. It's even better than the Warp Text feature in that you can customize your wrap, which makes the chore of mapping one image onto another a breeze.

Step One:

Open the photo that has an object you want to map another photo onto (in this case, I want to add a label to the wine bottle in the photo, and I want it to follow the curvature of the bottle realistically, so it doesn't look "stuck-on-in-Photoshop").

Step Two:

Open the photo you want to map onto the bottle (in this case, we're using a wine label created in Photoshop). You can create your own custom wine label in Photoshop, or of course, you can download the wine label shown here from this book's website. *Note:* If the label isn't on its own layer, press W to get the Magic Wand tool, click once on the white background, and then go under the Select menu and choose Inverse. This allows you to select just the label without the white background.

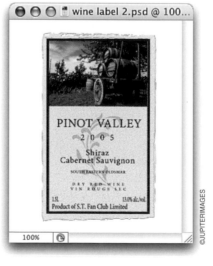

Step Three:
Press V to get the Move tool and drag the label onto your wine bottle image. Press Command-T (PC: Control-T) to bring up Free Transform. Press-and-hold the Shift key, grab the bottom-right corner point, and drag inward to scale the label down so it fits easily on the front of the bottle. Then, click-and-drag within the bounding box to position the label in the center of the bottle. As you can see, the label looks very flat, very "stuck-on-after-the-fact" because it doesn't follow the contours of the bottle, and it covers the highlights of the bottle. It couldn't look more "faked."

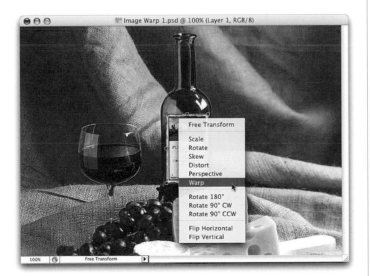

Step Four:
While Free Transform is still in place, Control-click (PC: Right-click) within the Free Transform bounding box and a contextual menu of transformations will appear. Choose Warp from the menu.

Continued

Step Five:

When you choose Warp, the Options Bar gives you a list of options for warping your image. From the Warp pop-up menu in the Options Bar, choose Arch. This will arch your label, adding the curvature you need, but the default arch has the label bending the wrong way (you'll fix that easily in the next step).

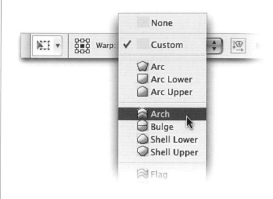

Step Six:

Once you choose Arch, a grid appears over your label, with a control point at the top center of the grid. This control point lets you drag the entire arch up or down (there's also a field in the Options Bar that lets you type in a number, but seriously, come on—we're Photoshop people. "We don't need no stinkin' numbers!"). Click on this center point and drag straight down. Keep dragging until the arch is bending downward. Now, you can see the effect coming together.

Step Seven:

You have only one control point—that point at the top center—but you can actually tweak every point on the grid individually using control handles (similar to the Pen tool's handles for controlling Beziér curves). To do this, go back up to the Warp pop-up menu in the Options Bar and choose Custom.

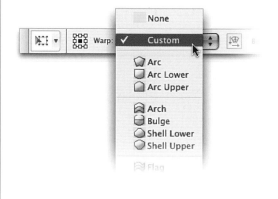

Step Eight:

Once you choose Custom, points appear at all the outer intersections, and you can adjust them individually, or you can just grab the grid in the center and start dragging it around (try this once—it's pretty darn slick). In the example shown here, I wanted to add more curve to the bottom of the label, so I clicked on the bottom control handles and dragged each down a little to add some bend.

TIP: If you're warping a photo and you need to switch back to Free Transform for just a moment to tweak something (like adjusting the overall size or perspective), you can do that by clicking on the little Warp icon that appears in the group of four icons on the right side of the Options Bar (while Warp is engaged). To toggle back to Warp from Free Transform, just click on the icon again.

Step Nine:

When you have the label warped to your satisfaction, press Return (PC: Enter) to lock in your warping. Then, to bring back some of the highlights on the bottle, go to the Layers palette and lower the Opacity setting of the label layer to around 80%, which completes the effect. This allows the highlights to show through and helps sell the idea that the label is really on there.

Fake Duotone

The duotone tinting look is all the rage right now, but creating a real two-color duotone, complete with curves, that will separate in just two colors on press is a bit of a chore (and if you're up for that chore, turn to Chapter 7 and you can give it a whirl). However, if you're outputting to an inkjet printer, or to a printing press as a full-color job, then you don't need all that complicated stuff—you can create a fake duotone that looks at least as good (if not better).

Step One:

Open the color RGB photo that you want to convert into a duotone (again, I'm calling it a duotone, but we're going to stay in RGB mode the whole time, so you can just treat this like any other color photo). Now, the hard part of this is choosing which color to make your duotone. I always see other people's duotones, and think "Yeah, that's the color I want!" but when I go to the Foreground color swatch and try to create a similar color in the Color Picker, it's always hit or miss (usually miss). That's why you'll want to know this next trick.

Step Two:

If you can find another duotone photo that has a color you like, you're set. So I usually go to a stock-photo website (like Photos.com) and search for "Duotones." When I find one I like, I return to Photoshop, press I to get the Eyedropper tool, click-and-hold anywhere within my image area, and then (while keeping the mouse button held down), I drag my cursor outside Photoshop and onto the photo in my Web browser to sample the color I want. Now, mind you, I did not and *would* not take a single pixel from someone else's photo—I'm just sampling a color.

Step Three:

Return to your image in Photoshop. Go to the Layers palette and click on the Create a New Layer icon. Then, press Option-Delete (PC: Alt-Backspace) to fill this new blank layer with your sampled color. The color will fill your image area, hiding your photo, but we'll fix that.

Step Four:

While still in the Layers palette, change the blend mode of this sampled color layer to Color.

Step Five:

If your duotone seems too dark, you can lessen the effect by clicking on the Background layer, and then going under the Image menu, under Adjustments, and choosing Desaturate. This removes the color from your RGB photo without changing its color mode, while lightening the overall image. Pretty sneaky, eh?

Replicating Traditional Photography Filters

This is a totally digital way to replicate some of the most popular photography filters, such as the 81A and 81B Color Correction filters used by many photographers. These are primarily used to warm photos, especially those taken outdoors where a bright sky radiates to give photos a bluish cast, but they can also be used to create a dramatic statement using color, as we'll do here.

Step One:
Open the photo that you want to apply a lens filter effect to. In this case, we have a shot taken along California's Pacific Coast Highway, but the image is kind of grayish and bland, so we'll add a photo filter (after the fact, in Photoshop) to give the photo more interest and life (basically, to make it look more like it did when I was actually there taking the shot. After all, while I was there I didn't say to myself, "Hey, this looks grayish and bland—let's shoot it!" It looked beautiful and spectacular, and I want to bring back the essence of what made me take that shot in the first place).

Step Two:
Choose Photo Filter from the Create New Adjustment Layer pop-up menu at the bottom of the Layers palette (it's the half-black/half-white circle icon).

Step Three:

The Photo Filter dialog will appear. Click-and-hold on the Filter pop-up menu and a list of filters will appear. Since we're trying to add a blue effect to our image, choose one of the Cooling Filters (in this example, I chose Cooling Filter [82] simply because I liked it best, after trying all three blue Cooling Filters). So, choose Cooling Filter (82) (or whichever one you like best).

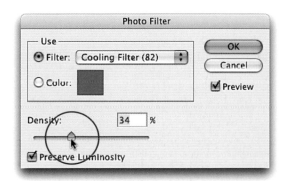

Step Four:

If you want a more intense effect than the default, drag the Density slider to the right. The default setting was 25%, so I cranked it up a little to 34% so the blue looked even more intense.

Step Five:

When you click OK, the entire photo gets a wonderful blue filtering effect. (The final effect is shown here, incorporating the "Poster Presentation" technique I show in Chapter 14.) If you decide you want this blue to affect only certain parts of your photo (for example, let's say you wanted to leave the mountains as they were before the filter), just press B to switch to the Brush tool, choose a soft-edged brush, press X to set black as your Foreground color, and paint over the areas you don't want cooled by the filter. As you paint, those areas will return to the original color (which is why it's so great that Adobe created Photo Filters as adjustment layers—they're adjustable!).

PACIFIC COAST HIGHWAY

Blending Photos Together

Photoshop collage techniques could easily fill a whole chapter, maybe a whole book; but the technique shown here (using layer masks) is probably the most popular—and one of the most powerful—used today by professionals. Best of all, it's easy, flexible, and even fun to blend photos together seamlessly.

Step One:
Open the photo that you want to use as your base (this will serve as the background of your collage).

Step Two:
Open the first photo that you want to collage with your background photo.

Step Three:
Press the letter V to switch to the Move tool, and then click-and-drag the photo from this document right onto your background photo. It will appear on its own layer in your background document.

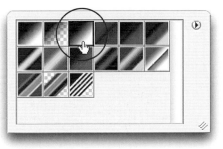

Step Four:
Click on the Add Layer Mask icon at the bottom of the Layers palette. Press the letter G to get the Gradient tool from the Toolbox, and then press Return (PC: Enter) to bring up the Gradient Picker (it appears at the location of your cursor within your image area). Choose the Black to White gradient (it's the third gradient in the Picker).

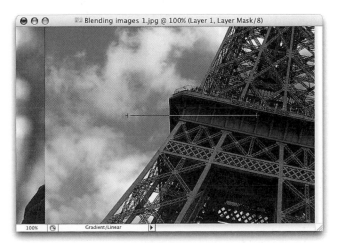

Step Five:
Click the Gradient tool at the point in your photo that you want to be transparent and drag (in this case, to the right), stopping at the point where you want the rest of the photo to be at 100% opacity.

Continued

Step Six:

When you release the mouse button, the photo on the top layer will smoothly blend from a solid image (on the right) to transparency (as it overlaps the woman's face). Once the blend is in place, if it seems like the Eiffel Tower covers too much of her face, just switch to the Move tool and drag the Eiffel Tower layer to the right until it just touches the edge of her cheek.

Step Seven:

Open another photo you'd like to blend in with your existing collage. Switch to the Move tool, and click-and-drag this photo onto the top of your "collage-in-progress."

Step Eight:

Click on the Add Layer Mask icon again at the bottom of the Layers palette to add a layer mask to this new layer.

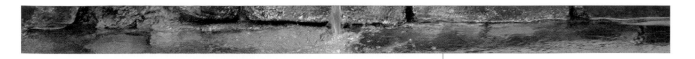

Step Nine:
Click the Gradient tool just past the letter R in the sign and drag to the left, to the center of the letter M in the sign to blend this new photo in with the other layers. When you release the mouse button, the solid-to-transparent blend appears.

Step Ten:
If the sign appears too close to the woman's face, get the Move tool, click on the sign, and drag it to the left a bit until the edge trails off just like you want it to. If you want to tweak the blend a bit, just press B to grab the Brush tool, choose a large, soft-edged brush, and start painting on your image. If you paint using the color white, more of the sign will appear. If you press the letter X to switch to black and start painting, less of the sign will appear.

Infrared Technique

Here's my digital twist on getting an infrared look from regular photos taken with your digital camera. The first few steps give you the standard infrared look (which makes it kinda look like you popped a Hoya R72 infrared filter on your lens), and the last steps let you bleed some color in for some really interesting looks.

Step One:

Open the RGB photo you want to apply an infrared effect to in Photoshop. Go to the Layers palette and choose Channel Mixer from the Create New Adjustment Layer pop-up menu (it's the half-black/half-white circle icon) at the bottom of the palette.

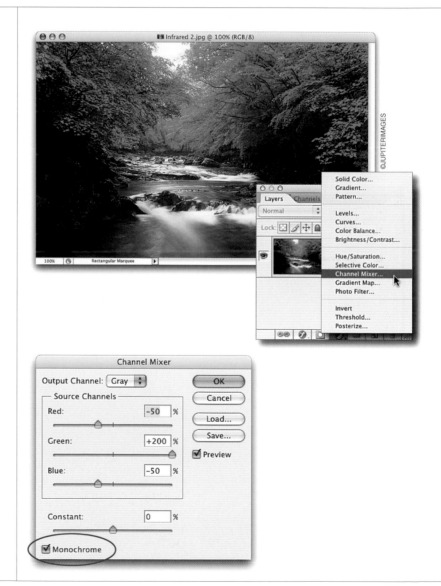

Step Two:

When the Channel Mixer dialog appears, turn on the Monochrome checkbox at the bottom of the dialog. Then, set the Red channel to -50% (you can just type it in the field or move the slider to the left until it reads -50%); set the Green channel to +200%; and set the Blue channel to -50%.

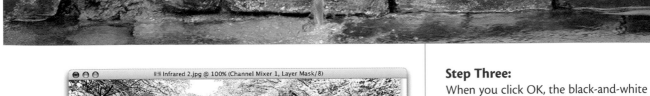

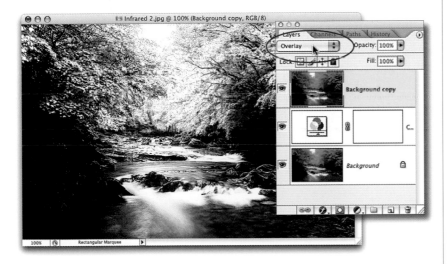

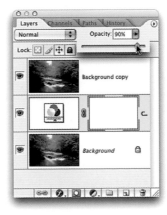

Step Three:

When you click OK, the black-and-white infrared effect is applied to your image. If you want to keep your photo in black and white, then you're done. If you want to add some muted color (which is a very popular technique these days), then go on to the next step.

Step Four:

Go to the Layers palette and drag-and-drop the Background layer onto the Create a New Layer icon to duplicate it. Then, drag this Background copy layer above the Channel Mixer layer at the top of the layer stack. Now, make two changes: (1) Change the layer blend mode from Normal to Overlay, and (2) lower the Opacity to 50%. You're not done yet.

Step Five:

In the Layers palette, click on the center layer (the Channel Mixer adjustment layer) and lower the Opacity to bring back more of the original color. In the example shown here, I only had to lower the Opacity by 10% to bring the color roaring back in.

Continued

Step Six:

Once you lower the Opacity on that Channel Mixer adjustment layer, you've got the final effect. Now that you know how to do this technique, want to try a little deviation from it, for a totally cool color effect? Good (I knew you'd be up for it). Start by dragging the Background copy layer and the Channel Mixer layer to the Trash icon at the bottom of the Layers palette to get back to your original, untouched Background layer.

Step Seven:

Now, choose Channel Mixer again from the Create New Adjustment Layer pop-up menu. You're going to enter the same settings (-50%, +200%, -50%), but this time *don't* turn on the Monochromatic checkbox, and you'll get the way-cool effect you see here. It's not infrared, but it doesn't have to be—it's just a totally cool color effect. Give it a shot and see what you think.

One of the most popular lens filters for outdoor photographers is the Neutral Density filter, because often (especially when shooting scenery, like sunsets) you wind up with a bright sky and a dark foreground. A Neutral Density gradient lens filter reduces the exposure in the sky by a stop or two, while leaving the ground unchanged (the top of the filter is gray, and it graduates down to transparent at the bottom). Well, if you forgot to use your ND gradient filter when you took the shot, you can create your own ND effect in Photoshop.

Neutral Density Gradient Filter

FOR PROS ONLY!

©DAVE MOSER

Step One:
Open the photo (preferably a landscape) where you exposed for the ground, which left the sky too light. Press the letter D to set your Foreground color to black. Then, go to the Layers palette and choose Gradient from the Create New Adjustment Layer pop up menu at the bottom of the palette.

Step Two:
When the Gradient Fill dialog appears, click on the little, black downward-facing arrow (it's immediately to the right of the Gradient thumbnail) to bring up the Gradient Picker. Double-click on the second gradient in the list, which is a gradient that goes from Foreground to Transparent. Don't click OK yet.

Continued

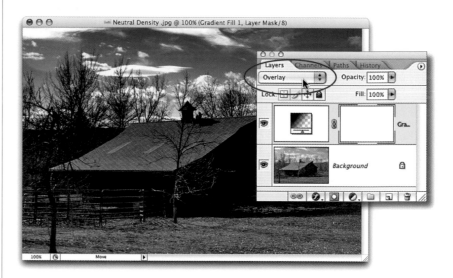

Step Three:

By default, this puts a dark area on the ground (rather than the sky), so click on the Reverse checkbox to reverse the gradient, putting the dark area of your gradient over the sky and the transparent part over the land. Your image will look pretty awful at this point, but you'll fix that in the next step, so just click OK.

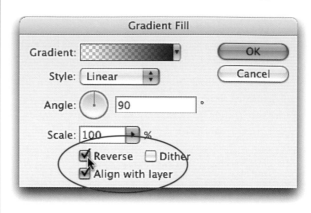

Step Four:

To make this gradient blend in with your photo, go to the Layers palette and change the blend mode of this adjustment layer from Normal to Overlay. This darkens the sky, but it gradually lightens until it reaches land, and then it slowly disappears. So, how does it know where the ground is? It doesn't. It puts a gradient across your entire photo, so in the next step, you'll basically show it where the ground is.

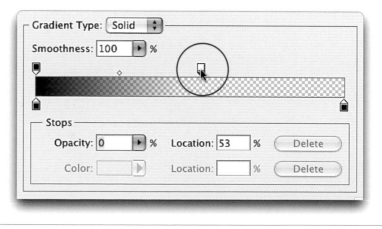

Step Five:

In the Layers palette, double-click on the thumbnail for the Gradient adjustment layer to bring up the Gradient Fill dialog again. To control how far down the darkening will extend from the top of your photo, just click once on the Gradient thumbnail at the top of the dialog. This brings up the Gradient Editor. Grab the top-right white color stop above the gradient ramp near the center of the dialog and drag the color stop to the left; the darkening will "roll up" from the bottom of your photo, so keep dragging to the left until only the sky is affected, and then click OK in the Editor.

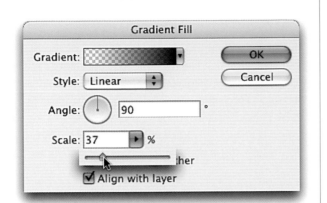

Step Six:

By default, the gradient you choose fills the entire image area, smoothly transitioning from a dark gray at the top center to transparent at the very top. It's a smooth, "soft-step" gradient. However, if you want a quicker change from black to transparent (a hard step between the two), you can lower the Scale amount in the Gradient Fill dialog.

Step Seven:

Also, if the photo you're working on doesn't have a perfectly straight horizon line (maybe you're photographing the sky over an angled roof), you also might have to use the Angle control by clicking on the line in the center of the Angle circle and dragging slowly in the direction that your horizon is tilted. This literally rotates your gradient, which enables you to have your gradient easily match the angle of your horizon. When it looks good to you, click OK to complete the effect.

Before: Exposing for the darn barn makes the sky too light.

After: The barn is the same, but the sky is now bluer and more intense.

Perspective Pasting with Vanishing Point

In Chapter 9, "Removing Unwanted Objects," we used Photoshop CS2's incredibly cool Vanishing Point filter to clone someone out of a picture, and Vanishing Point cloned him away in perfect perspective (and keeping that perspective would have been incredibly hard to do with just the regular Clone Stamp tool). Well, one of the things that makes Vanishing Point so "incredibly cool" is that it's not just for removing things—here's how to add a photo to an object in perfect perspective (by the way, this works great for type as well as photos).

Step One:

Open the photo you want to add an object into. In this case, it's an office building, and we're going to add a photo to the angled front side of the building—more importantly, we want it to perfectly match the perspective of the building. You start by adding a new blank layer by clicking on the Create a New Layer icon at the bottom of the Layers palette.

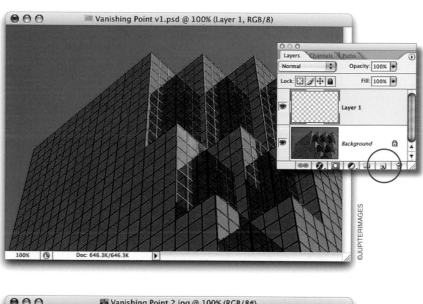

©JUPITERIMAGES

Step Two:

Now open the photo that you want to appear on the side of the building. Press Command-A (PC: Control-A) to put a selection around the entire photo, and then press Command-C (PC: Control-C) to copy this photo into memory. Since it's copied into memory, you can close this photo now.

©SCOTT KELBY

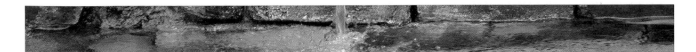

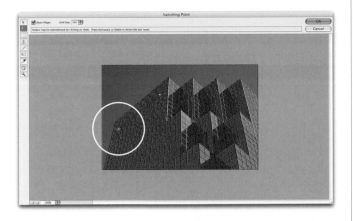

Step Three:

Go under the Filter menu and choose Vanishing Point. Here's what you're going to do: You have to tell Photoshop where you want the photo to go by mapping out the perspective (don't worry, it's easier than it sounds). Start by getting the Create Plane tool (it's the second tool from the top in the Toolbox on the left side of the dialog). Click once on the front-right side of the building (two windows in near the top-right corner), then drag across to the left side and click again to make an angled line.

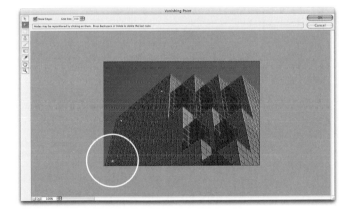

Step Four:

The Create Plane tool kind of acts like the Polygonal Lasso tool, so now you can just move down along the left side of the building, click again, and it will create a straight line back to your last point. You can pretty much see what you're going to do, and that's draw a rectangle along the side of the building. To make it easier, follow along the windowpane lines that separate the rows of windows.

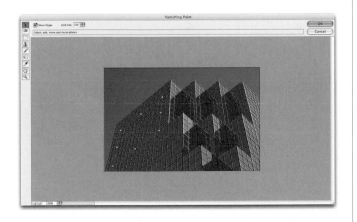

Step Five:

When you click the bottom-right corner, it finishes the other side for you, and a blue grid will appear (it's blue if you drew the perspective right). If it's yellow, get the Edit Plane tool (it looks like an arrow in the Toolbox) and adjust your points until it turns blue. If your grid outline turns red, it's a bad grid (your perspective isn't right), and you'll need to tweak the points a bit.

Continued

Step Six:

Once your grid is in place, it's time to bring in the photo you want placed on the building. Press Command-V (PC: Control-V) to paste the photo into Vanishing Point. In this example, the photo we pasted in is way too large to fit on the side of the building, but luckily Vanishing Point lets you resize your pasted image using Free Transform, so press Command-T (PC: Control-T) to bring up the Free Transform bounding box.

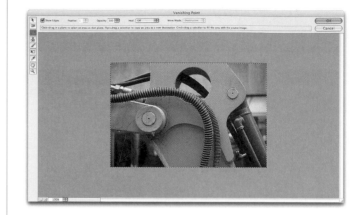

Step Seven:

Press-and-hold the Shift key, grab a corner point, and drag inward to adjust your photo to approximately the size you want (it doesn't have to be right on the money, because of course you can always tweak the size later). Now, *don't* hit Return or Enter, just get your image down to size and leave the Free Transform handles in place.

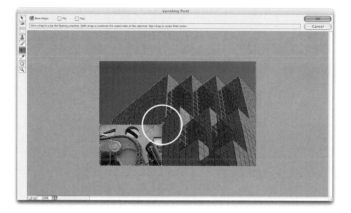

Step Eight:

Click in the center of your photo and drag it up to where the faint outline of the grid is. When your cursor enters the grid area, your photo will immediately snap onto the grid in perfect perspective. Since Free Transform is still in place, click on a corner point and scale the photo to fit into your grid area (it likely won't fit perfectly, so just get it close).

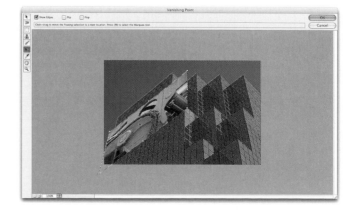

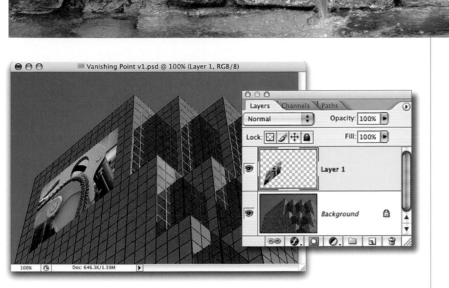

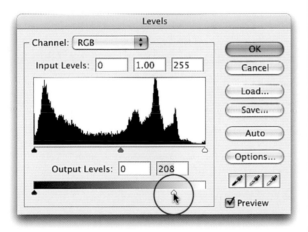

Step Nine:

When it's sized the way you want it, click the OK button and your photo is transformed with the proper perspective. You can now see why we created a new blank layer in Step 1. Without it, the perspective photo would be applied directly to the Background layer, and you'd have no real control over it after you applied Vanishing Point. On a separate layer, you can change blend modes, opacity, etc.

Step Ten:

To make the pasted-in photo better match the tone of the main photo, we're going to darken it up a bit (after all, we pasted it onto the side of a building that's in shadows). Press Command-L (PC: Control-L) to bring up Levels, then drag the bottom right-hand Output Levels slider to the left to darken the photo until you feel it matches the tone of the shadow side of the building.

Step Eleven:

Click OK and the final image is completed. The pasted photo matches both the perspective of the building and the overall tone of the image.

Exposure: 1/200s | Focal Length: 12mm | Aperture Value: f/4.0

Wide Receiver
creating panoramas

Before we get into this chapter, I think it's important that you acquaint yourself with some "insider" panorama jargon, some "panoterminology" (if you will), so the next time you're at one of those underground pano-parties, you don't create a panoramic-sized faux pas that gets you shunned from the panorama community at large. Let's begin. First, never, ever refer to a panorama as a "panorama." That's like getting caught using Photoshop's Paint Bucket tool—it brands you as a beginner, and once they think you're a weenie, you're always a weenie. From now on, always refer to them as "panos." You shoot panos. Now, the act of putting these panos together is called "stitchin'." So, when making small talk at a pano-party, just casually mention something like this, "I'm really beat. I've been stitchin' panos all day." They'll all nod in agreement, as if to say, "Me too, dude. I know where you're coming from." Now, each segment you shoot has a special name too. Don't make the mistake of calling them "the left segment" or "the center segment." They'll have security escort you from the premises. So, call the left pano segment "the flabengaffer," the center segment "the barfnoor," and the rightmost segment "the fleepinflopper." Also, never refer to Photoshop's Photomerge feature by its official name. Always refer to it as "Baabaaleepdonk," and don't even mention the Automate menu. Just call it "Slapumgoogoogonk." Use it, and you may even draw a gasp from the partygoers (don't be surprised if you're signing a few autographs before you leave the party). By the way, they always refer to the File menu as "the File menu." I don't know why.

Manually Stitching Panoramas Together

Stitching panoramas together in Photoshop is fairly easy, if you follow these two simple rules before you shoot your pano: (1) Use a tripod to keep things level. That's not to say you can't shoot panos handheld, but the consistency a tripod brings to panos makes a world of difference when you try to stitch the photos together. And (2), when you shoot each segment, make sure that part of the next segment overlaps at least 20% of your previous segment (you'll see why this is important in this tutorial). First we'll look at manually stitching panos together, and then we'll look at the automated version later in this chapter.

Step One:
Open the first segment of your pano. The photo shown here is the first of three segments that we'll be stitching together.

Step Two:
Next, go under the Image menu and choose Canvas Size (or in CS2, press Command-Option-C [PC: Control-Alt-C]). In the capture shown in the previous step, you can see the width of the first segment is about 5". We're stitching three segments together, so we'll need to add enough blank canvas to accommodate two more photos of the same size, so make sure the Relative checkbox is turned on, then enter 10" as the Width setting. This extra blank canvas needs to be added immediately to the right of your first segment, so in the Anchor grid (at the bottom of the dialog), click on the left-center grid square. Then, change the Canvas Extension Color pop-up menu to White.

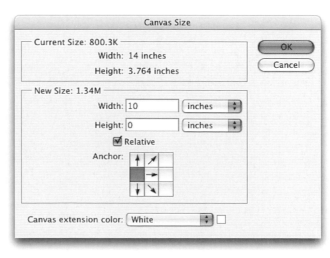

Step Three:

Click OK and about 10" of white canvas space is added to the right of your photo (if it doesn't look like the capture shown here, press Command-Z [PC: Control-Z] to undo, then go back and check your Anchor grid setting to make sure you clicked on the left-center grid square).

Step Four:

Now, open the second segment of your pano. Notice that part of the taxi on the far right of the first segment also appears on the left side of the second segment. That's absolutely necessary because now we have common objects that appear in both photos, and we can use the taxi as a target to align our panos.

Step Five:

Press the letter V to get the Move tool from the Toolbox, and click-and-drag your second segment into the first segment's document window. Drag the second segment over until it overlaps the first segment a bit. If needed, zoom in so you can see the two segments overlapping.

Continued

Step Six:

In the Layers palette, lower the Opacity of this second segment's layer to 50% so you can see through your top layer to the layer beneath it, which makes lining up the two taxis much easier. This is pretty much the secret of manually stitching panos. As the two taxis (your target objects) get closer in alignment, take your hand off the mouse and do the final aligning using the Left and Right Arrow keys on your keyboard. At first, the taxis will look blurry, but as the two target objects get closer to each other, the blur lessens.

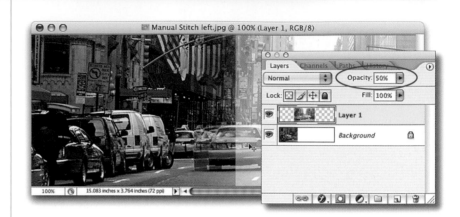

Step Seven:

If you're still having trouble lining things up, try this trick: raise the Opacity back to 100%, then change the layer blend mode of your top layer to Difference in the Layers palette. Now use the Arrow keys on your keyboard to align the taxi on the top layer with the one on the bottom. As long as you see color in the overlapping area (as you do here), it's not yet perfectly aligned.

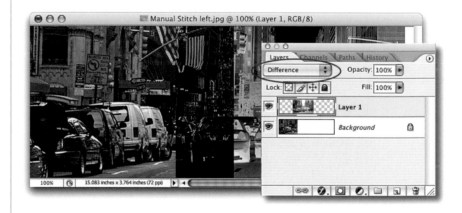

Step Eight:

Keep nudging with the Arrow keys until the overlapping area turns solid black. When it's black (meaning no colors are showing in the overlapping center area), it's perfectly aligned.

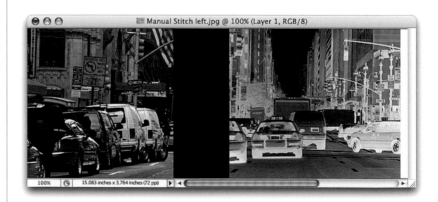

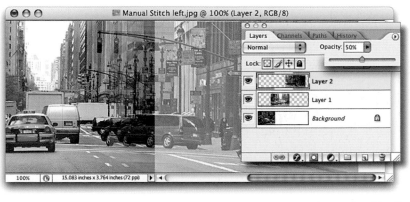

Step Nine:

Go to the Layers palette and change your blend mode back to Normal (that is, if you set it to Difference, otherwise just raise the Opacity to 100%) to see how your stitch looks. The two images should look like one (that is, if you shot them using a tripod and didn't bump the camera along the way).

TIP: If you see a hard edge along the left-hand side of the top layer, press E to switch to the Eraser tool; choose a 200-pixel, soft-edged brush by clicking on the Brush thumbnail in the Options Bar; and lightly erase over the edge. Since the photos overlap, as you erase the edge, the top photo should blend seamlessly into the bottom photo.

Step Ten:

Now, open the third segment of your three-segment pano.

Step Eleven:

Repeat the same technique of dragging this photo into your main pano, lowering the Opacity of this layer to 50%, and dragging the segment over your target object. (In this example, we're overlapping the van turning onto the street.)

Continued

Step Twelve:

Don't forget, as you get close to aligning the vans, take your hand off the mouse and use the Arrow keys on your keyboard to align these last two segments. (Don't forget to try changing the layer blend mode to help you align the two segments.) Again, after you raise the Opacity of the top layer back to 100% (or change the blend mode back to Normal), if you see a hard edge between the two, use a soft-edged Eraser to erase away any seam.

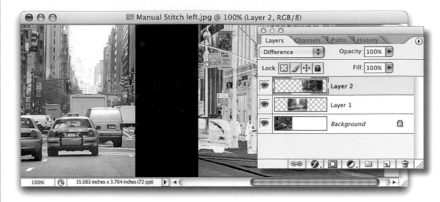

Step Thirteen:

Here the three segments are stitched together, but I overestimated how much canvas size we'd need, so there's some blank canvas space to the right of my pano. To quickly get rid of it, go under the Image menu and choose Trim to bring up the Trim dialog. The area we no longer need is on the right-hand side, so in the dialog, under Based On, choose Bottom Right Pixel Color, which will trim away everything outside your photo that is the color of your bottom-right pixel (which is white).

Step Fourteen:

Click OK in the Trim dialog, and the excess canvas area is trimmed away, completing your pano. Now, this was an ideal situation: You shot the panos on a tripod, so the stitching was easy; and you didn't use a fisheye, so there wasn't much stretching or distorting to deal with.

Automated Pano Stitching with Photomerge

If you've taken the time to get your pano set up right during the shoot (in other words, you used a tripod and overlapped the shots by about 20% to 30% each), you can have Photoshop's Photomerge feature automatically stitch your panoramic images together. If you handheld your camera for the pano shoot, you can still use Photomerge—you'll just have to do most of the work manually.

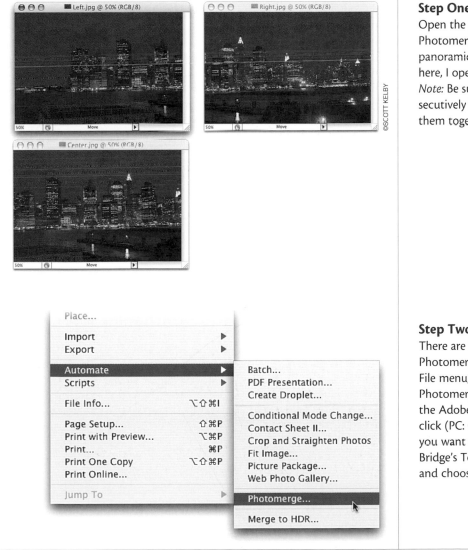

©SCOTT KELBY

Step One:
Open the photos that you want Photomerge to stitch together as one panoramic image. In the example shown here, I opened three shots in Photoshop. *Note:* Be sure to open your images consecutively in the order you want to stitch them together.

Step Two:
There are two ways to access Photomerge: (1) Go under Photoshop's File menu, under Automate, and choose Photomerge (as shown here), or (2) in the Adobe Bridge you can Command-click (PC: Control-click) on the photos you want to stitch, then go under the Bridge's Tools menu, under Photoshop, and choose Photomerge.

Continued

Step Three:

If you choose Photomerge from Photoshop's Automate menu (rather than the Bridge), a dialog appears asking which files you want to combine into a panorama. Any files you have open will appear in the window, or you can change the Use pop-up menu to Files, and then choose individual photos to open. When your file names appear in the window, Shift-click the top and bottom images to select them in the window. Make sure the Attempt to Automatically Arrange Source Images checkbox is on if you want Photomerge to try to build your pano for you, and then click OK.

Step Four:

If your pano images were shot correctly (as I mentioned in the introduction of this technique), the Photomerge dialog will appear and stitch your images together seamlessly (if not, skip to Step 12). *Note:* By default, Photomerge creates a flattened image, but if you want a layered file instead (great for creating panoramic video effects), turn on the Keep as Layers checkbox in the bottom right-hand corner of the dialog.

Step Five:

You might also try the Perspective Stitching to see if you like the results better. To turn this on, and see an instant preview of the results, go to the Settings section on the right side of the Photomerge dialog and click on the Perspective radio button. You can see how it adjusts the perspective, but it also creates a cropping issue (which you'll deal with a little later). So, click OK in the dialog, and Photomerge will create the pano.

Step Six:

In the pano shown here, the horizon line is a bit tilted to the left. Although you can rotate individual sections from right within Photomerge, it's easier if you correct an overall problem like this after you've created the pano, so start by choosing the Measure tool from the Toolbox (it's nested under the Eyedropper tool). Click-and-drag the Measure tool along the horizon (which is at the base of the Manhattan skyline, in this example), starting at the left and dragging to the right.

Step Seven:

Now, go under the Image menu, under Rotate Canvas, and choose Arbitrary. This brings up the Rotate Canvas dialog, and the amount of angle (as provided by the Measure tool) is already calculated. You just have to click OK to straighten your pano.

Step Eight:

Here's the straightened pano—now you just have to crop it down to size (this is a fairly common routine when using Photomerge to stitch your photos, so don't think you're doing it wrong, especially if you use the Perspective effect, as we have here—cropping is just part of the job).

Continued

Step Nine:

Now it's time to crop away the excess area. Press the letter C to get the Crop tool, then drag out your cropping border so the extra areas at the top, bottom, and sides will be cropped away, leaving a nice, clean, wide rectangular panorama.

Step Ten:

Press Return (PC: Enter) to apply your crop, and your panorama will appear as one image. Now it only needs one more thing—sharpening. Go under the Filter menu, under Sharpen, and choose Smart Sharpen. Try an Amount of 60% and a Radius setting of 1 pixel.

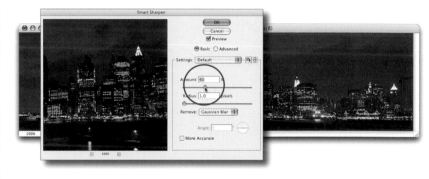

Step Eleven:

When you click OK, the sharpening is applied to the photo, and in this case it helps bring out the twinkling lights of the city, adding more contrast. Now, this pano stitch—even with having to rotate it after we were done—is what we call a "best-case scenario," where you shot the panos on a tripod and overlapped enough so Photomerge had no problems; it just did its thing, making it perfect the first time. But you know, and I know, life just isn't like that…

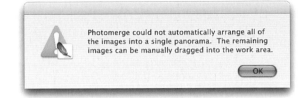

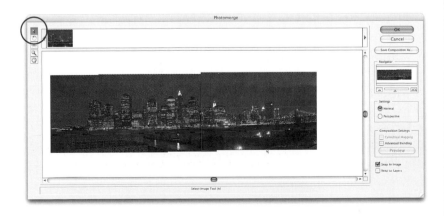

Step Twelve:

More likely what you'll get (especially if you handheld your camera or didn't allow enough overlap) is a warning dialog letting you know that Photomerge "ain't gonna do it for you" (that's a technical phrase coined by Adobe's Alabama tech office). In other words—it's up to you. So if you've had problems since Step 3, read on.

Step Thirteen:

Once you click OK in that warning dialog, Photomerge will try to merge as many segments together as possible. The segments it can't merge will be placed in the Lightbox (the horizontal row across the top of the dialog). Although Photomerge didn't do all the work for you, it can still help—just make sure the Snap to Image checkbox (in the bottom right-hand corner) is turned on.

Step Fourteen:

Using the Select Image tool (the hollow arrow at the top of the Toolbox on the left), drag a segment from the Lightbox into your work area near the first image. When you get close to the main image, release your mouse button. If Photomerge sees a common overlapping area, it will snap them together and blend any visible edges (thanks to Snap to Image). If you need to rotate a segment, click on it with the Select Image tool first, then switch to the Rotate Image tool (R), and click-and-drag within the segment to rotate it. When the images are stitched together, click OK. You'll have a little cropping to do, but outside of that, Photomerge does most of the work.

Using Match Color to Fix Pano Exposure Problems

When you're shooting panos, you can really get burned by using the automatic exposure setting on your camera because at least one of your segments will wind up either lighter or darker than the rest, creating very obvious seams in your pano. The way around this (when taking the shot) is to compose the first segment, hold the shutter half way down to set the exposure, then memorize that exposure setting, and switch to manual. Now shoot all the segments in manual mode, using that exact exposure. If you didn't do that, here's what to do in Photoshop CS2:

Step One:

Open the segments of your pano (taken using auto exposure mode) and examine them for color shifts. If you're not sure if the colors are off, do a quick Photomerge (go under the File menu, under Automate, and choose Photomerge), and when the photos are stitched together, the problem will be pretty obvious. In the example shown here, you can see that the third segment from the left is underexposed, making the seams obvious (and the pano unusable). In fact, it was off by so much, that Photomerge could only auto-stitch three sections—I had to place one manually from the Lightbox.

Step Two:

Go ahead and click Cancel to delete the test pano you just created, and then, from the segments you already have open, click on one of the photo segments that is properly exposed.

TIP: In the intro above, I recommended turning off auto exposure when shooting panos. Another tip that will make things easier is to turn off auto focus as well, and manually focus each segment—that way, both your exposure and focus will be consistent from segment to segment.

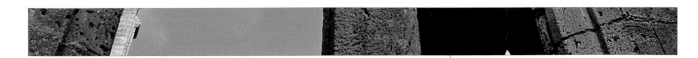

Step Three:
Click on the open photo segment with the exposure problem (this one is underexposed, compared to the other segments taken within seconds of each other).

Step Four:
Go under the Image menu, under Adjustments, and choose Match Color. When the Match Color dialog appears, from the Source pop up menu at the bottom of the dialog, choose the photo segment you clicked on in Step 2 (the one you want to match it to), and you'll instantly see an onscreen preview of how the tones have matched. In the example shown here, the match came out a little bit too purple, so you can drag the Color Intensity slider to the left just a little bit until the two images match even closer. You can now click OK, and the tone of the two segments will now match up pretty darn closely.

Step Five:
Now you can use Photomerge again to merge all four photos into one panorama, where all four segments match up perfectly. Incidentally, once I adjusted the tone of the third segment, Photomerge was able to stitch all four segments together automatically.

Advanced Blending in Photomerge

If you shoot everything perfectly (you used a tripod, you didn't shoot from an extreme angle, you were careful when panning the camera to the next segment so it didn't move up or down, etc.), then your pano will come together pretty easily, with little interaction from you. Ah, but if life were only that simple. Sometimes you're going to have a little camera movement, a little deviation in exposure, or some other problem that's not going to let Photomerge blend the edges of your photos perfectly. That's why we need to know about Advanced Blending.

Step One:
In the Adobe Bridge, select the photos you shot for your panorama by Command-clicking (PC: Control-clicking) on them. Now, go under the Bridge's Tools menu, under Photoshop, and choose Photomerge. *Note:* We're not going to do any color correction or sharpening yet—we'll save that for after our pano has been created, so we're working with one single image.

Step Two:
When the Photomerge dialog opens, by default it will try to stitch your panorama together. In the example shown here, it did just that, but because the exposures are off by a little bit, you can see a distinct diagonal line between each of the four photos (in other words, they didn't blend together well). (*Note:* Press Z to switch to the Zoom tool in the dialog and zoom into the preview window to see the merge better.) This is when it's time to try Photomerge's Advanced Blending option.

Step Three:
On the right side of the Photomerge dialog, in the Composition Settings section, turn on the checkbox for Advanced Blending. When you turn this on, nothing happens onscreen until you click on the Preview button that appears just below the Advanced Blending checkbox.

Step Four:
Now Photomerge will re-blend the edges, and display the results in this Preview Mode. Notice that the blend between photos is much smoother, even though the top edges are a bit frayed between each image, but you can pretty much ignore that because you're going to crop away those "stairsteps" soon—so just be concerned with the difference in tone between the four images, which is minimal now (at least, compared to what it was in Step 2). By the way, while you're in Preview Mode, you can only view the pano—not make any changes to it. You have to click Exit Preview to be able to make changes.

Step Five:
When you click OK, Photomerge creates the panorama for you in a separate document. You can still see the "stairstepped" areas along the top and bottom, so in the next step you'll need to crop that away.

Continued

Step Six:
Press the letter C to get the Crop tool, and click-and-drag a cropping border with the top border landing just below the stairsteps in the top of the image and the border ending just above the stairstepped edges along the bottom.

Step Seven:
Press Return (PC: Enter) to complete your crop, leaving the photo cropped down to size without the stairstepped edges. If you look closely, you can see we still have some work to do (that's because the original pano wasn't shot perfectly—the angle and exposure were all off by a little bit, and that makes our job a little bit harder).

Step Eight:
Press Z to get the Zoom tool and zoom in on the rocks along the top center of the image. You'll see that there are two areas that didn't blend perfectly. The quickest way to fix this is to use the Clone Stamp tool to clone some sky over the smudged rocks.

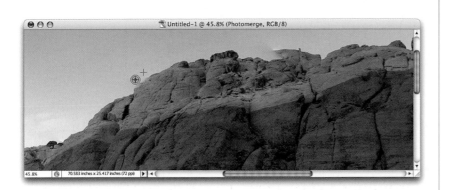

Step Nine:
Press S to switch to the Clone Stamp tool. In the Options Bar, click on the thumbnail to the right of the word "Brush", and choose a soft-edged brush from the Picker. Now, Option-click (PC: Alt-click) in the sky near the rock problem area to sample the sky, and then paint (clone) blue sky over the smudged edge of the rock. You may need to zoom in even closer (with the Zoom tool), then switch to a smaller, hard-edged brush and clone along the rocks so the edge looks hard, rather than soft.

Step Ten:
You'll use the same technique to fix the other smudged rock areas: Option-click (PC: Alt-click) in the sky beside the smudged rock, clone nearby sky right over the edge of the rock, and use a smaller, hard-edged brush to touch up the edges. With the problem areas cloned away, it's time to adjust the pano.

Step Eleven:
Double-click the Zoom tool to view your image at 100% zoom. Now, use Curves (press Command-M [PC: Control-M]) to balance the overall color of the shot (see "Color Correcting Digital Images" in Chapter 6). Then, to get the sky looking richer and bluer, I used the "Neutral Density Gradient Filter" technique from Chapter 11, and then chose Flatten Image from the Layers palette's flyout menu. Finally, I applied Photoshop CS2's Smart Sharpen filter (found under the Filter menu, under Sharpen) with the Amount set at 58% and the Radius set to 1 pixel to complete the photo.

Exposure: 1/100s   Focal Length: 18mm   Aperture Value: f/3.5

Look Sharp
sharpening techniques

Thus far, we've been sticking to song names, movie titles, and a TV title here or there. I'm pushing the paradigm here a bit by going with an album name, "Look Sharp!," from the '90s pop band Roxette, but I knew you'd understand. That's because you can feel my pain. You sense my struggle and how I must suffer to find just the right title, just the right name, or the whole chapter just doesn't work. Of course, none of that is true, but let's just pretend for a moment that it is. Nah. Let's not. Hey, instead, let's do a sharpening quiz, because there's a lot of misinformation about sharpening out there, and this quiz will go a long way in dispelling some of the longstanding myths about sharpening, many of which have held us back from growing as a society. Question 1: Which one of these filters is *not* used as a sharpening filter: (a) Colored Pencil, (b) Stained Glass, (c) Lens Flare, or (d) Clouds. This is tougher than you thought, eh? Well, I'll give you a hint—this is a trick question, because all four are used for sharpening an image. See, you needed this chapter more than you thought. No, wait, I think I messed up. Oh that's right, none of those filters are used for sharpening an image. Okay, you can skip this chapter altogether (unless you answered a, b, c, or d, in which case, you do need this chapter. But if you answered either b or c, you only need to read the first 11 pages; however, if you answered a or d, then you need to read all but the last three pages. If you answered a, b, or d, then read it back to front, skipping every third technique). Are you still reading this? Just checking.

Basic Sharpening

After you've color corrected your photos and right before you save your file, you'll definitely want to sharpen your photos. I sharpen every digital camera photo, either to help bring back some of the original crispness that gets lost during the correction process, or to help fix a photo that's slightly out of focus. Either way, I haven't met a digital camera (or scanned) photo that I didn't think needed a little sharpening. Here's a basic technique for sharpening the entire photo.

Step One:

Open the photo you want to sharpen. Because Photoshop displays your photo in different ways at different magnifications, it's absolutely critical that you view your photo at 100% when sharpening. To ensure that you're viewing at 100%, once your photo is open, double-click on the Zoom tool in the Toolbox, and your photo will jump to a 100% view (look in the image window's title bar to see the actual percentage of zoom).

Step Two:

Go under the Filter menu, under Sharpen, and choose Unsharp Mask. (If you're familiar with traditional darkroom techniques, you probably recognize the term "unsharp mask" from when you would make a blurred copy of the original photo and an "unsharp" version to use as a mask to create a new photo whose edges appeared sharper.) Of Photoshop's sharpening filters, Unsharp Mask is the undisputed choice of professionals because it offers the most control over the sharpening process.

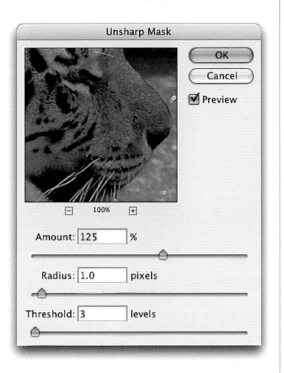

Step Three:

When the Unsharp Mask dialog appears, you'll see three sliders. The Amount slider determines the amount of sharpening applied to the photo; the Radius slider determines how many pixels out from the edge the sharpening will affect; and the Threshold slider works the opposite of what you might think—the lower the number, the more intense the sharpening effect. Threshold determines how different a pixel must be from the surrounding area before it's considered an edge pixel and sharpened by the filter. So what numbers do you enter? I'll give you some great starting points on the following pages, but for now, we'll just use these settings: Amount 125%, Radius 1, and Threshold 3. Click OK and the sharpening is applied to the photo.

Before

After

Continued

Sharpening soft subjects:

Here is an Unsharp Mask setting (Amount 150%, Radius 1, Threshold 10) that works well for images where the subject is of a softer nature (e.g., flowers, puppies, people, rainbows, etc.). It's a subtle application of sharpening that is very well suited to these types of subjects.

Sharpening portraits:

If you're sharpening close-up portraits (a bust for example), try this setting (Amount 75%, Radius 2, Threshold 3), which applies another form of subtle sharpening.

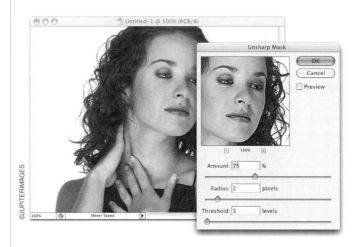

Moderate sharpening:

This is a moderate amount of sharpening that works nicely on product shots, photos of home interiors and exteriors, and landscapes. If you're shooting along these lines, try applying this setting (Amount 225%, Radius 0.5, Threshold 0), and see how you like it (my guess is, you will).

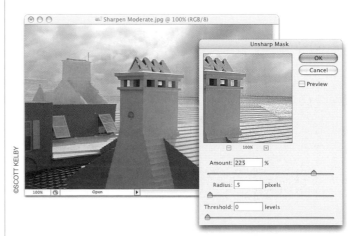

Maximum sharpening:

I use these settings (Amount 65%, Radius 4, Threshold 3) in only two situations: (1) The photo is visibly out of focus and it needs a heavy application of sharpening to try to bring it back into focus. (2) The photo contains lots of well-defined edges (e.g., buildings, coins, cars, machinery, etc.).

All-purpose sharpening:

This is probably my all-around favorite sharpening setting (Amount 85%, Radius 1, Threshold 4), and I use this one most of the time. It's not a "knock-you-over-the-head" type of sharpening—maybe that's why I like it. It's subtle enough that you can apply it twice if your photo doesn't seem sharp enough the first time you run it, but once will usually do the trick.

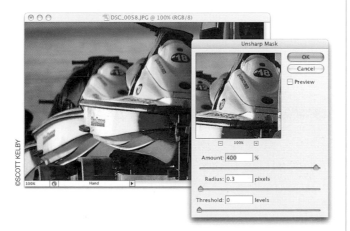

Web sharpening:

I use this setting (Amount 400%, Radius 0.3, Threshold 0) for Web graphics that look blurry. (When you drop the resolution from a high-res, 300-ppi photo down to 72 ppi for the Web, the photo often gets a bit blurry and soft.) If the effect seems too intense, try dropping the Amount to 200%. I also use this same setting (Amount 400%) on out-of-focus photos. It adds some noise, but I've seen it rescue photos that I would otherwise have thrown away.

Continued

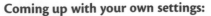

Coming up with your own settings:

If you want to experiment and come up with your own custom blend of sharpening, I'll give you some typical ranges for each adjustment so you can find your own sharpening "sweet spot."

Amount

Typical ranges run anywhere from 50% to 150%. This isn't a hard-and-fast rule—just a typical range for adjusting the Amount, when going below 50% won't have enough effect, and going above 150% might get you into sharpening trouble (depending on how you set the Radius and Threshold). You're fairly safe staying under 150%. (In the example here, I reset my Radius and Threshold to 1 and 4, respectively.)

Radius

Most of the time, you'll use just 1 pixel, but you can go as high as (get ready)— 2 pixels. You saw one setting I gave you earlier for extreme situations, where you can take the Radius as high as 4 pixels. I once heard tell of a man in Cincinnati who used 5, but I'm not sure I believe it. (Incidentally, Adobe allows you to raise the Radius amount to [get this] 250! If you ask me, anyone caught using 250 as their Radius setting should be incarcerated for a period not to exceed one year and a penalty not to exceed $2,500.)

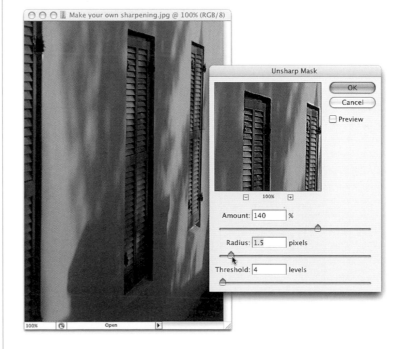

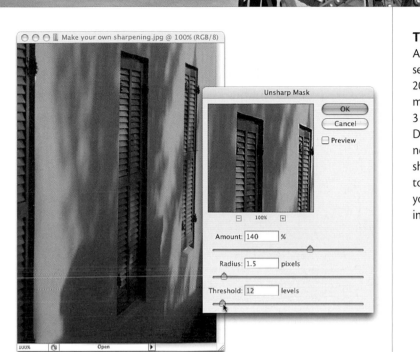

Threshold

A pretty safe range for the Threshold setting is anywhere from 3 to around 20 (3 being the most intense, 20 being much more subtle. I know, shouldn't 3 be more subtle and 20 more intense? Don't get me started). If you really need to increase the intensity of your sharpening, you can lower the Threshold to 0, but keep a good eye on what you're doing (watch for noise appearing in your photo).

Lab Color Sharpening

This sharpening technique is probably the most popular technique with professional photographers because it helps to avoid the color halos that appear when you add a lot of sharpening to a photo. And because it avoids those halos, it allows you to apply more sharpening than you normally could get away with.

Step One:
Open the RGB photo you want to sharpen using Lab sharpening. Go to the Channels palette (found under the Window menu), and you can see that your RGB photo is made up of three channels—Red, Green, and Blue. Combining the data on these three channels creates a full-color RGB image (and you can see that represented in the RGB thumbnail at the top of the palette).

Step Two:
Go under the Image menu, under Mode, and choose Lab Color. In the Channels palette, you'll see that although your photo still looks the same onscreen, the channels have changed. There are still three channels (besides your full-color composite channel), but now there's a Lightness channel (the luminosity and detail of the photo) with "a" and "b" channels, which hold the color data.

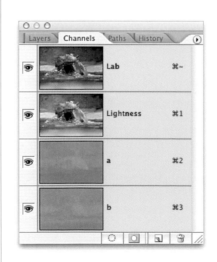

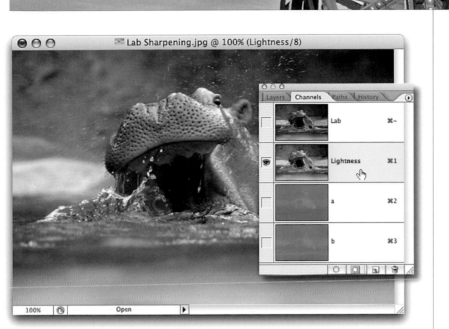

Step Three:

By switching to Lab Color, you've separated the detail (Lightness channel) from the color info (the a and b channels), so click on the Lightness channel to select it. Now you'll go to the Filter menu, choose Sharpen, and apply the Unsharp Mask filter to just this black-and-white Lightness channel, thereby avoiding the color halos, because you're not sharpening the color (pretty tricky, eh?). *Note:* If you need some settings for using Unsharp Mask, look in the previous tutorial called "Basic Sharpening"; however, I recommend these settings: Amount 85%, Radius 1 pixel, and Threshold 4.

Step Four:

Once you've sharpened the Lightness channel, you may want to apply the sharpening again by pressing the keyboard shortcut Command-F (PC: Control-F) for a crisper look. Then, go under the Image menu, under Mode, and choose RGB Color to switch your photo back to RGB. Now, should you apply this brand of sharpening to every digital camera photo you take? I would. In fact, I do, and since I perform this function quite often, I automate the process (as you'll see in the next step).

Continued

Step Five:

Open a new RGB photo, and let's do the whole Lab sharpening thing again, but this time before you start the process, go under the Window menu and choose Actions to bring up the Actions palette. The Actions palette is a "steps recorder" that records any set of repetitive steps and lets you instantly play them back (apply them to another photo) by simply pressing one button. You'll dig this.

Step Six:

From the Actions palette's flyout menu, choose New Action to bring up the New Action dialog. The Name field is automatically highlighted, so go ahead and give this new Action a name. (I named mine "Lab Sharpen." I know—how original!) Then, from the Function Key pop-up menu, choose the number of the Function key (F-key) on your keyboard that you want to assign to the action (this is the key you'll hit to make the action do its thing). I've assigned mine F12, but you can choose any open F-key that suits you (but everybody knows F12 is, in fact, the coolest of all F-keys— just ask anyone). You'll notice that the New Actions dialog has no OK button. Instead, there's a Record button, because once you exit this dialog, Photoshop CS2 starts recording your steps. So go ahead and click Record.

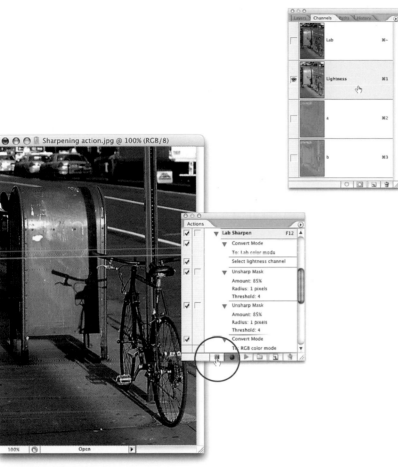

Step Seven:

With Photoshop recording every move you make, you can now convert your photo to Lab color, click on the Lightness channel, and apply your favorite Unsharp Mask setting to it (basically repeating Steps 2–4). If you generally like a second helping of sharpening, run the filter again (as I did in Step 4), and then switch back to RGB mode.

Step Eight:

Now, in the Actions palette, click on the Stop button at the bottom of the palette (it's the square button, first from the left). This stops the recording process. If you look in the Actions palette, you'll see all your steps recorded in the order you did them. Also, if you expand the right-facing triangle beside each step, you'll see more detail, including individual settings, for the steps it recorded.

Step Nine:

Now, open a new RGB photo and press the F-key you assigned to your action (you chose F12, right? I knew it!). Photoshop immediately applies the sharpening to the Lab channel for you (complete with conversions from Lab back to RGB) and does it all faster than you could ever do manually, because it takes place behind the scenes with no dialogs popping up.

©SCOTT KELBY

Continued

Step Ten:

Now that you have an action that will apply Lab sharpening, we're going to put this baby to work. You could open each photo, press F12 to sharpen it, and then close it; but there's a better way: Once you've written an action, Photoshop will let you apply that action to multiple photos—and Photoshop will totally automate the whole process. You can literally have it open every photo, apply your Lab sharpening, and then close every photo—all automatically. How cool is that? This is called Batch Processing, and here's how it works: Go under the File menu, under Automate, and choose Batch to bring up the Batch dialog (or you can choose Batch from the Tools menu's Photoshop submenu within the Adobe Bridge). At the top of the dialog under the Play section, choose your Lab Sharpen action from the Action pop-up menu.

Step Eleven:

In the Source section of the Batch dialog, you can tell Photoshop where to locate the photos that you want to Lab sharpen. We're doing a folder in this example, so choose Folder from the Source pop-up menu (or you can select photos batched from the Bridge, or you can import photos from another source, or choose images that are already open). Then, click on the Choose button. A standard Open-style dialog will appear in which you can navigate to your desired folder of photos. Now click on the Choose button (or OK button on a PC).

Step Twelve:

In the Destination section of the Batch dialog, you can tell Photoshop where you want to put these photos once the action has completed. If you choose Save and Close from the Destination pop-up menu, Photoshop will save the images in the same folder they're in. If you select Folder from the Destination pop-up menu, Photoshop will place your Lab-sharpened photos into a totally different folder. To do this, click on the Choose button in the Destination section, navigate to your target folder (or create a new one), and click Choose (or OK on a PC).

Step Thirteen:

You might also want to rename your photos. In short, here's how the file naming works: In the first field under the File Naming section, you type the basic name you want all the files to have. In the other fields, you can choose (from a pop-up menu) the automatic numbering scheme to use (adding a 1-digit number, 2-digit number, etc.) or what file extension (.jpg, .tiff, etc.). There's also a field where you can choose the starting serial number. At the bottom of the dialog, there's a row of checkboxes for choosing compatibility with other operating systems. I generally turn all of these on, because ya never know. When you're finally done in the Batch dialog, click OK and Photoshop will automatically Lab Sharpen and save all your photos for you. (*Note:* If you want detailed information on how Photoshop's automated file naming works, look in Chapter 1 for details.)

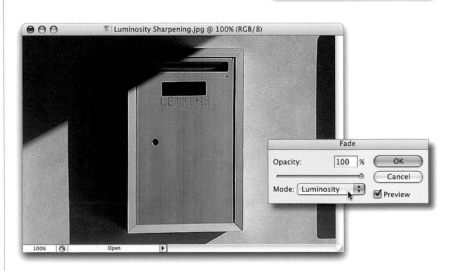

Luminosity Sharpening

This is another sharpening technique popular with professionals, and one that sparks debate among photographers who prefer it to the Lab Color sharpening technique. Both sharpen just the luminosity (rather than the color data), so theoretically they do the same thing, but you'll hear pros argue that one method produces better results than the other. That's why I'm including both in the book, so you can decide which you like best (and then argue about it with other photographers. This is what we do for fun).

Step One:

Open an RGB photo that needs some moderate sharpening. Go under the Filter menu, under Sharpen, and choose Unsharp Mask. Apply the filter directly to your RGB photo (don't switch to Lab Color, etc.). (*Note:* If you're looking for some sample settings for different types of images, look at the "Basic Sharpening" tutorial at the beginning of this chapter; however, I used Amount 225%, Radius 0.5 pixels, and Threshold 0.) When you have the image looking the way you want, click OK to apply the Unsharp Mask filter.

Step Two:

Go under the Edit menu and choose Fade Unsharp Mask. When the Fade dialog appears, change the Mode pop-up menu from Normal to Luminosity. When you click OK, the sharpening is applied only to the luminosity of the photo—not to the color data. This enables you to apply a higher amount of sharpening without getting unwanted halos that often appear.

A lot of people (myself included) are predicting that Photoshop CS2's new Smart Sharpen filter will actually replace Unsharp Mask as the sharpening filter of choice. Here's why: (1) It does a better job of avoiding those nasty color halos, so you can apply more sharpening without damaging your photo; (2) it lets you apply sharpening to just the highlights or just the shadows; (3) you can save and reuse your favorite settings; (4) it has a "More Accurate" feature that applies multiple iterations of sharpening; and (5) it's easier to use and has a larger preview.

Using CS2's Smart Sharpen Filter

Step One:
Open the photo you want to sharpen using this new Smart Sharpen filter. (By the way, although most of this chapter focuses on the Unsharp Mask filter, I only do that because it's the current industry standard. If you find you prefer the Smart Sharpen filter, from here on out, when I say to apply the Unsharp Mask filter, you can substitute the Smart Sharpen filter instead. Don't worry. I won't tell anybody.)

Step Two:
Go under the Filter menu, under Sharpen, and choose Smart Sharpen. In the resulting dialog, the filter is in Basic mode by default, so there are only two sliders: Amount (which controls the amount of sharpening—sorry, I had to explain that) and Radius, which determines how many pixels the sharpening will affect. I generally leave this setting at 1 pixel, but if a photo is visibly blurry, I'll pump it up to 2. (Very rarely do I ever try to rescue an image that's so blurry that I would have to use a 3- or 4-pixel setting.)

Continued

Step Three:

Below the Radius slider is the Remove pop-up menu, which lists the three types of blurs you can reduce using Smart Sharpen. Gaussian Blur (the default) applies a brand of sharpening that's pretty much like what you get using the regular Unsharp Mask filter (it uses a similar algorithm). Another Remove menu choice is Motion Blur, but unless you can determine the angle of blur that appears in your image, it's tough to get really good results with this one. So, which one do I recommend? The other choice—Lens Blur. It's better at detecting edges, so it creates less color halos than you'd get with the other choices, and overall I think it just gives you better sharpening for most images. The downside? Choosing Lens Blur makes the filter take a little longer to "do its thing."

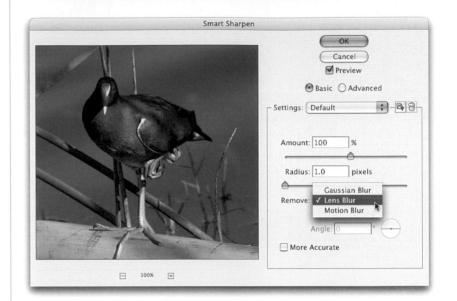

Step Four:

At the bottom of the dialog, there's a checkbox named "More Accurate." It gives you (according to Adobe) more accurate sharpening by applying multiple iterations of the sharpening. I leave More Accurate turned on nearly all the time. (After all, who wants "less accurate" sharpening?) *Note:* If you're working on a large file, the More Accurate option can cause the filter to process slower, so it's up to you if it's worth the wait.

Step Five:
I've found with the Smart Sharpen filter that I use a lower Amount setting than with the Unsharp Mask filter to get a similar amount of sharpening (as I did in this example), especially if I'm working with low-res images.

TIP: If you find yourself applying a setting such as this over and over again, you can save those settings by clicking on the floppy disk icon to the right of the Settings pop-up menu. (Why a floppy disk icon? I have no idea.) This brings up a dialog for you to name your saved settings, so name your settings and click OK. Now, the next time you're in the Smart Sharpen filter dialog and you want to instantly call up your saved settings, just choose your saved settings from the Settings pop-up menu.

Continued

Step Six:

Another advantage of using Smart Sharpen is that you can limit how much sharpening is applied to the Shadow and Highlight areas. You do this by first applying your regular sharpening, then click on the Advanced radio button. Two additional tabs will appear with controls for reducing the sharpening in just the Shadow or just the Highlight areas. When you tweak the settings in this Advanced section, you're really further adjusting the settings you chose in the Basic section. That's why in the Shadow and Highlight tabs, the top slider says "Fade Amount" rather than just "Amount." So, when you drag the Fade Amount slider to the right, you're really reducing the amount of sharpening already applied, rather than increasing it.

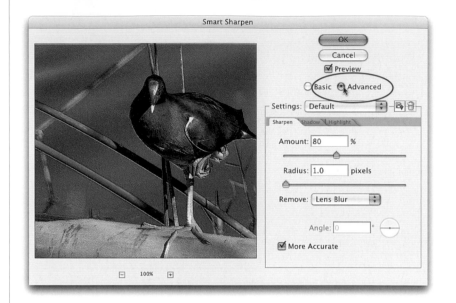

Step Seven:

Click on the Highlight tab to view those options. Now drag the Fade Amount slider to the right to reduce the amount of sharpening in the highlight areas of the photo (this can help reduce halos in the highlights). By the way, without increasing the amount of fade, you can't tweak the Tonal Width and Radius amounts. They only "kick in" when you increase the Fade Amount.

Step Eight:
The Shadow tab works the same way—click on it to make the shadow options visible, and then increase the Fade Amount to lessen the sharpening in the shadow areas. You can then tweak those settings using the Tonal Width and Radius sliders.

Before

After (using the Basic sharpening mode)

Edge-Sharpening Technique

This is a sharpening technique that doesn't use the Unsharp Mask filter, but still leaves you with a lot of control over the sharpening, even after the sharpening is applied. It's ideal to use when you have an image (with a lot of edges) that can hold a lot of sharpening or one that really needs it.

Step One:

Open a photo that needs edge sharpening. Duplicate the Background layer by pressing Command-J (PC: Control-J). The copy will be named Layer 1 in the Layers palette.

Step Two:

Go under the Filter menu, under Stylize, and choose Emboss. You're going to use this filter to accentuate the edges in the photo. You can leave the Angle and Amount settings at their defaults (135° and 100%), but for low-res images, you'll want to lower the Height setting to 2 pixels (for high-res images, you can raise it to 4 pixels). Click OK to apply the filter, and your photo will turn gray with neon-colored highlights along the edges. To remove those neon-colored edges, press Shift-Command-U (PC: Shift-Control-U) to desaturate the color from this layer.

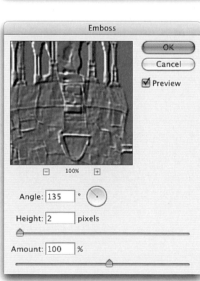

Step Three:
In the Layers palette, change the layer blend mode of this layer from Normal to Hard Light. This removes the gray color from the layer, but leaves the edges accentuated, making the entire photo appear much sharper.

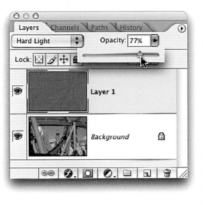

Step Four:
If the sharpening seems too intense, you can control the amount of the effect by simply lowering the Opacity of this layer in the Layers palette.

Before

After

Extreme Edge Sharpening

This edge-sharpening technique is great when you want to apply some intense sharpening to a particular object in your photo, but there are other areas that you won't want sharpened at all. This technique is different because you're going to actually enhance the edge areas yourself, by using some tricks to put a selection around only those edges that you want to sharpen.

Step One:

Open the RGB photo to which you want to apply edge sharpening (in this example, I want to sharpen the prominent fence, but I don't want to sharpen the soft background). Press Command-A (PC: Control-A) to put a selection around the entire photo, then press Command-C (PC: Control-C) to copy the photo into memory.

Step Two:

Go to the Channels palette (found under the Window menu) and click on the Create New Channel icon at the bottom of the palette. When the new channel appears, press Command-V (PC: Control-V) to paste a grayscale version of your photo into this new channel. Now, deselect by pressing Command-D (PC: Control-D).

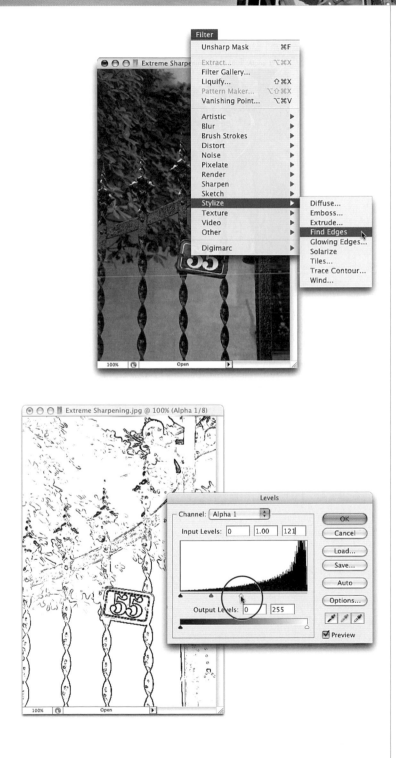

Step Three:
Go under the Filter menu, under Stylize, and choose Find Edges. There's no dialog, no settings to enter—the filter is simply applied and it accentuates any visible edges in your photo. The problem you'll likely encounter is that it accentuates too many edges, so you'll want to tweak things a bit so only the most defined edges remain visible.

Step Four:
Press Command-L (PC: Control-L) to bring up Levels. When the dialog appears, drag the top-right Input Levels slider (the highlights) to the left. As you do, you'll be "cleaning up" the excess lines—the lines that aren't very well defined and don't need to be sharpened. When the edges look cleaner, click OK. Defining the edge areas within your photo is very important for this method of sharpening to be effective, so we're going to further define those edges.

Continued

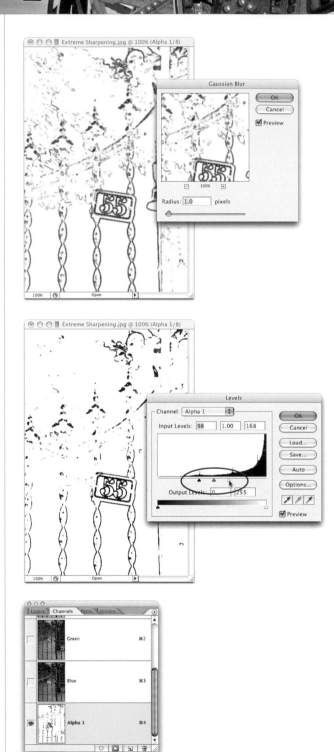

Step Five:

It's going to sound kind of counter-productive, but you're going to blur the existing lines (don't worry, you'll remove the blur in the next step). Go under the Filter menu, under Blur, and choose Gaussian Blur. Enter a Radius setting of 1 pixel and click OK to slightly blur your channel.

Step Six:

Press Command-L (PC: Control-L) to bring up the Levels dialog again. This time, you're going to use Levels to remove the blurring, and by doing so, further accentuate the edges. All you have to do is drag the Input Levels sliders at each end (the left shadow slider and the right highlight slider) toward the middle until the blurring is gone. You'll drag them until they almost meet the center midtones slider, or until the blurring is gone and the lines look much more defined. When it looks good to you, click OK.

Step Seven:

Go to the Channels palette, press-and-hold the Command key (PC: Control key), and click on the thumbnail for the Alpha 1 channel to load it as a selection.

Step Eight:
In the Channels palette, click on the RGB channel to see your full-color image. Your selection is loaded, but it has selected everything but the edges, so you'll need to go under the Select menu and choose Inverse to invert the selection (so that only the well-defined edges in the photo are selected). Before you apply your Unsharp Mask, press Command-H (PC: Control-H) to hide the selection border, so you can really see the results of your sharpening as you apply it. Now, go to the Filter menu, under Sharpen, and apply the Unsharp Mask filter. Move the Amount slider to the right, and when you do, only the selected edge areas will be affected, leaving the trees in the background virtually unsharpened. Press Command-D (PC: Control-D) to deselect, completing the sharpening.

Before   *After*

Advanced Sharpening for Portraits of Women

This is a more advanced technique for sharpening portraits of women that I learned (not surprisingly) from fashion photographer Kevin Ames. It does a great job of allowing you to create an overall feeling of sharpness, without emphasizing the texture of the skin. It takes a few extra steps, but the final effect is worth it.

Step One:
Open the portrait you want to sharpen without accentuating the skin texture. Duplicate the Background layer by pressing Command-J (PC: Control-J).

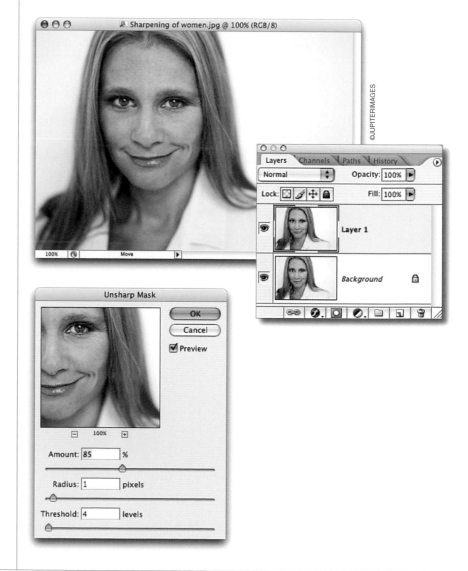

©JUPITERIMAGES

Step Two:
Go under the Filter menu, under Sharpen, and apply the Unsharp Mask filter to this layer. Use these settings: Amount 85%, Radius 1 pixel, and Threshold 4. Although you'll see the texture in the skin appear to be accentuated as a result of the sharpening, it's okay—in the next step we'll fix that.

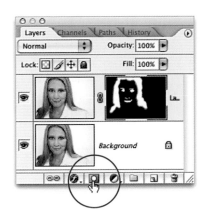

Step Three:

Press-and-hold the Option (PC: Alt) key and click on the Add Layer Mask icon at the bottom of the Layers palette. Holding the Option/Alt key fills the layer mask with black, hiding the Unsharp Mask filter you just applied. Press B to get the Brush tool, and in the Options Bar, click on the thumbnail to the right of the word "Brush" to choose a medium-sized, soft-edged brush in the Picker. Press the letter D to switch your Foreground color to white (if it isn't already white), and then begin to paint over the areas on her face where you want to apply detail (lips, eyes, eyelashes, eyebrows). Using the Brush tool, you're actually going to paint the sharpening back in, so avoid any skin areas (that's the whole point of sharpening using this method) and only paint over detail areas. You can also paint over hair and other areas outside the face that you want to sharpen.

Before

After

Exposure: 1/80s   Focal Length: 70mm   Aperture Value: f/4.4

Men at Work
how to show your work

This one was easy—the Australian band Men at Work just jumped into my head. Oh sure, I could've gone with The Beatles tune "We Can Work It Out," but it just didn't seem to fit as well. Although the Men at Work title does sound a little bit sexist (hey, take off the last three letters. Cha-ching!), it's still better than Michael Jackson's "Workin' Day and Night." Now, I struggled back and forth with the real name of this chapter. Should it be "How to Show Your Work" or "How to Present Your Work"? It's an important chapter, because when it comes to photography, presentation is everything these days. Incidentally, this chapter is based on one of my most popular sessions that I teach at the Photoshop World Conference & Expo (if you've never been to Photoshop World, check it out at photoshopworld.com). That's a blatant plug. Don't tell my editors, though—they hate it when you sneak in plugs (they might not mind if I sneak one in; they don't like it if *you* sneak one in). I'm not worried about them catching the plug themselves, as they don't bother to read these chapter intros. If they did, I'd be fired for wasting paper. You see, they have to pay for the paper. Well, sometimes they shoplift it from Office Depot, but occasionally they buy it just like everybody else, so they get kind of cranky when you write copy that doesn't directly relate to the tutorial at hand. They want everything to "make sense" and "support the technique." Also, they get all weird about a word or two being misspelled. Freaks.

Creating Photo-Grid Posters

After you've separated your photos into five-, four-, and three-star ratings in the Adobe Bridge, you pretty much know which ones are going to wind up in your portfolio and which will never see the light of day. Well, this is a great technique for giving some of those three-star photos a new life, by close-cropping them and arranging them on a grid to create a poster-style layout. Again, don't waste your best shots on this technique, but it's an ideal way to save the ones that "got away."

Step One:

In Photoshop, go under the File menu and choose New. In the resulting dialog, choose 8x10 from the Preset pop-up menu and click OK to create a blank 8x10" document (I'm using the default 300-ppi resolution here, but you can enter any resolution you want at this point).

Step Two:

Now, open nine of your three-star-rated photos from a recent shoot (technically, these should all be from the same location or of the same basic subject, like "trip to Bermuda" or "close-up shots of baby," etc.).

©SCOTT KELBY

Step Three:

Click back on your 8x10" document to make it active (if you can't see it to click on it, choose it from the bottom of the Window menu; it's likely named "Untitled 1"). Then, go under the View menu, under Show, and choose Grid (if you don't see the grid appear over your blank document, go back under the View menu and choose Extras). An alignment grid will appear over your blank document. This grid is just there to help you align things, so don't worry—it won't appear on your photo when you print it out.

Step Four:

Switch to the first photo you want to place on your grid (choose it from the bottom of the Window menu if needed). From a design standpoint, one of the key points to this technique is that all the photos appear perfectly square, so press M to get the Rectangular Marquee tool, press-and-hold the Shift key, and drag out a perfectly square selection (this will be your cropping border, so choose an area that you want to appear within your poster).

Continued

Step Five:

Press V to get the Move tool and drag-and-drop your photo onto your 8x10" grid document. Depending on the size of your original, when you drag it over, it may appear really large (or really small), so you'll need to scale it to fit on the grid with eight other photos (which you'll do in the next step).

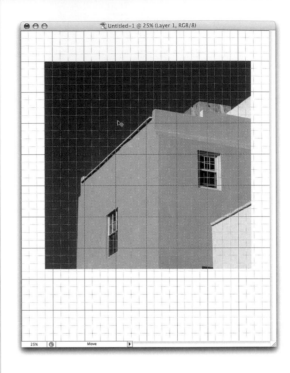

Step Six:

Press Command-T (PC: Control-T) to bring up Free Transform. Hold the Shift key, grab the bottom-right corner point and drag inward to scale your photo in size. Once you get it close to the size you see here, you'll need to move your cursor inside the Free Transform bounding box and position it so there are three grid squares to the left of the photo, four grid squares above it, and then ensure the image itself is eight squares wide. (*Note:* When dragging within the Free Transform bounding box, avoid clicking on the bounding box's center point.) When it's lined up and sized to fit, press Return (PC: Enter) to lock in your transformation. Now, if that seemed like a lot of "grid-square counting," don't worry—much of the rest of this resizing process is automated (as you'll see in a moment).

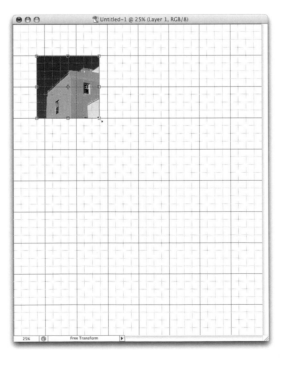

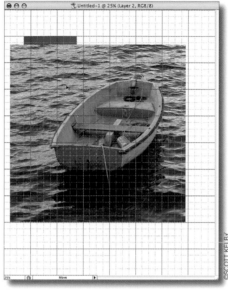

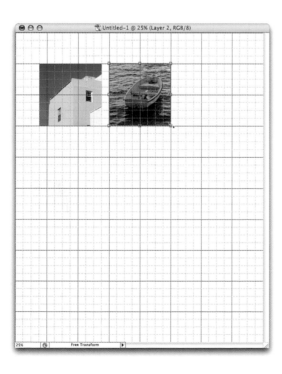

Step Seven:
Choose the second photo you want to appear on the grid from the Window menu. Again, switch to the Rectangular Marquee tool, press-and-hold the Shift key, and drag a perfectly square selection around the focal point of your image. Switch to the Move tool again, click within the selected area, and drag-and-drop it onto your grid document.

Step Eight:
Since you've already used Free Transform to scale the first photo, you can now take advantage of a Photoshop command called "Transform Again." Just press Shift-Command-T (PC: Shift-Control-T), and the exact same resizing that was applied to the previous photo will be applied to this one. Just press Return (PC: Enter) to lock in your transformation, and then use the Move tool to position this photo to the right of your first photo, with just one grid square separating them.

Continued

Step Nine:

Now all you have to do is repeat this process with the remaining seven photos: Open a photo, make a square selection over the best part of the photo, drag it onto your grid document, press the Transform Again keyboard shortcut, and then position the photo on the grid, leaving one space between photos and one grid space between vertical rows. *Note:* The Transform Again command can get rather lazy, so you may have to use Free Transform on another image to refresh the command's settings. Also, it sizes images based on their physical size, so if you drag in a smaller-sized image, the Transform Again command may adjust the image incorrectly—just use Free Transform (while holding the Shift key if needed) to adjust them accordingly.

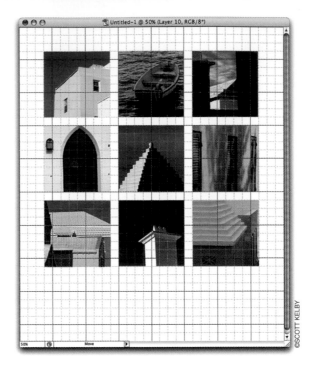

Step Ten:

Once you've got all nine photos placed on the grid, you don't need the grid anymore, so you can turn it off by going back under the View menu, under Show, and choose Grid. Now, to give it the full "poster" effect, you can add a title at the bottom (the font used here is Gil Sans Light). To complete the effect, I also added the date and a credit under the bottom corners of the grid using the font ITC Grimshaw Hand. Now, getting color photos to work well together in a layout like this can sometimes be a real challenge, but I've got a trick that will get around that if you want to take it a few steps further….

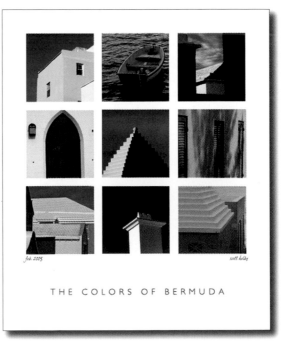

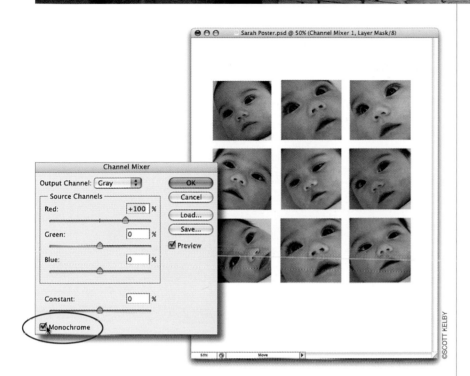

©SCOTT KELBY

Step Eleven:

Here's another example of the nine-photo grid technique, using close-up shots of my cute little niece, Sarah. Although the color is fairly similar in the images, the composition looks kind of flat overall because the colors are so neutral. To fix that, we're going to convert it to black and white to give it more of an artistic look. In the Layers palette, ensure the top layer is active, then choose Channel Mixer from the Create New Adjustment Layer pop-up menu at the bottom of the Layers palette. When the dialog appears, turn on the Monochrome checkbox.

Step Twelve:

When you click OK, all the photos appear in black and white, giving the composition that unifying little "something" that just makes it work. Although it works well here, you'll find it even more useful when trying to combine photos where the colors don't match up nicely. Just add that grayscale Channel Mixer adjustment layer, and suddenly everything just "works."

SARAH MCKENNA CRIST

Mothers's Day • April 9, 2004

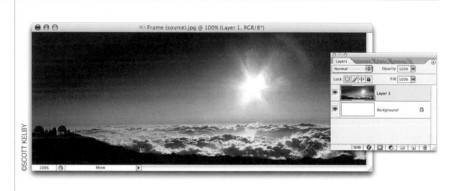

Creating a Digital Frame

This is a great technique for displaying your images in online galleries or in PDF presentations for clients. It gives your photos that finished "gallery" look, but without the time or costs involved in framing your prints and then shooting the framed work—it's totally a digital illusion created from scratch in Photoshop.

Step One:

Open the photo you want to frame digitally. Press D to set your Foreground/Background colors to their defaults. Press Command-A (PC: Control-A) to put a selection around your entire photo, and then press Shift-Command-J (PC: Shift-Control-J) to cut your photo from the Background layer and put it on its own separate layer (Layer 1).

Step Two:

Go under the Image menu and choose Canvas Size (or in CS2 you can now just press Option-Command-C [PC: Alt-Control-C]). When the dialog appears, turn on the Relative checkbox, set the Canvas Extension Color pop-up menu to White, and then enter 4 inches for both Width and Height. Click OK to add white space around your photo.

Step Three:

Press-and-hold the Command key (PC: Control key) and click on the Create a New Layer icon at the bottom of the Layers palette. By pressing this key, the new layer you're creating appears below your photo layer, rather than above it.

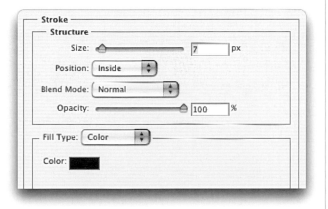

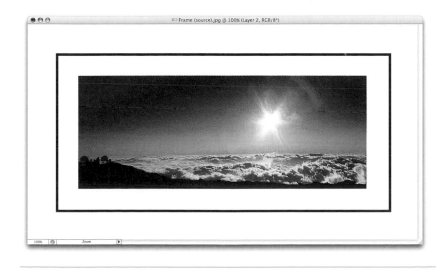

Step Four:

Press M to get the Rectangular Marquee tool. Draw a selection that's a couple of inches larger than your photo (this will be the edge of your frame, so you'll want to make this selection as big as you want your frame). Next, press the letter D and then X to set your Foreground color to white, and press Option-Delete (PC: Alt-Backspace) to fill this selection with white. Now press Command-D (PC: Control-D) to deselect.

Step Five:

At this point, there's nothing much to see (after all, you have a white box over a white background). To add the edge of your frame, choose Stroke from the Add a Layer Style pop-up menu at the bottom of the Layers palette. When the dialog appears, set your Size to 7 pixels, set the Position to Inside, and click on the Color swatch and choose black in the resulting Color Picker. (*Note:* If you're working with high-res, 300-ppi images, you'll need to increase your Size setting.)

Step Six:

When you click OK, a black border will appear around the outside edge of your white-filled rectangle. The reason the corners of the frame are so nice and sharp is because you chose Inside for your Position. If you left it at the default setting of Outside, the corners would've been rounded, and it wouldn't look like a real frame. Now, on to adding some depth….

Continued

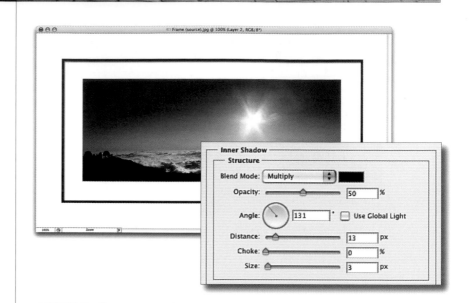

Step Seven:

Choose Inner Shadow from the Add a Layer Style pop-up menu. When the dialog appears, lower the Opacity to 50%, uncheck the Use Global Light checkbox, set the Angle to 131°, increase the Distance to 13 pixels, and lower the Size to 3 pixels, and then click OK. This adds a small shadow inside the left and top of your frame, which gives the illusion of depth by creating distance between the white top mat and the frame. (*Note:* Again, increase the Distance and Size settings for high-res, 300-ppi images.)

Step Eight:

Go back to the Layers palette and click on the Create a New Layer icon. You're going to create a thin bottom mat on this layer, so get the Rectangular Marquee tool again, but this time draw a selection that's just slightly larger than your image. Fill this selection with white by pressing Option-Delete (PC: Alt-Backspace), and then deselect by pressing Command-D (PC: Control-D).

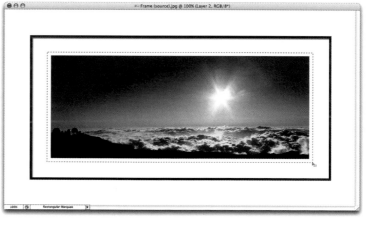

Step Nine:

Again, there's not much to see yet because you created a white box over a white background, but that'll change now as you choose Inner Glow from the Add a Layer Style pop-up menu. Change the Blend Mode pop-up menu to Normal, lower the Opacity to 20%, then click on the color swatch and change the glow color to black in the Color Picker.

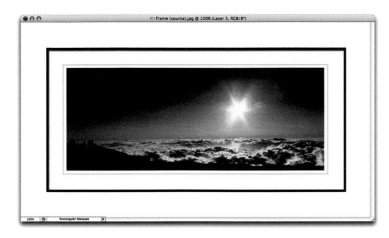

Step Ten:
When you click OK in the dialog, a soft shadow will appear along the edge of your inner frame, which makes it look like an inner mat. There's one last thing we need to do to add some depth, so let's add a drop shadow to the outer frame layer. In the Layers palette, click on the outer frame layer (the layer with the black stroke).

Step Eleven:
Choose Drop Shadow from the Add a Layer Style pop-up menu. Lower the Opacity to 60%, turn off the Use Global Light checkbox, increase the Size (which is the softness of the shadow) to 9 pixels, and then click OK. (*Note:* If you're working with high-res, 300-ppi images, increase the Size setting.)

Step Twelve:
This adds a soft shadow around the bottom and right side of the frame. Since your mats are white and your frame is on a white background, you may want to create some additional contrast between the background and your frame. In the example shown here, I clicked on the Background layer, clicked on the Foreground color swatch, chose a light gray in the Color Picker, and then filled it with the light gray by pressing Option-Delete (PC: Alt-Backspace). This added contrast between the background and the frame, which completes the effect.

Poster Presentation

This technique gives your work the layout of a professional poster, yet it's incredibly easy to do. In fact, once you learn how to do it, this is the perfect technique to turn into a Photoshop action. That way, anytime you want to give your image the poster look, you can do it at the press of a button.

Step One:

Open the photo you want to turn into a poster layout.

Step Two:

Go under the Image menu and choose Canvas Size (or press Option-Command-C [PC: Alt-Control-C]). When the dialog appears, turn on the Relative checkbox, enter 1 inch for both the Width and the Height fields, and choose White in the Canvas Extension Color pop-up menu.

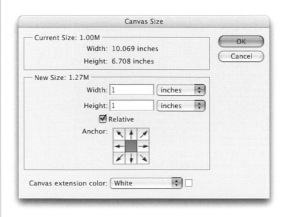

Step Three:

When you click OK, an inch of white canvas space will be added around your photo.

Step Four:

Now you're going to go back to the Canvas Size dialog, so press the keyboard shortcut again. Add another inch of white canvas but only to the bottom of your image. In the Canvas Size dialog, enter 1 inch in the Height field, and then in the Anchor grid, click on the top-center anchor (which makes the area you're adding appear below the current image).

Step Five:

Click OK and an additional inch of white canvas area is added below your photo.

Continued

Step Six:

In this extra inch of white space, you'll add some type. Press T to get the Type tool to add your type (i.e., the name of your studio, the name of the poster, whatever you'd like). I chose the font Gil Sans Light in all caps at a size of 14 points. The extra space between the letters adds an elegant look to the type. To do that, highlight your type with the Type tool, then go to the Character palette (found under the Window menu), and in the Tracking field enter 800. Now, to keep your type from overpowering the photo, go to the Layers palette and lower the Opacity of your Type layer to 60%.

Step Seven:

To center your text perfectly within your image area, click on the Background layer in the Layers palette, and then, pressing-and-holding the Shift key, click on the Type layer so both layers are selected. Press V to get the Move tool, and in the Options Bar, you'll see four sets of alignment icons. In the second set from the left, click on the Align Horizontal Centers icon to center your text beneath your image.

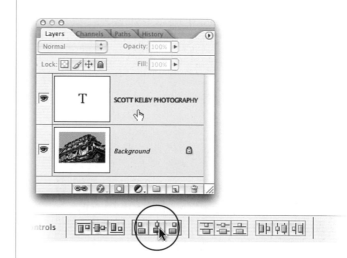

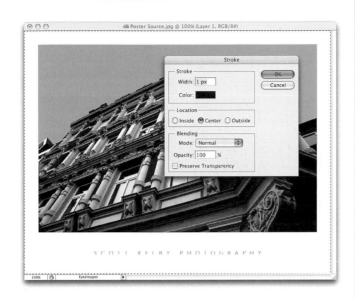

Step Eight:

Now, we'll add a thin outside border. Click on the Create a New Layer icon in the bottom of the Layers palette, and then press Command-A (PC: Control-A) to put a selection around your entire image area. Go under the Edit menu and choose Stroke. When the Stroke dialog appears, set black as your stroke Color, set the Width to 1 pixel, set the Location to Center, and click OK. Now you can press Command-D (PC: Control-D) to deselect.

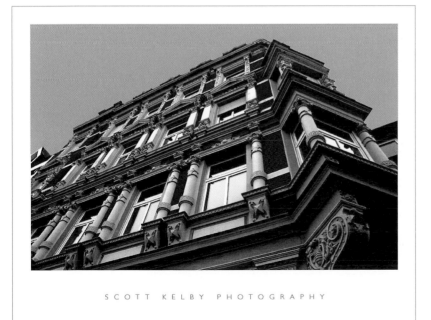

Step Nine:

To make the outside border thinner and less obtrusive, go to the Layers palette and lower the Opacity setting for this layer to around 30%, giving you the final poster layout shown here.

Creating Gallery Prints

This is basically an upscale version of the previous poster technique, but like photography in general—it's the little things—and in this case, some little things can make your regular poster look much more elegant. By the way, in this technique I have you convert your photo to black and white using Channel Mixer. You don't have to convert to black and white at all; but if you do, you can substitute one of the black-and-white conversion techniques from Chapter 7 (they're better).

Step One:

Open the photo you want to turn into a gallery-print poster. Press the letter D to set your Foreground/Background colors to their defaults, and then press Command-A (PC: Control-A) to put a selection around the entire photo. With your selection in place, press Shift-Command-J (PC: Shift-Control-J) to cut the photo from the Background layer and put it on its own separate layer.

Step Two:

You're going to add white canvas space around your photo (like you did in the previous tutorial, but this time you're going to add more space). So, go under the Image menu and choose Canvas Size (or press Option-Command-C [PC: Alt-Control-C]). Turn on the Relative checkbox, enter 3 inches for both Width and Height, choose White in the Canvas Extension Color pop-up menu, and click OK to add white space around your photo. Go back to the Canvas Size dialog once again, and then enter 1 inch for Height, click on the top-center square in the Anchor grid (so the space is only added below your photo), and click OK.

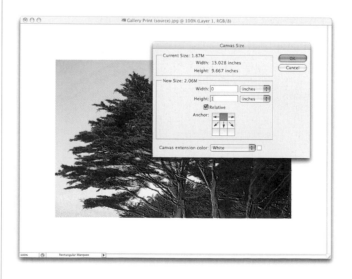

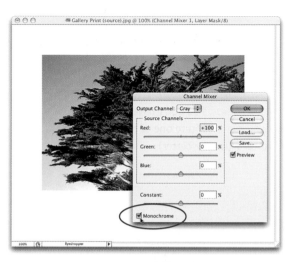

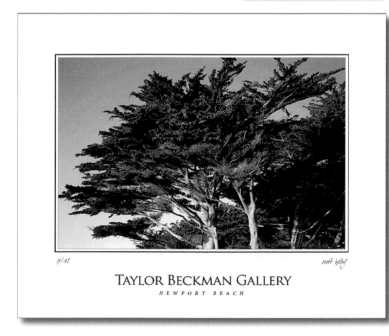

TAYLOR BECKMAN GALLERY

NEWPORT BEACH

Step Three:
To convert your color photo to black and white, choose Channel Mixer from the Create New Adjustment Layer pop-up menu at the bottom of the Layers palette. When the dialog appears, click on the Monochrome checkbox and click OK. In the Layers palette, click on the Create a New Layer icon to create a new layer above your Channel Mixer layer. Do *not* switch layers, but hold the Command (PC: Control) key and click directly on your photo layer's thumbnail (Layer 1) to put a selection around *just* your photo.

Step Four:
Go under the Edit menu and choose Stroke. For Width choose 1 pixel, for Location choose Center, for Color choose a light gray, and click OK to put a thin gray stroke around your photo. Press Command-D (PC: Control-D) to deselect. Now, press M to switch to the Rectangular Marquee tool and draw a selection that's slightly larger than your photo.

Step Five:
Press the letter D to set your Foreground color to black, and then go under the Edit menu and choose Stroke. Enter 2 pixels for Width, leave the Location set to Center, and click OK to add a thin black stroke around your selection. Press Command-D (PC: Control-D) to deselect. To finish off the project, add type using the Type tool (T). The gallery name is set in the font Trajan Pro, the location is set in Minion Pro, and the artist's name and numbering is set in Dear Joe Italic with the Opacity lowered to 50% in the Layers palette.

ADVANCED TECHNIQUES
FOR PROS
ONLY!

Medium Format Frames

This is a popular technique that brings a real "pro-photographer" style to showing your work, as it incorporates the look of a slide. I've seen this used everywhere from photographers' online galleries and postcards for studios, to prints in wedding albums. Although it's got a few steps, it's very easy to do.

Step One:

From the File menu, create a new document set at approximately 9x7" at 300 ppi. Create a new layer by clicking on the Create a New Layer icon at the bottom of the Layers palette. Press M to get the Rectangular Marquee tool, press-and-hold the Shift key, and draw a square selection in the center of the image area.

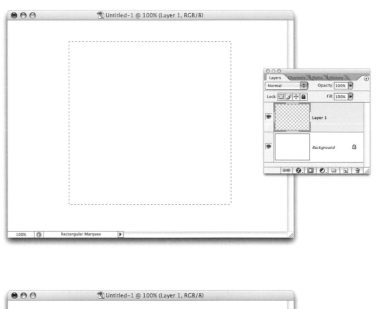

Step Two:

Press D to set your Foreground color to black, and then press Option-Delete (PC: Alt-Backspace) to fill your square selection with black. Deselect by pressing Command-D (PC: Control-D). Now, you'll need to make another square selection using the Rectangular Marquee tool inside the borders of your black square. Just for the sake of authenticity, I usually make this selection a little off-center, with a tiny bit more space on the left side than the right (which comes in handy later when you're adding text).

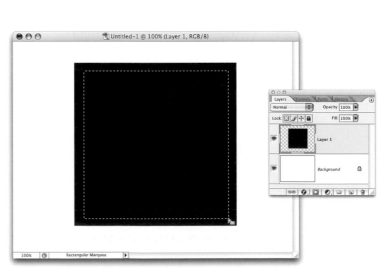

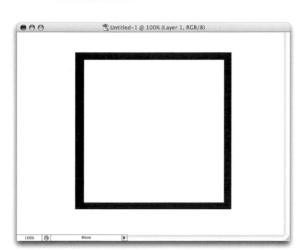

Step Three:

Press Delete (PC: Backspace) to knock a hole out of your black square, and then press Command-D (PC: Control-D) to deselect. To make it into a realistic-looking image slide, you're going to add text in the next step, but first, click on your Foreground color swatch and choose a dirty yellowish color in the Color Picker (I used R: 199, G: 185, B: 91).

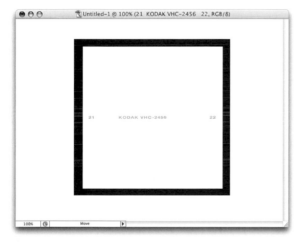

Step Four:

Press T to get the Type tool, and in the Font pop-up menu in the Options Bar, choose either Helvetica Bold or Arial Bold as your font, and then choose a small size in the Font Size pop-up menu (adjust your tracking if needed in the Character palette, found under the Window menu). Now, click near the left side of your frame and type any two-digit number as your frame number (I chose 21). Press the Spacebar eight or nine times, type "KODAK VHC-2456," and then hit the Spacebar another eight or nine times and type the sequential two-digit number (22 in this case). Press Enter to set your type.

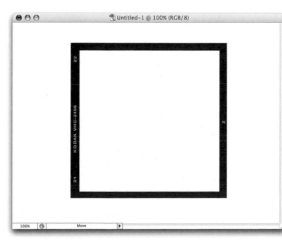

Step Five:

Go under the Edit menu, under Transform, and choose Rotate 90° CCW. This turns your type vertically. Press V to get the Move tool, and then position your type over the left side of the frame. Then, get the Type tool again, type the number "2," press Enter, rotate it 90° CCW, and use the Move tool again to position it on the right side of your frame.

Continued

Step Six:

Click on the Create a New Layer icon in the Layers palette. Press Shift-L until you have the Polygonal Lasso tool, and then draw a tiny triangle pointing upward on the right side of your frame below the number 2. Press Option-Delete (PC: Alt-Backspace) to fill it with your Foreground color, and then press Command-J (PC: Control-J) to duplicate it. Using the Move tool, drag this second triangle near the top-right side of your frame. Now, you're going to merge all those Type and triangle layers into just one layer—the frame layer. Hide the Background layer from view by clicking on its Eye icon, and then, in the Layers palette's flyout menu, choose Merge Visible.

Step Seven:

Open the photo you want to apply the effect to. Go back to your frame document, get the Move tool, and drag-and-drop your frame onto your photo. Press Command-T (PC: Control-T) to get Free Transform, press-and-hold the Shift key, and scale the frame down within the document (if needed, press Command-0 [zero] [PC: Control-0] to see your bounding box). Click inside your frame to drag it into position, and then move your cursor outside the bounding box to rotate the frame a little. Press Return (PC: Enter).

Step Eight:

Press Command-J (PC: Control-J) two more times to create the other two frames. Use Free Transform to reposition and rotate them slightly in opposite directions. Press Return (PC: Enter) to lock in your transformation. (*Note:* Make sure all three frames overlap a bit.)

©SCOTT KELBY

Step Nine:

Get the Polygonal Lasso tool again, click somewhere within one of the black frames, and begin tracing around the outside of your frames. You just click once, move your mouse to the next corner, click again, and the tool draws a straight line between the two points. You want to click around all the frame edges, avoiding the areas where the frames intersect in the center. Once you get all the way around to the first point where you started, you'll see a tiny circle appear in the bottom right-hand corner of your Polygonal Lasso cursor, letting you know "you've come full circle." Click on that first point, and the lines will join to create a selection (you will have all the frames and their contents selected). Now, go under the Select menu and choose Inverse, so you have everything *but* the frame selected.

Step Ten:

In the Layers palette, click on the Background layer, and then hit Delete (PC: Backspace) to remove all of the background photo surrounding your frames, which creates the impression that you've pieced together three medium format images to create this one image. Press Command-D (PC: Control-D) to deselect. See, I told you this was gonna be easy.

Showtime
showing your client

Okay, technically Showtime isn't a movie title, TV show, or song. It's not a band either. It's a TV network, but this is the last chapter, so I figured I'd slip one past the goalie, right? So riddle me this, Batman: What makes "Showing Your Client" different from "How to Show Your Work"? They're actually the exact same chapter, but I came up about 36 pages short on the promised page count for this book, and rather than anger my publisher, I just ran the same chapter twice with a different intro. Now, does that sound like something I would do? Okay, let me rephrase that. Did I do that? No. Actually, the "How to Show Your Work" chapter was about how to display your work like a pro. The finished product. Your portfolio. This chapter is about how to show your client what you've done for them in a professional format—whether it be in your office, via email, or on the Web—before it becomes your finished, billable work. Now, I know what you're thinking: "Scott, that makes sense. But this very sensible thing appears within a chapter intro at the very back of the book, mind you. What gives?" You know, there comes a point in every man's life when he has to shed his sophomoric ways, strip away the hyperbole, and get down to the essence of what he came here to do. Part of it is that I'm just tired. I spent a whole day stitchin' panos, and when I was working on the barfnoor, I couldn't get it to align properly with the fleepinflopper, so I went under the Slapumgoogoogonk menu, launched Baabaaleepdonk, and by then I was so tired I just went under the File menu and saved it. See, when it comes down to it, that's what it's really all about.

Watermarking and Adding Copyright Info

This two-part technique is particularly important if you're putting your proofs on the Web for client approval. In the first part of this technique, you'll add a see-through watermark, so you can post larger proofs without fear of the client downloading and printing them; and secondly, you'll embed your personal copyright info, so if your photos are used anywhere on the Web, your copyright info will go right along with the file.

Step One:
First, we'll tackle the see-through watermark: Open the image for watermarking. Choose the Custom Shape tool from the Toolbox (or just press Shift-U until you have the tool).

Step Two:
Once you have the Custom Shape tool, go up to the Options Bar and click on the thumbnail to the right of the word "Shape" to bring up the Custom Shape Picker. Choose the Copyright symbol, which is included in the default set of the Custom Shape library.

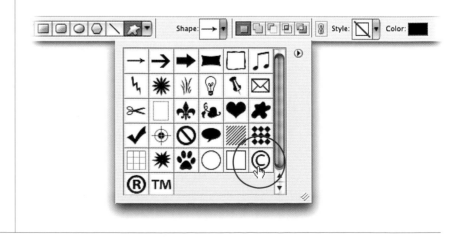

Step Three:
Create a new blank layer by clicking on the Create a New Layer icon at the bottom of the Layers palette. Press the letter D to set your Foreground color to black. Now, press-and-hold the Shift key and click-and-drag the Copyright symbol over your photo (use your own judgment as to size and placement, but the Shift key will ensure the symbol remains in proportion). *Note:* If you end up with a Shape layer or a path, look in the Options Bar to make sure that you have Fill Pixels selected (it's the third icon from the left in the first group of icons) before you draw the Copyright symbol.

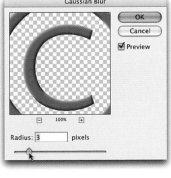

Step Four:
Go under the Filter menu, under Stylize, and choose Emboss. Apply the Emboss filter set at Angle 135°, Height 3 pixels, and Amount 100% (you can increase the Height setting to 5 pixels if you want the effect to be more pronounced), and then click OK.

Step Five:
To smooth the edges of the Copyright symbol, go to the Layers palette, turn on Lock Transparent Pixels (it's the first icon from the left in the Lock section at the top of the palette), and then go under Filter, under Blur, and add a 2- or 3-pixel Gaussian Blur.

Continued

Step Six:
Go to the Layers palette and change the layer blend mode of this Copyright symbol layer from Normal to Hard Light, which makes the watermark transparent.

Step Seven:
Press T to switch to the Type tool, click on your document where you want your studio name to appear, and then enter the name of your studio. (*Note:* Highlight your type with the Type tool and choose the Character palette from the Window menu to set your type if needed.) Once your type is set, press Enter.

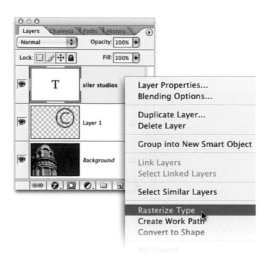

Step Eight:
You're going to apply the same filter to your type that you applied to the Copyright logo. But to apply a filter to type, you first have to convert your Type layer into a regular Photoshop image layer by Control-clicking (PC: Right-clicking) on the Type layer (in the Layers palette) and choosing Rasterize Type from the resulting contextual menu.

Step Nine:

Apply the Emboss filter to your raster-ized text layer (using the same settings you used in Step 4). Then, change the layer blend mode from Normal to Hard Light to make the text transparent, and lower the Opacity of both of these layers to around 40% so the watermark isn't overwhelming. That completes the first part of this two-part technique. The next part is embedding the copyright info into the file.

Step Ten:

To embed the copyright, go under the File menu and choose File Info to bring up the File Info dialog. This is where you enter information that you want embed-ded into the file itself. This embedding of info is supported by all Macintosh file formats (except GIF), but on Windows only the major file formats are supp-orted, such as TIFF, JPEG, EPS, PDF, and Photoshop's native PSD.

Step Eleven:

In the File Info dialog, change the Copyright Status pop-up menu to Copyrighted. In the Copyright Notice field, enter your personal copyright info, and then under Copyright Info URL, enter your full Web address. That way, when clients open your file in Photoshop, they can go to File Info, click on the Go To URL button, and then their Web browser will launch, taking them directly to your website. Click OK and the info is embedded into the file.

Continued

Step Twelve:

Once copyright info has been added to a file, Photoshop automatically puts a copyright symbol before the file's name, which appears in the photo's title bar. It also adds the symbol in the Info Bar at the bottom left of the document window. Now, flatten the image by choosing Flatten Image from the Layers palette's flyout menu.

Step Thirteen:

You can automate the entire process with the press of a button or two. Start by opening a new photo, then go to the Actions palette (found under the Window menu) and click on the Create New Action icon at the bottom of the palette. When the New Action dialog appears, name the action and choose the Function key (F-key) that you want to use to apply the action. (*Note:* I added the Command key to my F-key shortcut, but you can really choose any F-key with or without a modifying key.)

Step Fourteen:

Click on the Record button, and then repeat the whole process of adding the Copyright symbol and File Info, starting at Step 1 and ending at Step 11 (we stop at Step 11 because you may want to reposition your watermark on your other images; otherwise, go ahead and include Step 12 to flatten your image). As you do, Photoshop will record all your steps. (I know, you're thinking, "Shouldn't you have told me this in Step 1?" Probably, but it wouldn't be as much fun as telling you now.)

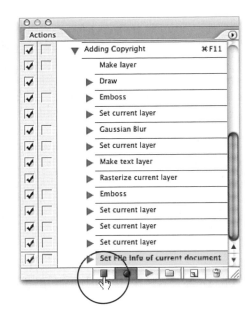

Step Fifteen:
When you're done, click on the Stop icon (it looks like a tiny square) at the bottom of the Actions palette. You can close the Actions palette now, because you can apply the watermark, studio name, and copyright info just by pressing the F-key shortcut you chose in the New Action dialog.

Step Sixteen:
If you want to apply this action to a whole folder full of photos, just go under the File menu, under Automate, and choose Batch to bring up the Batch dialog (or from the Adobe Bridge, go under Tools, under Photoshop, and choose Batch). This command lets you pick one action and automatically apply it to multiple photos. In the Play section (at the top), for Action, choose your action's name. Under Source, choose Folder from the pop-up menu and click on the Choose button, navigate to your folder full of photos, then under Destination choose Save and Close. This will apply the watermark, studio name, and copyright info to your images, and then save and close the documents. If you want to save them to a different folder, or rename them, choose Folder under the Destination section.

Creating Your Own Custom Copyright Brush

If you want a quick way to apply your copyright watermark to an image, check out this trick I learned from portrait photographer (and Photoshop guru) Todd Morrison. He showed me how to turn your copyright info into a brush, so you're only one click away from applying your mark to any photo. My thanks to Todd for letting me share his ingenious technique.

Step One:
Create a new document, and then click on the Create a New Layer icon at the bottom of the Layers palette to create a new blank layer. Press Shift-U until you get the Custom Shape tool (it's in the flyout menu of Shape tools right below the Type tool in the Toolbox). In the Options Bar (in the group of three icons), click on the third icon from the left (which creates your custom shape using pixels rather than paths). Then, press the Enter key to bring up the Custom Shape Picker onscreen, and choose the Copyright symbol from the default set of shapes. Press the letter D to set black as your Foreground color and drag out a copyright symbol in the center of your document.

Step Two:
Press T to switch to the Type tool, and then type your copyright info. The Type tool will create a Type layer above the copyright layer. (*Note:* When you set your type, go up to the Options Bar and make sure your justification is set to Center Text [click on the center of the three align icons]). Then, type a few spaces between the copyright date and the name of your studio. This enables you to put the large copyright symbol in the center of your type.

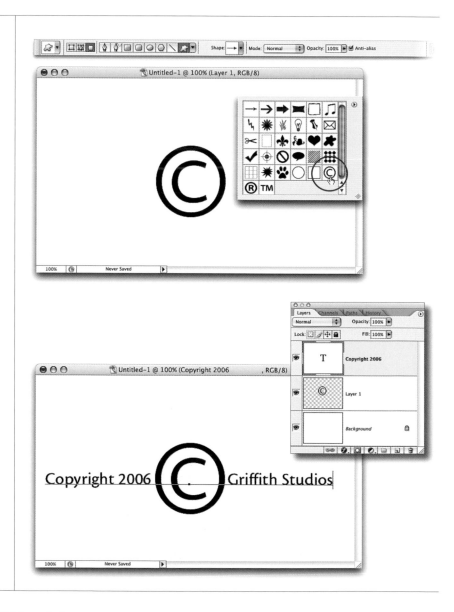

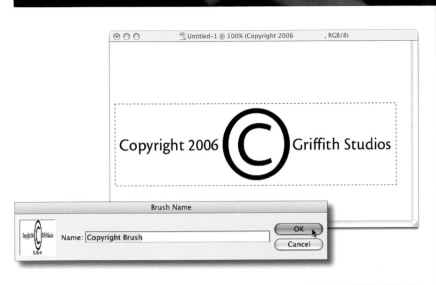

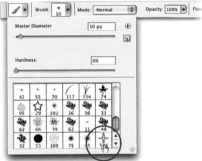

Step Three:
Press M to get the Rectangular Marquee tool, and click-and-drag a selection around your type and your copyright symbol. Then, go under the Edit menu and choose Define Brush Preset. When the Brush Name dialog appears, name your brush and click OK. This adds your type as a custom brush in your Brush Presets library. *Note:* Don't worry—the preview of the brush that appears in the Brush Name dialog may look squished, but the brush won't be.

Step Four:
Press B to get the Brush tool, and in the Options Bar, click on the thumbnail to the right of the word "Brush," and in the resulting Brush Picker, scroll to the bottom of the brushes. The last brush in the set is the custom copyright brush you just created.

Step Five:
Now that you've created your copyright brush, it's time to put it to use. Open a photo that you want to use as a client proof. Click on the Create a New Layer icon in the Layers palette, and then get the Brush tool, choose your copyright brush from the Brush Picker, and click once where you want your copyright info to appear. Lower the Opacity in the Layers palette to around 20% so you can see through the copyright. Two things to keep in mind: (1) If the photo is dark, try white as your Foreground color. (2) You can use the Brush palette's or Brush Picker's Master Diameter slider to change the size of your brush.

Embedding Digimarc Digital Copyright Info

ADVANCED TECHNIQUES **FOR PROS ONLY!**

Digimarc is a digital copyright watermarking system that is applied to your photos right within Photoshop using the Digimarc filter, which appears at the bottom of the Filter menu. (You always wondered what that filter was for, didn't you?) The system is pretty ingenious, and although it requires an annual subscription to the Digimarc service, you can do that online right from the filter's dialog. Here's how the process is done (and how to prepare your files for digital watermarking).

Step One:

Open a photo for digital watermarking. This watermark is applied directly to your photo, and as long as the photo isn't one big solid color (there are some variations in color and detail in the image), the digital watermark is imperceptible to the human eye (however, dogs can see it, no sweat, but they see it in black and white).

Step Two:

The embedding should take place right before you save the file, so do all your color correction, retouching, sharpening, and special effects before you get ready to embed the watermark. Also, this Digimarc embedding only works on a flattened photo, so if you have a layered document, duplicate it (by going under the Image menu and choosing Duplicate), and then flatten the duplicate, layered document by choosing Flatten Image from the Layers palette's flyout menu.

Step Three:
Go under the Filter menu, under Digimarc, and choose Embed Watermark. This brings up the Embed Watermark dialog. I'm assuming at this point you don't have a Digimarc account set up, so click on the Personalize button. If you do have a Digimarc account, click on the same button, and it will ask for your Digimarc ID and PIN. If not, you'll have a chance to get yours in the next dialog.

Step Four:
The Personalize Digimarc ID dialog is where you enter your Digimarc ID and PIN. If you don't have one, then click on the Get Info button. As long as you have an Internet connection, it will launch your Web browser and take you to Digimarc's website, where you can choose which subscription plan best suits your needs. At the time of this writing, the service started at $49 for a one-year basic subscription and went up from there based on how many photos you want to protect, and other options you might want to purchase. See their site for details.

Step Five:
At the Digimarc site, the registration process is very simple (pretty much like any other e-commerce site these days), and immediately after you hit the Submit button (with your payment info), you're presented with your Digimarc ID and PIN. Enter these in the Personalize Digimarc ID dialog. Needless to say, that's not my real Digimarc ID number and PIN. Or is it? Hmmmm.

Continued

Step Six:
Click OK to return to the Embed Watermark dialog. In the Image Information pop-up menu, leave the Copyright Year selected, and then enter the year the photo is copyrighted. For Image Attributes, select the information you'd like to appear on the file. You also need to choose a Target Output, which helps determine how strongly the watermark will be applied to your photo (for example, Web images that will go through compression will need more durability than photos saved in lossless formats like TIFF or PSD). Look under the Watermark Durability slider in the dialog to see the relationship between visibility and durability (kind of like the compression relationship in JPEG images, where higher quality means larger file sizes and lower quality means smaller file sizes).

Step Seven:
Click the Verify checkbox at the bottom left of the dialog if you want to check the strength of the watermark immediately after you apply it.

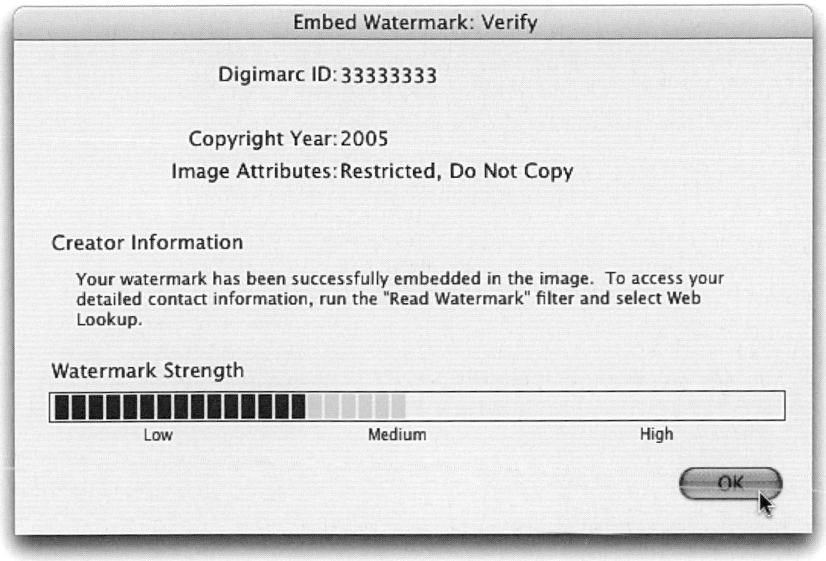

Embed Watermark: Verify

Digimarc ID: 33333333

Copyright Year: 2005

Image Attributes: Restricted, Do Not Copy

Creator Information

Your watermark has been successfully embedded in the image. To access your detailed contact information, run the "Read Watermark" filter and select Web Lookup.

Watermark Strength

| Low | Medium | High |

OK

Watermark Information

Digimarc ID: 33333333

Copyright Year: 2005

Image Attributes: Restricted, Do Not Copy

Creator Information

For information about the creator of this image, click the Web Lookup button to connect to Digimarc's MarcCentre® locator service.

Watermark Strength

| Low | Medium | High |

Web Lookup   OK

Step Eight:

When you click OK (with Verify turned on), Digimarc immediately verifies the strength of the watermark, and whether it was successful. Click OK in this dialog, and the process is complete—a copyright symbol appears next to your file's name when viewed in Photoshop. Also, your website URL, your contact info, and your copyright info are embedded into the file. Now it's okay to save the file. (*Note:* If you're saving as a JPEG, to preserve the watermark, it's recommended that you don't use a compression Quality lower than 4 in the JPEG Options dialog.)

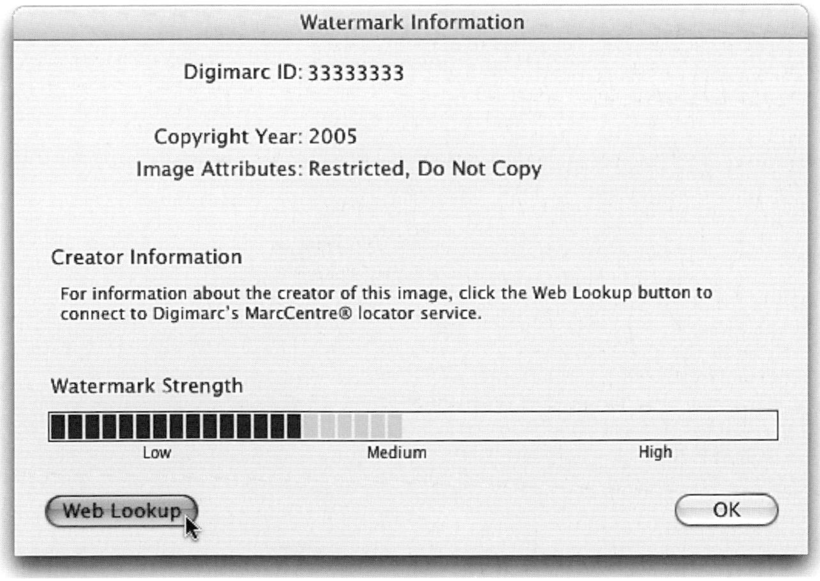

Step Nine:

Now that the info is embedded, if somebody opens your copyrighted photo in Photoshop, the watermark will be detected. You can check the watermark manually by going under the Filter menu, under Digimarc, and choosing Read Watermark. This brings up the Watermark Information dialog, which shows that the photo is copyrighted and whether the image is restricted. In the bottom left-hand corner of the dialog is a Web Lookup button, so if clients who downloaded your photo click on this button, it will launch their Web browser and take them directly to your copyright and contact info. Pretty slick stuff!

Showing a Client Your Work on Your Computer

Any time I'm showing clients my work onscreen, I use this technique because it quickly tucks Photoshop out of the way so the palettes, menus, etc., don't distract the clients. They can focus on just the image, and not on the software I'm using. Also, it does a nice job of presenting each photo in almost a museum setting—perfectly centered on a black background with no distractions.

Step One:
Open the photo you want to show to your client in Photoshop.

Step Two:
Press the letter F key twice and then press the Tab key. The first F centers your photo onscreen, surrounding it with gray canvas area. The second time you press F, the background changes to black, and Photoshop's menu bar is hidden. Then, when you press Tab, Photoshop hides the Toolbox, Options Bar, and any open palettes, presenting your photo onscreen.

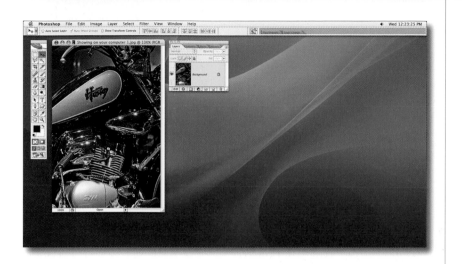

Step Three:
To return quickly to your normal display layout, just press F, then Tab. Now that you know these two shortcuts, you can use a variation of them to create a slide show right within Photoshop.

Step Four:
Go under the File menu and choose Open. In the Open dialog, click on the first new photo you want to open, press-and-hold the Command key (PC: Control key), and then click on all the other photos you want to open. *Note:* If the images that you want to open are contiguous, simply hold the Shift key and then click on the first and last image in the Open dialog to select them all.

Continued

Step Five:

Click the Open button and Photoshop will open all the photos, one right after the other. Once all the photos you want in your slide show are open, press-and-hold the Shift key and click on the Full Screen Mode icon at the bottom of the Toolbox (it's the third icon in the group of three icons along the bottom).

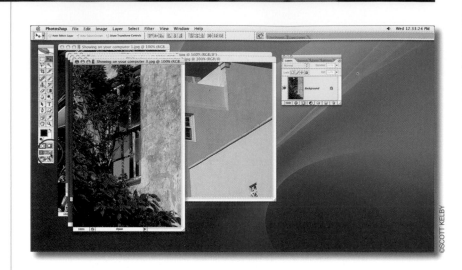

Step Six:

Shift-clicking the Full Screen Mode icon centers all the open photos and puts them on a black background (starting with the top photo in the stack), but your palettes and Options Bar will still be visible, so press the Tab key to hide them.

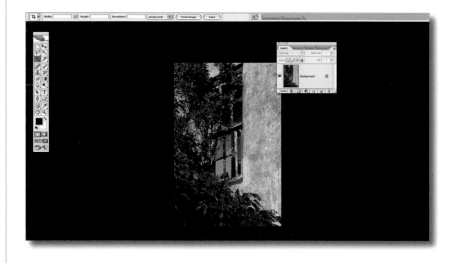

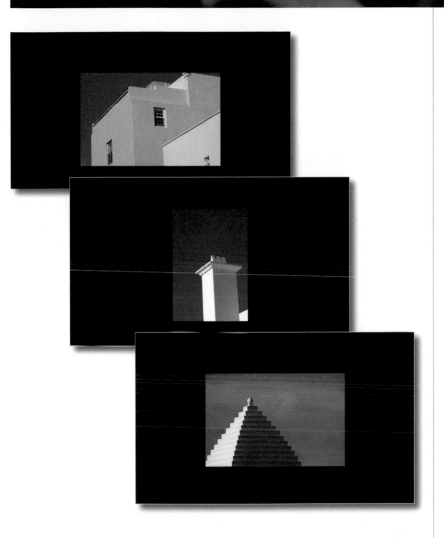

Step Seven:
Once your palettes are hidden, your slide show is ready. To view the next "slide," just press Control-Tab and the next photo in the stack will open. Because you held the Shift key when you switched to Full Screen Mode, the previous picture will automatically be hidden when the next photo appears. Continue through the stack by pressing Control-Tab. The slide show will automatically loop, so scroll through as many times as you'd like.

Step Eight:
When you're done with your slide show and want to return to the standard Photoshop interface, press the Tab key to make the Toolbox visible again, press-and-hold the Shift key, and then click on the Standard Screen Mode icon at the bottom of the Toolbox (it's the first icon in the group of three along the bottom).

Letting Your Clients Proof on the Web

Giving your clients the ability to proof online has many advantages, and that's probably why it's become so popular with professionals. Luckily, Photoshop has a built-in feature that not only automatically optimizes your photos for the Web, it actually builds a real HTML document for you, complete with small thumbnail images, links to large, full-size proofs, your e-mail contact info, and more. All you have to do is upload it to the Web, and give your client the Web address for your new site. Here's how to make your own:

Step One:
Create a new blank folder on your desktop (you will later store your Web gallery images here).

Step Two:
In the Adobe Bridge, navigate to a folder of images, and then Command-click (PC: Control-click) on all the photos you want to appear on your Web page (or Shift-click the first and last photos in your folder). Now, go under the Tools menu, under Photoshop, and choose Web Photo Gallery. *Note:* You can also get to the Web Photo Gallery from within Photoshop—it's under the File menu, under Automate.

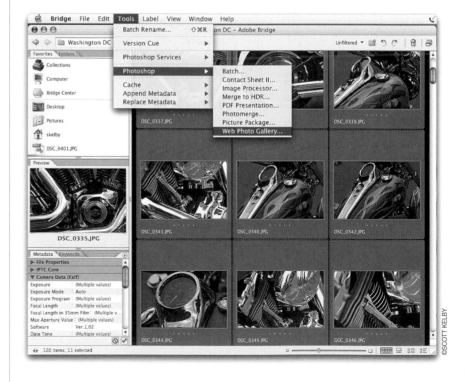

©SCOTT KELBY

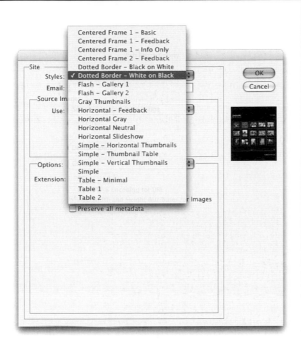

Step Three:

This brings up the Web Photo Gallery dialog. At the top is a Styles pop-up menu of presets that you can choose as different Web page layouts. As you choose a style, a thumbnail preview of each template appears in the far-right column of the dialog (below the Cancel button). In this example, I chose Dotted Border—White on Black, which creates a website with rows of thumbnails that display full size (on their own separate pages) when they're clicked on. Just below the Styles pop-up menu is a field for entering your e-mail address (which will appear prominently on your Web page) so your client can easily contact you with choices from the online proofs.

Step Four:

In the Source Images section of the Web Photo Gallery dialog, specify the location of the photos you want to put on the Web (the Bridge in this case), and then determine which folder these Web-optimized images will reside in for uploading (the folder you created in Step 1). When you click on the Destination button, a dialog appears that lets you navigate to the folder in which you want to save your images. Choose the folder you created in Step 1 and click Choose (or OK on a PC). *Note:* Although we're using images from the Bridge for this technique, you can also create a Web Photo Gallery using a folder of photos on your hard disk. To do this, choose Folder (instead of Selected Images from Bridge) under the Source Images section.

Continued

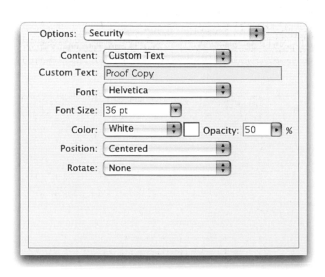

Step Five:
In the Options section of the dialog, choose Banner from the pop-up menu to enter the headlines and subheads for the site.

Step Six:
Go to the Options pop-up menu again and choose Large Images. Options will appear allowing you to choose the final size and quality of the full-size photos displayed on your Web page. You can also choose titles to appear under each photo in the Titles Use section. I recommend checking the Copyright checkbox, which will display your copyright info under each photo. *Note:* For this to work, you have to embed your copyright info in the photo first by going under the File menu, choosing File Info, and entering your copyright text in the Copyright categories.

Step Seven:
Change the Options pop-up menu to Security, and then in the Content pop-up menu choose Custom Text. This makes fields available where you can enter text that will appear right across your large-sized photos. This is where you might add things like "Proof Copy," "Not for Printing," or "Not for Duplication." You can also specify the Font Size, Font Color (I chose White), Opacity (which I lowered here), and Position in this section.

TIP: When you add custom text, here's an example of how the text will appear over your photo.

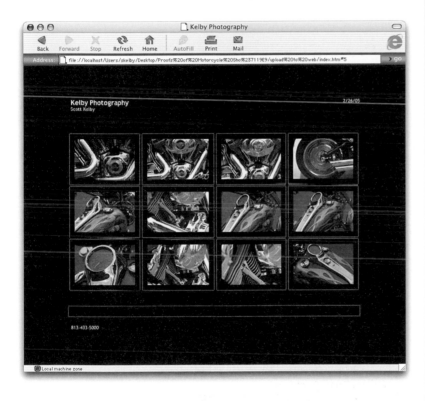

Step Eight:
Click OK and Photoshop will do its thing—resizing the photos, adding custom text, making thumbnails, etc. Then it will automatically launch your Web browser and display the HTML Web page it created for you. If you click on any of the thumbnails, it will take you to a page with a larger version of that photo, and there you'll find buttons to move to the next photo, previous photo, and back to the home page (which is shown here). Your contact info appears at the bottom, and if you've included an email address, a live email link will be included as well. *Note:* In the example shown here, I made the thumbnails larger—125 pixels to be exact—by choosing Thumbnails in the Options pop-up menu.

Step Nine:
If you look in that folder you created earlier, you'll find that Photoshop automatically created all the files and folders you'll need to put your Web Photo Gallery live on the Web, including your home page (index.htm). *Note:* If your browser didn't launch automatically in the previous step, open this index document using your Web browser to see your gallery.

Getting One 5x7", Two 2.5x3.5", and Four Wallet Size on One Print

When it's time to deliver final prints to your client, you can save a lot of time and money by creating a "Picture Package," which lets you gang-print common final sizes together on one sheet. Luckily, Photoshop does all the work for you. All you have to do is open the photo you want ganged and then Photoshop will take it from there, except the manual cutting of the final print, which is actually beyond Photoshop's capabilities. So far.

Step One:

Open the photo you want to appear in a variety of sizes on one page, and then go under the File menu, under Automate, and choose Picture Package. (In Photoshop CS2, you can also choose Picture Package from the Photoshop submenu, under Tools, from right within the Adobe Bridge.) At the top of the dialog, the Source Images section is where you choose your source photo. By default, if you have a photo open, Photoshop assumes that's the one you want to use (your Frontmost Document), but you can choose from the Use pop-up menu to pick photos in a folder or an individual file on your drive. By default, Picture Package chooses an 8x10" page size for you, but you can also choose either a 10x16" or 11x17" page size.

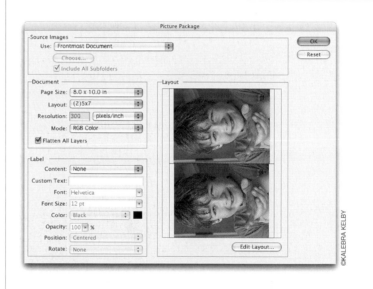

Step Two:

You choose the sizes and layout for your Picture Package from the Layout pop-up menu. In this example, I chose (1) 5x7 (2) 2.5x3.5 (4) 2x2.5, but you can choose any combination you like. When you choose a layout, a large preview of that layout appears in the right column of the dialog.

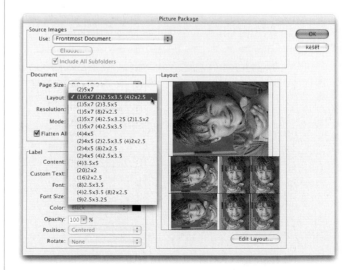

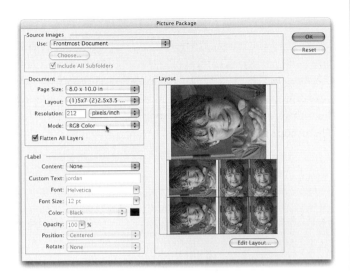

Step Three:

You can also choose the final resolution output in the Resolution field (which I lowered to 212 ppi here, because you don't really need a high resolution when you're not printing to a commercial press). Then, you can pick the color mode you'd like for your final output (in this case, I chose RGB in the Mode pop-up menu because I'll be printing to a color inkjet printer). The bottom-left section of the dialog is for labeling your photos, but be forewarned— these labels appear printed right across your photos, so use them only if you're creating client proof sheets—not the final prints. *Note:* Like the Web Photo Gallery, with the exception of adding your own custom text, this information is pulled from embedded info you enter in the File Info dialog, found under the File menu.

Step Four:

Click OK and Photoshop automatically resizes, rotates, and compiles your photos into one document. The one thing many photographers have complained about is that Picture Package doesn't offer you a way to add a white border around each photo in the package, but we've got a workaround for that, so close this document without saving it.

Step Five:

To have a white border appear around your photos in Picture Package, you have to first add that space manually. Start by pressing the letter D to set your Background color to white, and with your photo still open, go under the Image menu and choose Canvas Size (or press Option-Command-C [PC: Alt-Control-C]). Make sure the Relative checkbox is selected and enter the amount of white border you'd like in the Width and Height fields (I used a quarter of an inch).

Continued

Step Six:

When you click OK in the Canvas Size dialog, a white border will appear around your photo. Now you're ready to go under the File menu, under Automate, and choose Picture Package.

Step Seven:

Your previous settings should still be in place in the Picture Package dialog, so just click OK. Here's how your final Picture Package output will look, with a border added around each photo (compare it with the Picture Package output in Step 4 with no border). Remember, although the final print sizes will be correct (a 5x7" will still measure 5x7" including the border), adding this white border does make the photo itself a little bit smaller in order to compensate.

Step Eight:

Another feature of Picture Package is that you can use more than one photo. For example, to change one of the 2.5x3.5" prints to a different photo (while keeping the rest intact), just click on the preview of the image that you want to change in the Layout section.

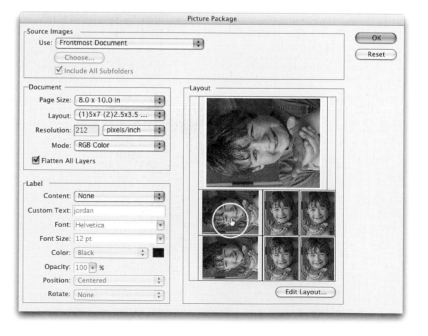

Step Nine:
When you click on this photo, a dialog will appear prompting you to Select an Image File. Navigate to the photo you want to appear at this size and location on your print sheet.

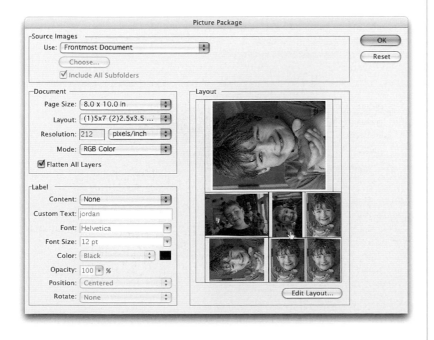

Step Ten:
Click on the Open button and that photo will appear within your Picture Package in the dialog's Layout section. You can replace any other photo (or all the photos) using the same method. When the Picture Package looks the way you want, click OK to create your document, and then print it out from the File menu.

Creating Your Own Custom Picture Package Layouts

As cool as Picture Package is, I don't think there's a Photoshop user alive who hasn't used it and thought, "This is cool, I just wish there was a layout that had...." In other words, although most of the popular layout choices are already there as presets, the one you really want isn't there, because that's just the way life works. Although technically you could edit the text file that controlled these presets back in Photoshop 7, it was a tricky, tedious task. Not so in Photoshop CS2, thanks to a clever visual layout editor.

Step One:

Open a photo (it doesn't matter which one; you're just using it as a placeholder to build your template), and then go under the File menu, under Automate, and choose Picture Package. (*Note:* You can also access Picture Package from directly within the Adobe Bridge by choosing Tools and going under the Photoshop submenu.) When the Picture Package dialog opens, click on the Edit Layout button (located in the bottom-right corner of the Layout section).

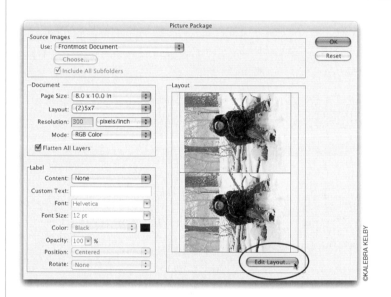

Step Two:

When the Picture Package Edit Layout dialog opens, go to the Layout section in the top-left corner and give your new custom layout a name (this name will later appear in the pop-up menu of preset layouts within the Picture Package dialog). Choose your page size and your desired ruler units from this Layout section.

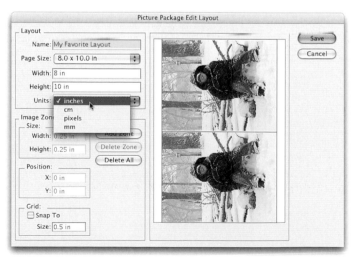

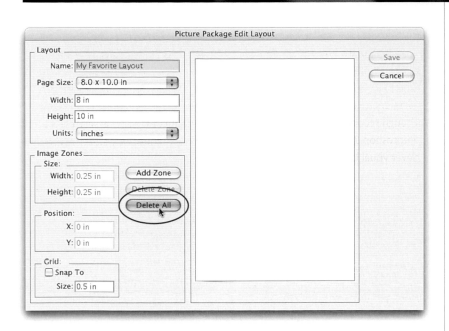

Step Three:

You'll probably find it easier to create your custom layout if you start from scratch (unless the layout you're creating is very similar to an existing layout, in which case, choose that layout before you enter the Edit Layout mode). To start from scratch, click the Delete All button to remove all the existing photo thumbnails from the preview window. (*Note:* Adobe calls these areas "Zones," so we might as well get used to calling them that too so we sound cool at Photoshop parties.)

Step Four:

Click the Add Zone button to add your first Zone. A bounding box appears around your photo, so you can resize your Zone by dragging the adjustment handles that appear on the corners and sides of the bounding box. To move the Zone around within the preview area, just click-and-drag inside the bounding box.

Continued

Step Five:

Since the idea behind Picture Package is "multiple copies of the same image on one page," it's easy to create duplicate Zones. Just Option-click (PC: Alt-click) within a Zone's bounding box and a contextual menu appears, where you can choose to duplicate the Zone, delete the current Zone, or create a duplicate of a Zone in one of the preset sizes. Choosing one of these sizes from the contextual menu doesn't affect the current Zone; it makes a duplicate in the size you choose.

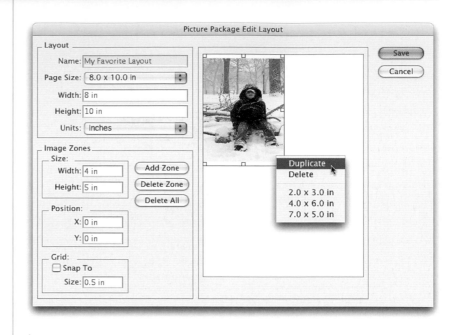

TIP: If you've been looking in the dialog for a button called "Make Horizontal" or "Flip on Side," forget it—those are too descriptive, and if Adobe named buttons like that, you'd easily figure it out, and then where would we be? Instead, when you want to change the orientation of a photo from portrait to landscape, just click on a corner point and drag the box until it's wider than it is tall (or vice versa for landscape-to-portrait images). When you do this, the Layout Editor will automatically flip your photo on its side. It sounds clunky, but try it once and you'll see it's really not.

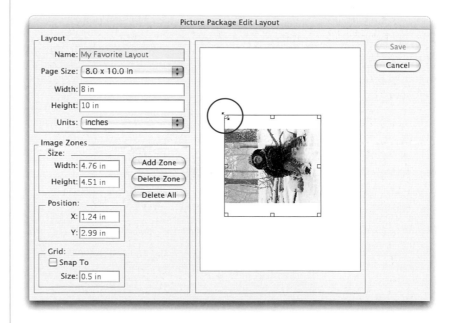

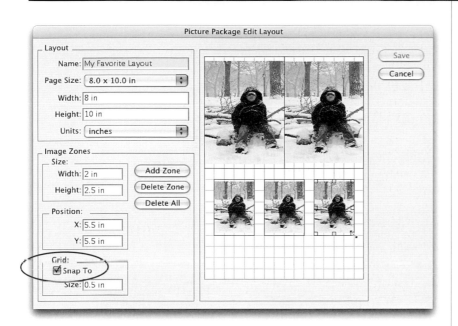

ANOTHER TIP: Another thing you might find helpful when creating your layout is to turn on a placement grid. You do this at the bottom of the Image Zones section of the dialog (in the bottom-left corner) by turning on the Snap To option. This also makes your Zones snap to the grid, which makes precise positioning much easier.

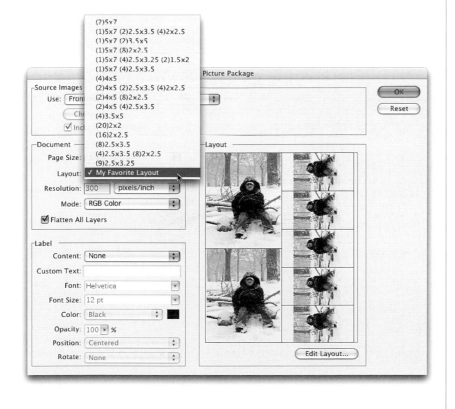

Step Six:

When you click OK, a standard Save-style dialog will appear, asking you to name your new layout. (This is just the name of the file on your hard drive, not the name that will appear in the Layout pop-up menu within Picture Package, so just give it a name that you'll recognize if you decide to delete this layout one day.) Click Save, and your newly named layout will now appear in the Layout pop-up menu of the Picture Package dialog, where you can access it anytime from here on out.

How to Email Photos

Believe it or not, this is one of those "most-asked questions," and I guess it's because there are no official guidelines for emailing photos. Perhaps there should be, because there are photographers who routinely send me high-res photos that either (a) get bounced back to them because of size restrictions, (b) take all day to download, or (c) never get here at all because "there are no official guidelines on how to email photos." In the absence of such rules, consider these the "official unofficial rules."

Step One:

Open the photo that you want to email. Before you go any further, you have some decisions to make based on whom you're sending the photo to. If you're sending it to friends and family, you want to make sure the file downloads fast, and (this is important) can be viewed within their email window. I run into people daily (clients) who have no idea how to download an attachment from an email. If it doesn't show up in their email window, they're stuck, and even if they could download it, they don't have a program that will open the file. So the goal: Make it fit in their email browser.

Step Two:

Go under the Image menu and choose Image Size (or in CS2, press Option-Command-I [PC: Alt-Control-I]). To play it safe, enter a resolution of 72 ppi and a physical dimension no wider than 8" and no higher than 5" (but the height isn't the big concern, it's the width, so make sure you stay within the 8" width).
By limiting your emailed photo to this size, you're ensuring that friends and family will be able to download it quickly, and it will fit comfortably within their email window.

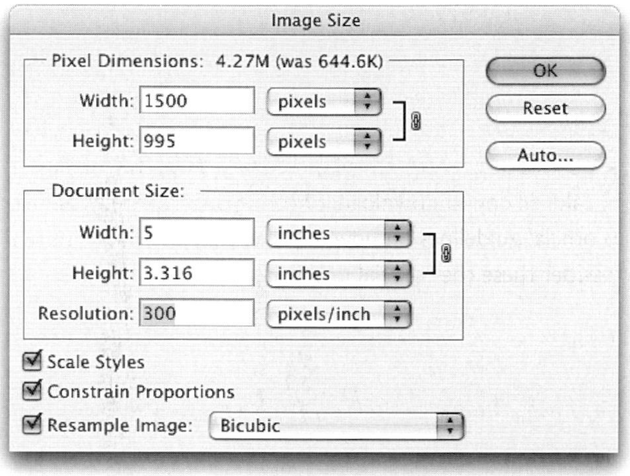

Image Size

Pixel Dimensions: 4.27M (was 644.6K)

Width: 1500 pixels

Height: 995 pixels

Document Size:

Width: 5 inches

Height: 3.316 inches

Resolution: 300 pixels/inch

☑ Scale Styles
☑ Constrain Proportions
☑ Resample Image: Bicubic

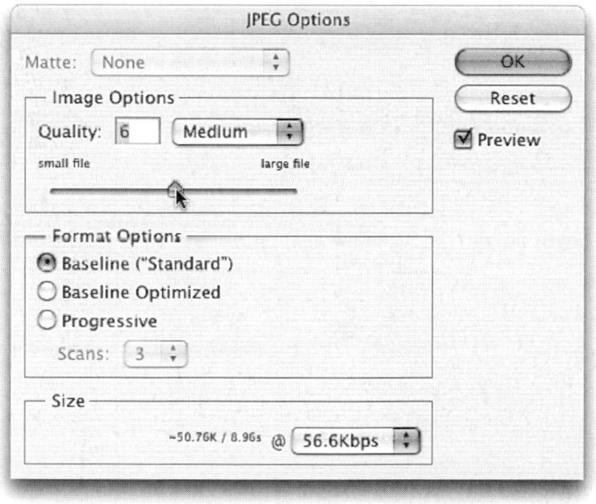

OK
Reset
Auto...

JPEG Options

Matte: None

Image Options

Quality: 6 Medium

small file   large file

Format Options
⦿ Baseline ("Standard")
○ Baseline Optimized
○ Progressive

Scans: 3

Size

~50.76K / 8.96s @ 56.6Kbps

OK
Reset
☑ Preview

5x7 photo @ 300 Resolution
Saved as a JPEG with 12 Quality
= 2.2MB (download time: nearly 7 minutes)

5x7 photo @ 150 Resolution
Saved as a JPEG with 12 Quality
= 656K (download time: Less than 2 minutes)

5x7 photo @ 300 Resolution
Saved as a JPEG with 6 Quality
= 253K (download time: Less than 1 minute)

5x7 photo @ 150 Resolution
Saved as a JPEG with 6 Quality
= 100K (download time: 18 seconds)

Step Three:
If you're sending this to a client who does know how to download the file and print it, you'll need a bit more resolution (at least 150 ppi and as much as 300 ppi, depending on how picky you are), but the photo's physical dimensions are no longer a concern because the client will be downloading and printing out the file, rather than just viewing it onscreen in their email program (where 72 ppi is enough resolution).

Step Four:
As a general rule, JPEG is the best file format for sending photos by email. To save the file as a JPEG, go under the Edit menu and choose Save As. In the Save As dialog, choose JPEG in the Format pop-up menu, and then click Save. This brings up the JPEG Options dialog. This format compresses the file size, while maintaining a reasonable amount of quality. How much quality? That's up to you, because you choose the Quality setting in the JPEG Options dialog. Just remember the golden rule: The higher the quality, the larger the file size, and the longer it will take your client to download it.

Step Five:
Your goal is to email your client a photo that is small in file size (so it downloads quickly), yet still looks as good as possible. (Remember, the faster the download, the lower the quality, so you have to be a little realistic and flexible with this.) The chart shown here gives you a breakdown of how large the file size and download time would be for a 5x7" saved with different resolutions and different amounts of JPEG compression. It's hard to beat that last one—with an 18-second download on a standard dial-up modem.

Sending a Portfolio Presentation to a Client

In Photoshop CS2, there's a feature that takes a folder full of images, creates a slide show (complete with transitions), and compresses it into PDF format so you can email it easily to a client for proofing. This is perfect for showing your portfolio to clients, sending clients proofs of wedding shots or portrait sittings, and any of a dozen other uses, none of which I can happen to think of right at this particular moment, but I'm sure later today, when I'm at the mall or driving to the office, they'll come to me.

Step One:
Open the photos you want to use in your PDF presentation (you actually have the choice of using photos you already have open in Photoshop or choosing a folder, but for this example, we'll start by simply opening a few photos).

Step Two:
There are two ways to access PDF Presentation: (1) Go under Photoshop's File menu, under Automate, and choose PDF Presentation (as I chose here), or (2) choose PDF Presentation from within the Adobe Bridge by going under the Tools menu, under Photoshop, and choosing PDF Presentation.

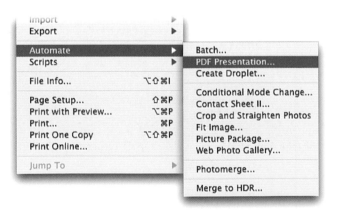

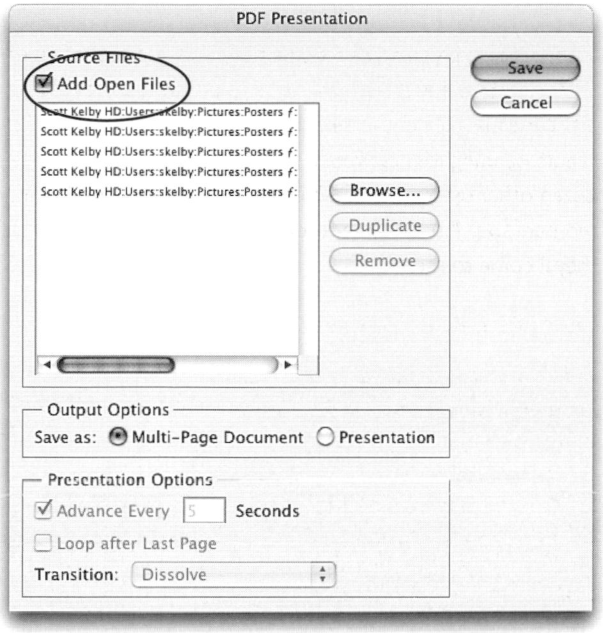

Step Three:

This brings up the PDF Presentation dialog. To create a presentation using the photos you already have open in Photoshop, click on the Add Open Files checkbox at the top of the dialog, and a list of your open files will appear in the window by default. If you have a photo open that you don't want in your presentation, just click on the photo (in the list) and then click the Remove button (you can also add an image by clicking on the Browse button).

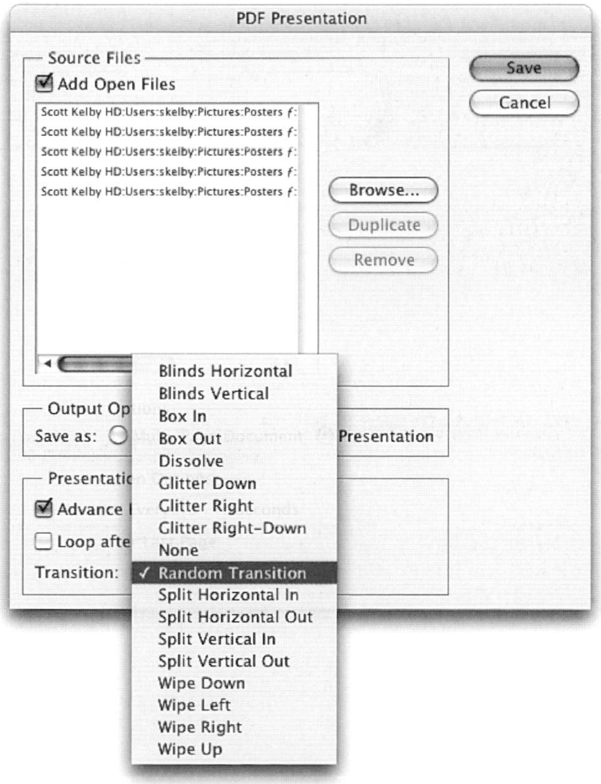

Step Four:

In the Output Options section of the dialog, click on the Presentation radio button. Under the Presentation Options section of the dialog is one of the coolest things about the PDF Presentation: You can choose a transition between slides, and they've got a pretty decent selection. A good way to find out which ones you like best is to create a test presentation and choose Random Transition from the Transition pop-up menu. That way, once you take a look at your test presentation, you'll quickly know which ones fit your style. In this Options section, you can also choose how many seconds you want each image to appear onscreen before advancing to the next image, and you can choose whether you want the presentation to loop (repeat) when it reaches the end.

Continued

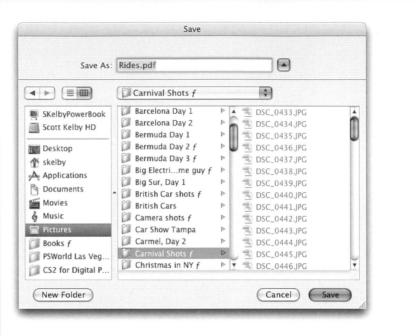

Step Five:
When you click the Save button, a standard Save dialog appears, where you need to name your file. Now, you'd think this is where the story ends, but actually clicking the Save button here brings up another dialog.

Step Six:
When the Save Adobe PDF dialog appears, from the Adobe PDF Preset pop-up menu, choose Smallest File Size (since you're sending these to a client via email, you probably want to keep your file size small so it transfers quickly, and so the email doesn't bounce back because your attachment is too large). Also, I would turn on the View PDF After Saving checkbox (under the General Options section). You don't have to view the PDF after saving, but it's always a good idea to see exactly what you're sending the client before you send it, just in case something didn't come out the way you wanted.

Step Seven:
In the list of categories on the left side of the dialog, click on Compression. This category shows the quality of the JPEG images that your client will see. Because we chose Small File Size in the previous step, the Image Quality is automatically set to Medium Low. Although this setting doesn't create the cleanest, most pristine images, that's okay because we don't want to send final high-res images this way. (Remember, this is just for proofing—if you sent high-quality images, your client might find a way to cut you out of the picture, so to speak, because the proofs are "good enough.")

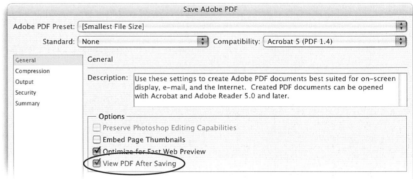

Step Eight:

Return to the list of categories on the left side of the dialog and click on Security. Since you're emailing this presentation to clients, it's important to protect your images from being "liberated" by your clients, which lets them sidestep any payment to you, the photographer. So, in the Permissions section, I recommend turning on the checkbox that reads "Use a password to restrict printing, editing and other tasks," and then enter a password in the Permissions Password field. Then, from the Printing Allowed pop-up menu, choose None. By doing this, you're protecting yourself because now your clients can't just print out full-color prints of your PDF to their color inkjet, or copy your photographs out of the PDF and place them into another application for printing. It pretty much ensures that your low-res proofs remain in your PDF and that you get paid for your work.

Step Nine:

When you click on the Save PDF button, a pop-up dialog will appear asking you to confirm your password. Enter your password, click OK, and Photoshop CS2 creates a PDF file for you, ready to email to your clients. When your clients open your emailed PDF, it launches Adobe Reader, goes into Full Screen mode (displaying your photos on a black background), and the presentation begins. And because you set up security preferences on this PDF, your clients won't be able to access the printing and photo-editing options in Reader. (*Note:* To return to Adobe Reader and end your slide show, just press the Escape key on your keyboard.)

The capture here shows the first slide in a PDF presentation, right before it transitions to the next photo.

Index

COLOPHON

The book was produced by the author and the design team using all Macintosh computers, including a Power Mac G4 733-MHz, a Power Mac G4 Dual Processor 1.25-GHz, a Power Mac G4 Dual Processor 500-MHz, a Power Mac G4 400-MHz, and an iMac. We use LaCie, Sony, and Apple monitors.

Page layout was done using Adobe InDesign CS. The headers for each technique are set in 20-point CronosMM700 Bold with the Horizontal Scaling set to 95%. Body copy is set using CronosMM408 Regular at 10 points on 13-point leading, with the Horizontal Scaling set to 95%.

Screen captures were made with Snapz Pro X and were placed and sized within InDesign. The book was output at 150-line screen, and all in-house proofing was done using a Tektronix Phaser 7700 by Xerox.

ADDITIONAL PHOTOSHOP RESOURCES

ScottKelbyBooks.com
For information on Scott's other books, visit his book site. For background info on Scott, visit www.scottkelby.com.

http://www.scottkelbybooks.com

National Association of Photoshop Professionals (NAPP)
The industry trade association for Adobe® Photoshop® users and the world's leading resource for Photoshop training, education, and news.

http://www.photoshopuser.com

KW Computer Training Videos
Scott Kelby is featured in a series of more than 20 Photoshop training videos and DVDs, each on a particular Photoshop topic, available from KW Computer Training. Visit the website or call 813-433-5000 for orders or more information.

http://www.photoshopvideos.com

Adobe Photoshop Seminar Tour
See Scott live at the Adobe Photoshop Seminar Tour, the nation's most popular Photoshop seminars. For upcoming tour dates and class schedules, visit the tour website.

http://www.photoshopseminars.com

Photoshop World Conference & Expo
The convention for Adobe Photoshop users has now become the largest Photoshop-only event in the world. Scott Kelby is technical chair and education director for the event, as well as one of the instructors.

http://www.photoshopworld.com

PlanetPhotoshop.com
"The Ultimate Photoshop Site" features Photoshop news, tutorials, reviews, and articles posted daily. The site also contains the Web's most up-to-date resource on other Photoshop-related websites and information.

http://www.planetphotoshop.com

Photoshop Hall of Fame
Created to honor and recognize those individuals whose contributions to the art and business of Adobe Photoshop have had a major impact on the application or the Photoshop community itself.

http://www.photoshophalloffame.com

Kelby's Notes
Now you can get the answers to the top 100 most-asked Photoshop questions with Kelby's Notes, the plug-in from Scott Kelby. Simply go to the How Do I? menu while in Photoshop, find your question, and the answer appears in an easy-to-read dialog. Finally, help is just one click away.

http://www.kelbysnotes.com

Layers magazine
Layers—The How-To Magazine for Everything Adobe—is the foremost authority on Adobe's design, digital video, digital photography, and education applications. Each issue features timely product news, plus the quick tips, hidden shortcuts, and step-by-step tutorials for working in today's digital market. America's top-selling computer book author for 2004, Scott Kelby, is editor-in-chief of *Layers*.

www.layersmagazine.com

Photoshop CS Down & Dirty Tricks
Scott is also author of the best-selling book *Photoshop CS Down & Dirty Tricks,* an amazing new collection of Photoshop techniques, including how to create the same effects you see every day in magazines, on TV, at the movies, and on the Web. It's available now at bookstores around the country.

http://www.scottkelbybooks.com

IMAGE 22474024
PRINT up to
8" x 6"
at 300dpi
PAY ONE FEE.
DOWNLOAD WHAT YOU NEED.
Royalty-free stock photography by subscription.
PHOTOS.COM™
$200 OFF 1-year subscriptions!
Regularly $599.95 - YOU PAY ONLY $399.95
Go to www.photos.com/promo/reminder
Expires July 15, 2006.
©2005 JupiterImages, a division of Jupitermedia Corporation. All Rights Reserved.